AF511720

(Translations of the three Inscriptions on the Cover.)

1. Arabic.

"These are our works which prove
what we have done;
Look, therefore, at our works
when we are gone."

2. Turkish.

"His genius cast its shadow o'er the world,
And in brief time he much achieved and
wrought:
The Age's Sun was he, and ageing suns
Cast lengthy shadows, though their time be
short."

(*Kemál Páshá-zádé.*)

3. Persian.

*"When we are dead, seek for our
resting-place
Not in the earth, but in the
hearts of men."*

(*Jalálu'd-Dín Rúmí.*)

"E. J. W GIBB MEMORIAL'

SERIES.

JURJI ZAYADAN'S

HISTORY OF ISLAMIC CIVILIZATION

UMAYYADS AND 'ABBASIDS

Translated by

D.S. MARGOLIOUTH,
D. LITT
Laudian Professor of Arabic in the University of Oxford

KITAB BHAVAN
New Delhi-110002

History of Islamic Civilization

KITAB BHAVAN

Publishers, Distributors, Exporters & Importers
1784, Kalan Mahal, Darya Ganj,
New Delhi - 1100 02 (India)

Phones :91-11-23277392, 23274686
Fax :(91-11) 23263383
Mob. :9910114484
Website : www.kitabbhavan.net
E-mail : info@kitabbhavan.net
:nasri@vsnl.com

I[st] Published in India :1981
V[th] Edition: 2018

ISBN :81-7151-057-4

Book Code No. :H00045

Printed & Published in India by :
Nusrat Ali Nasri for KITAB BHAVAN
Moonis Ali Nasri for KITAB BHAVAN
1784, Kalan Mahal, Darya Ganj,
New Delhi - 1100 02 [India]

TRANSLATOR'S PREFACE.

THE prosperous condition of Egypt, due to the British occupation and Lord CROMER'S statesmanlike administration. has led to a renaissance of Arabic literature and learning in that country, surpassing all that might have been imagined. Societies formed for the encouragement of Arabic literature are constantly bringing to light important texts bearing on Mohammedan history, antiquities, and religion ; and a whole series of magazines and reviews, such as the Muḳtaṭaf, the Hilál, the Muḳtabis, the Manár, the Muḥíṭ, the Diyá, and others, while providing lighter entertainment for the educated in Egypt, also devote some of their pages to the study of works which interest European Orientalists. The results and the methods of the latter are steadily making way among native scholars, to many of whom treatises in English, French, and Italian are accessible, while a smaller number have taken the trouble to familiarize themselves with German and Latin. Should the projected Cairene University be ultimately established, the admission of Egypt into the international republic of learning will be an accomplished fact.

The author of the present work, Mr. G. ZAIDAN, a Syrian by birth, but for many years resident in Cairo, where he edits the monthly magazine Hilal which has already been mentioned, is one of those Orientals who have taken pains to acquaint themselves with the works of European scholars. His " History of

Islamic Civilization" has received favourable notice from the doyen of our studies, Professor M. DE GOEJE, of Leyden, and other Orientalists of eminence have in letters to him or elsewhere expressed their approval of it, and their belief that it might with advantage be rendered accessible to those who cannot read Arabic. These opinions justified the present writer in gratifying the wish of the author that the former should—at any rate for part of the work—undertake the task of translation: a service which on the ground of personal friendship the author had the right to demand. Should the part selected meet with a favourable reception, translators will easily be found for the remainder. The Gibb Trustees, by signifying their willingness to let the book appear among their publications, have both solved all difficulties connected with the printing and given it otherwise a favourable start.

The translator has endeavoured throughout to give a faithful rendering of the text before him,[1] and must not be held responsible for either the statements or the opinions expressed therein.

[1] Occasionally the poems quoted have been abridged. It should be observed that the texts quoted in the notes are cited according to Oriental editions, which, however, are nearly as much used in Europe as Occidental editions, where such exist. After the precedent set by Dozy the authors' names have been abridged by the omission of 'Ibn' and similar prefixes. The translator must apologize for the spelling Khíllikán. He was not aware till too late that Dr. Wright had proved on the evidence of an autograph (reproduced in the Palæographical Society's publications) that the right spelling is Khallikán. The work cited as "Faraj" is Tanúkhí's al-Faraj ba'd al-shiddah, Cairo, 1903-4; that cited as "Wuzará" is Hilál al-Sábi's work, edited by H. F. Amedroz, Leyden, 1904. The author has acknowledged the use of Mr. Lane Poole's "Mohammedan Dynasties" for some of his tables.

CONTENTS.

INTRODUCTION.

FIRST ARABIAN PERIOD.

WE mean by this time the period during which the Islamic empire was in the hands of the Arabs, its policy Arabian, and its generals and governors Arabs, the Arabic element having the predominance. This period extends from the commencement of Islam to the end of the Umayyad dynasty; and it is divided into two portions, the dynasty of the Pious Caliphs and the dynasty of the Umayyads. Each of the two had its own political principles and methods of government, as will be explained. By way of introduction we must give a statement of the condition of the Arabs before Islam, so far as concerns our present subject.

§ 1. BEDOUINS AND TOWNSFOLK.

The life of the Bedouin has for its basis either agriculture or the rearing of animals. The Bedouin cultivator is compelled to stay in the same place, as he must wait for his crop. Such persons formed the population of hamlets, villages, and mountains; there were no large number of them in the deserts of Arabia; it is only in the Berber country, in North Africa, that they abound, as well as in the neighbourhood of the large towns in Egypt, Syria, Persia, and elsewhere. The Bedouins, on the other hand, who rear animals are accustomed to migrate in search of forage and water for their beasts. Of these there are two classes: the cattle-rearers, who look after sheep and cattle, and go no long distance into the desert, owing to the want of good pasturage, sometimes called sheepmen ; examples are the Berbers in North Africa, the Turks, their relations the Turcomans, the Ṣaḳálibah, and others who inhabit the deserts of Turkestan, Khorasan, etc.

The other sort, the camel-rearers, are chiefly represented by the Bedouins of Arabia, and they wander more and go further into the desert than the cattle-rearers, because the pastures, plants, and trees of the hills are not sufficient to maintain the life of the camel, which requires to feed on the desert trees, and to drink brackish water, and to wander in winter-time about the desert, in order to keep warm : the desert sand being required by this creature for dropping its young, since no other creature suffers more at that period, or requires more warmth. Hence the camel-rearing Bedouin is compelled to wander far into the desert, and bears to the townsfolk the relation of a wild and untameable beast to a tame one ; so averse are these folks to society, and so isolated are they in their deserts, and so ready to defend themselves. They always carry arms, look about on the roads, sleep only in snatches, where they sit, or on their saddles or frames. They isolate themselves in the wilderness, relying on their bravery, which becomes part of their character ; and indeed the further a Bedouin ventures into the desert the more courageous and hardy does he become.

The chief population of Arabia are nomad Bedouins, and hence cities were few in the peninsula, especially in the interior. The most famous Arabian cities before Islam were Meccah, Medinah, and Ṭá'if in the Ḥijáz, and Ma'rib and Ṣan'á in Yemen. The inhabitants were a mixture of Arabs, Persians, Jews, etc., who made their living by trading with their Bedouin visitors.

§ 2. Arab Patriotism before Islam.

Patriotism is a necessary characteristic of Bedouin peoples such as were the Arabs. Mankind are naturally greedy, and inclined to quarrels and disputes; these in towns are settled by judges and rulers, who prevent mutual injury, and also avert the attacks of external enemies by walls, armies, and munitions of war; but the Bedouins have to submit to the judgment of sheikhs and chieftains, whose authority rests on the respect felt for them in the tribe or clan; and indeed reverence for age is a Bedouin characteristic. When an enemy attacks from outside, the settlement is defended by the young and brave, who, however, will only do their duty if nerved by patriotism.

The inhabitants of any country or republic must have some bond capable of uniting the individuals; and the nature of such bond varies with the circumstances of the nation. In some cases the bond is the land, in others a religion, in others pedigree or language; now the Bedouins, as we have seen, have no land, and before Islam they had no common religion; hence there was nothing to keep them together except pedigree or language, both of which hang together, especially among the Bedouins.[1]

The chief causes of patriotism among them were the relations of brotherhood, parentage, and avunculate. Out of persons in this relation to each other was composed the family, and from the families the clan, e.g. that of Abú Ṭálib or 'Abbás; each of these being a unit composed of a number of families, and each of them belonging to the Banú Háshim. Of a number of clans was composed the *fakhidh*, e.g. the Banú Háshim and Banú Umayyah both belonged to the Banú 'Abd Manáf; a number of *fakhidhs* went to a *baṭn*, e.g. the Banú 'Abd Manáf, and the Banú Makhzúm were included in the *baṭn* Ḳuraish; a number of *baṭns* went to an *'imárah*, e.g. Ḳuraish and Kinánah were both included in Muḍar. A number of *'imárahs* went to a *ḳabílah*, e.g. Rabí'ah and Muḍar were both included in 'Adnán. A number of *ḳabílahs* were included in a *sha'b*, which represents the extreme end of the pedigree, e.g. that in which both 'Adnán and Kahtan were included.[2]

[1] On Arabic pedigrees and their value see Sprenger, *Das Leben, etc., des Muḥammad*, vol. iii, Introduction; Robertson Smith, *Kinship and Marriage, etc.*

[2] For the meaning of these terms see Robertson Smith, loc. cit.

§ 3. PATRIOTISM OF THE TRIBE.

Between the members of each of the divisions which we have enumerated there was patriotism, or clan-feeling, uniting them to each other, and varying with the nearness of the relationship. Thus the two divisions of a single *fakhidh* would be united against another *fakhidh*, though both *fakhidhs* might belong to one *baṭn*. Similarly two *baṭns* of one *'imárah* might be united against another *'imárah*, though both *'imárahs* belonged to a single *ḳabílah*. The principle is that contained in the proverb "I and my brother go against my cousin; and I and my cousin against the stranger." So a Ḳaḥṭanite would out of tribal feeling go against an 'Adnánite; this indeed being the most extensive form of patriotism. A similar feeling would be found in each *ḳabílah* against each, in each *'imárah* against each, in the *baṭns*, *fakhidhs*, and finally in the *faṣílahs* (clans) and families. Thus we find a feud raging between the Banú 'Abbás and the Banú Abí Ṭálib, though both these families were of the Háshim clan. A similar feud raged between the Banú Háshim and the Banú Umayyah, though both were of the clan Banú 'Abd Manáf.

Each *ḳabílah*, *baṭn*, and *fakhidh* would boast against the others of the prowess of its members, and make mention of its rival's defects. This gave rise to boasting matches, too long to be recorded here The most famous case of inter-tribal rivalry is that between the Ḳaḥṭánite or Yemenite and 'Adnánite sections. Mention of this is often made in the histories without attracting the reader's attention, because the historians rarely record the genealogy of the tribes. Thus we read "War broke out between Ḳais and Kalb," without being told that Ḳais was 'Adnánite and Kalb Ḳaḥṭánite, the reader being supposed to know it already. Similarly we are told without further explanation of boasting-matches between Ḳaḥṭán and Nizár, Ma'add and Yemen, Mudar and Ḥimyar, Hawázin and Kahlán, Kais and Hamdán, etc.

§ 4. THE ARABS AND THE PERSIANS BEFORE ISLAM.

Both Ḳaḥṭánites and 'Adnánites, it must be observed, would unite against non-Arabs, such as Persians, Turks, etc., whom they called 'Ajam, i.e. barbarians, the word meaning 'dumb,' whether the word came from the name or inversely. Against these they would boast of the superiority of their own descent and language, and they would treat the Barbarians generally with disdain. The word *akhzar*,[1] meaning 'narrow-eyed,' was applied by them to the Barbarians, an insulting epithet, which, if addressed to an Arab, was thought to imply that he was no true Arab. Properly the word *'Ajamí* applies only to the Persians, the first nation speaking a foreign language that mixed with the Arabs, but it was afterwards applied to any foreign people.

The rivalry between Arabs and Persians is of ancient date. During the Persian empire the Persians many a time had to drive the Arabs out of their country with the sword, and the Arabs would attack the cities of the Persians—even in the days of Sapor, some generations before the rise of Islam. This king wished to annoy the Arabs and drive them out of his country, especially the tribe Iyád. To this there is an allusion in a verse:—

> "Though Sabur the king son of Sabur forbad,
> There were horses and flocks round the tents of Iyad."

Nevertheless Sabur got possession of their persons by the force of his army, and slew many of them, those who escaped crossing the border into Roman territory. He also dealt in the same way with the Tamímites in Baḥrain; nor did the enmity between the Arabs and Persians cease till the Yemenite Arabs were compelled to invoke the help of Kisra against the Abyssinians in the fifth century A.D. He sent an army which drove them out and installed itself in their place, ruling the

[1] 'Iḳd Faríd, iii, 229.

Arabs till Islam came, when the Arabs recovered the sovereignty and lorded it over the Persians, to the vexation of the latter, especially in the days of the Umayyads, who were haters of all non-Arabs. Hence arose the sect called *Shu'ûbiyyah,* who attacked the Arabs, as shall be explained.

§ 5. MOTHERHOOD AND AVUNCULATE.

The principal source of clan-feeling among the Arabs is the paternal relation and derivation from a common father, just as is the case with other progressive peoples. Still, motherhood was of great consequence with them also, and affinity by marriage was a great source of clan-feeling. This was not due to the exalted station of woman in general, but owing to the respect felt for maternity. A woman was indeed held in contempt till she became a mother, when her importance would increase, and she would form a bond of unity. A man would respect his mother more than his wife, the latter's relation to him being less permanent than the former's. A story which illustrates this is that of Ṣakhr son of 'Amr son of Al-Sharíd, brother of Al-Khansá. In a war with the Banú Asad he was wounded by Rabí'ah son of Thaur the Asadite, and some of the links of his mail entered his side, occasioning him a severe illness which lasted for a year, during which he was attended by his mother and his wife Sulaima. His wife grew tired of acting nurse, and when asked by another woman how her husband was progressing, replied that he was not alive, and likely to be of use, or dead, so that he might be forgotten. Ṣakhr, hearing this, recited a poem, of which the following are verses:—

> "The mother of Sakhr through Ṣakhr's long ailing
> Tires not: 'tis his consort whose patience is failing.
> May that man live in trouble and shame all his life
> Who prizes his mother no more than his wife." [1]

In accordance with this, condolence was expressed only for such women as were mothers.[2] This was not only the case with

[1] Ibn Khillikán, i, 132. [2] 'Iḳd Faríd, ii, 264.

the Arabs, but the Greek view about women was the same. A woman was regarded by them as a servant, to be kept screened from men's gaze both before and after marriage, and to be occupied with household work, sewing, weaving, and nursing. The Persians treated their women in the same way till one became a mother, when her importance increased and she had the right to command and forbid in her own house. With the Bedouins this principle still holds good ; and it gave rise to the clan-feeling of the avunculate, i.e. the practice by which persons in this relationship were accustomed to aid their nephews, and indeed that by which the brothers of a woman would aid her husband's clan, even in cases where the father belonged to an 'Adnánite clan and the mother to a Yemenite, or *vice versâ*.

Prior to Islam the maternal uncle played an important *rôle*. The most obvious illustration is the aid afforded by the people of Medinah to the Prophet when he migrated thither ; the fact that the people of Medinah stood in this relation to the Prophet was one of their most potent motives in aiding him The Prophet's mother was of the Banú Najjár, a branch of the Khazraj, a Ḳaḥṭánite clan, whereas his father was of Ḳuraish, a Muḍarite clan. After his father's death, his mother took him to Medinah to take refuge with his maternal uncles, the numerous tribe of the Banú Najjár. They were religiously disposed more than others, and in the days of ignorance one of them had turned monk, put on sackcloth, and abandoned idolatry, also adopting the practice of ablution after pollution. This person was near adopting Christianity, but abandoned the idea. However, he made of his own house a place of worship. The Prophet's mother remained at Medinah in comfort and ease, and presently took him with her to his paternal uncles at Meccah, dying, however, on the journey. When he proclaimed his message, and endured persecution at the hands of his paternal uncles, he fled to his maternal uncles at Medinah, where his relations acknowledged his kinship, inasmuch as his connexion with the Banú Najjár involved the whole of the Khazraj group in the relationship of maternal uncle to him. When he arrived at Medinah his relatives welcomed him, and the first of his adherents there were his maternal uncles or persons of kin to them. These were his most earnest champions and defenders.[1] Presently the people of Medinah joined him *en masse.* In his campaigns when the fight became severe he would place himself under the standard of the Helpers,[2] who would offer their lives in his behalf, especially the Banú Najjar. When the enemies of the Helpers satirized them, they would bestow their chief attention to the Banu Najjar owing to the prominent part they played in the propagation of Islam. An example is to be found in a poem composed by 'Amr son of Al-'Áṣ on the day of Uhud, before his conversion:

> " Najjár desired to meet us by the side
> Of Sal' in battle, and were gratified." [3]

After the spread of Islam the avunculate was still reverenced by the Arabs, and was an important factor in patriotism and in directing the course of politics; so when Mu'áwiyah sought to obtain the Caliphate by the pretext of avenging the blood of 'Uthmán son of 'Affan, he was aided by the Yemenite tribe Kalb, to whom Ná'ilah, 'Uthman's wife, belonged—her fingers had been bespattered with blood when her husband was slain. Their assistance greatly helped his success, and he himself married a woman of the same tribe, who bore him his son and successor, Yazíd. When Yazid became Caliph he had on his side the whole tribe of Kalb on the ground of this relationship. Similar cases are to be found elsewhere in the history of Islam. So Al-Ma'mún was aided by the Persians owing to his mother having been Persian, whereas his rival Amín had an Arabian faction behind him, owing to his mother having been an Arab. Ma'mun retreated to Khorasan and took refuge with his mother's relatives at Merv, and they wrested the Caliphate from Amín and bestowed it

[1] Hishám, i, 189. [2] Ibid., ii, 81. [3] Ibid., ii, 110.

on him. Al-Mu'taṣim had a Turkish mother, and was attached to the Turks, out of whom he established a force which aided him against the Persians. Further details will be given later on illustrating the influence of the Queen-mother on the Empire. Kings, generals, and other administrators of public affairs used to strengthen themselves by marrying into different tribes and so secure the help of the clan-feeling of their wives' relations.

§ 6. Results of the Arabian Clan-feeling.

The clan-feeling of the Arabs was based on relationship by descent from one father in the first place, in the second by descent from one mother. There were besides others bonds of union, such as confederacy between tribes, not unlike the political confederations or leagues of our own times. The most famous confederations of Pagan days were those of the Muṭayyabin and the Fuḍúl; such a confederation could unite tribes however distant, such as 'Adnánites and Ḳaḥṭánites. Confederation could also take place between the Arabs and foreign settlers, in which case it took the form of clientship: thus of the Jewish tribes at Medinah, Naḍír, Kainuká', etc., some were confederates of the Aus, others of the Khazraj. The Jews of Wádi al-Kura were confederates of the Banú Háshim. These will again be mentioned when we treat of clientship.

A confederacy was the result of certain causes or conditions. Such a cause might be the presence of a prisoner who was unable to ransom himself. He might then be branded with the mark of the captor tribe, and reckoned confederate with it.[1] A confederate inherited in the tribe just like a genuine member.[2] When he was killed, however, the blood-money paid for him was the half of what was paid for a genuine member of the tribe.[3]

[1] Agháni, vii, 110. [2] Wuzará, 251. [3] Aghani, ii, 167.

§ 7. ADOPTION.

Adoption was a practice which resulted from the clan-feeling characteristic of Arabia before Islam. In such a case a man introduced into his family a slave, prisoner, or client, the last name being employed in all cases, and treated him as a member of his family. The most famous case of adoption in pre-Islamic times was that of Umayyah, eponymus of the Umayyads, adopting a slave named Dhakwán, to whom he gave the patronymic Abú 'Amr, and who was regarded as Umayyah's son. A descendant of this man was Al-Walíd Ibn 'Ukbah, brother of 'Uthmán Ibn 'Affán on the mother's side, and a distinguished Companion of the Prophet.

The most celebrated case of adoption in Islam was that of Ziyád, "his father's son," into the family of Abú Sufyán, father of Mu'áwiyah the Arabian Sisyphus. The story is told in the histories. Ziyád was the son of a woman named Sumayyah, who was in slavery, and bore Ziyád to a Greek client of the tribe Thakíf, named 'Ubaid. This fact was not generally known, and Ziyád's parentage was generally supposed to be uncertain, whence he was called "his father's son." When Mu'áwiyah became a candidate for the Caliphate and required help, he endeavoured to enroll among his adherents a number of the most sagacious of the Arabs. Among these was Ziyád, whom he determined to adopt. He therefore obtained an affidavit from a wine-dealer of Tá'if named Abú Maryam al-Salúlí, to the effect that Abú Sufyán had come to his tavern and demanded a prostitute: that Sumayyah had been brought by him to Abú Sufyán, and that Sumayyah in consequence gave birth to Ziyád. The best historians disbelieve this story, which they suppose to have been a fabrication of Mu'áwiyah got up with the intention of securing the services of Ziyád, an intention which was realized. Ziyád in consequence came to be called son of Abú Sufyán, after having been called son of Sumayyah,[1]

[1] Athir, iii, 225.

or "his father's son." Ziyád's family continued to count as members of the tribe Ḳuraish till they were expelled from it by the Caliph Mahdí in 160 A.H., when they were again affiliated to the above-mentioned 'Ubaid, and placed among the clients of the tribe Thaḳíf[1] A similar case was that of the family of Abu Bakrah, who, having been clients of the Prophet, became enrolled in the tribe Thaḳíf; the same Caliph reduced them to their former condition.

An adopted member of a tribe was called *da'í*, 'supposititious.' A man might be doubly supposititious, his clan bearing that relation to a tribe, and he himself bearing it to the clan. Such a case was that of the poet Ibn Harmah, who was an adoptive member of the clan Khalj, which was itself adoptive in the tribe Kuraish. Cases were common in which a whole clan or tribe was adopted at once by another, owing to the former having settled among the latter, or having aided the latter. Such a case was that of the 'Cousins' at Baṣrah. In the days of Omar I they settled among the Tamím, adopted Islam, and raided with the Moslems. Their comrades said to them, "Though you are not born Arabs, still you are our brethren and kinsmen, and our helpers, so we will call you *cousins*," and this name they retained, counting thenceforth as Arabs.[2]

An adoptive member of a clan or family was reckoned as one of themselves, and inherited or was inherited like true-born members of it.[3] The Arabs were often inclined to adopt their clients, hoping to inherit their property. If a client perceived their intention, he would often refuse to be adopted. Thus Nuṣaib, the famous singer, refused to be adopted by his patrons. "I had rather," said he, "be a decent client than an adopted hanger-on, and I know that all you want is my property."[4]

A source of clan-feeling, resembling confederation, was confraternity which might be instituted between tribes or individuals. This sort of relationship is still common among

[1] Ibid., vi, 20. [2] Aghání, iii, 76. [3] Ibid., xvii, 94. [4] Ibid., i, 134.

Bedouins. Once become the brother of an Arab, he will help you and defend you as if the tie between you were one of blood.

§ 8. Repudiation.

This is the opposite of adoption in their nomenclature. If a man were offended for any reason with his son, genuine or adoptive, he could repudiate, i.e. disown him, and thereby cease to be responsible for the mischief wrought by that son. This could also be done by a family or clan, a deputation of which would go to the Market of 'Ukáẓ, taking with them the repudiand, where they would publicly declare that they disowned him, and a crier would be employed to proclaim the same. Such a tribe would no longer be responsible for the acts of the repudiated member, nor exact compensation for mischief done to him. The tribe Khuzá'ah dealt thus with the pre-Islamic poet Kais Ibn al-Ḥaddádiyyah.[1] The act of repudiation was at times made out in a document.

The most famous case of repudiation in pre-Islamic times was that of 'Amr Ibn al-'As by his clan. He had gone on business to Abyssinia with 'Umarah son of al-Walíd the Makhzumite, and the two fell out on the way. 'Umarah did some mischief to 'Amr, who was of the tribe Sahm. 'Amr cherished a grudge against 'Umarah, and wrote to his father, requesting to be repudiated, so that his father should not be answerable for any vengeance that he took on the other. This was done. Both clans repudiated the disputants, and a herald was sent to Meccah to proclaim the fact.[2]

Such repudiated persons used to gather together in the deserts and form gangs of desperadoes, who would infest the roads and annoy their former tribesmen. In Islamic times they found themselves in antagonism to the government. So Ya'li al-Aḥwal, a poet of Umayyad times, was a repudiate, who collected the destitute Azdites and the persons whom they had repudiated, and out of them formed a gang with which he

[1] Agháni, xiii, 2. [2] Ibid., viii, 52.

annoyed the Arab tribes, and infested the caravan routes. Some slave-dealers used to purchase repudiates and take them into the Roman empire.

§ 9. SLAVES IN PRE-ISLAMIC TIMES.

Slavery is as ancient as mankind itself, for it is natural for man to endeavour to tyrannize over others, and for the strong to enslave the weak; at the commencement of civilization, indeed, when a man had overcome his enemy and got him in his power, he did not make a slave of him, but killed him: except, indeed, in the case of women, who were preserved for concubinage. At a later period they took to making slaves of captives and employing them to till the fields or to mind sheep, or practise some handicraft, unless indeed they sold them as chattels. This was the practice of the ancient civilizations of Assyria, Babylon, and Egypt; but the slave-trade also flourished in the Roman empire, slaves being bought by the hundred and the thousand, sold like sheep, and treated like quadrupeds. In the best days of the Roman empire the practice of marrying slave-girls was common; and whereas the Roman at first could beat or kill his slaves at pleasure, he presently became accountable for his conduct to the judges, and could be punished for ill-treatment of slaves.

Slaves existed in large numbers in the Roman empire, and were to be found in every house. Most of them had originally been captives of war, or were the progeny of such captives. They were employed in domestic duties or were taught some trade. There was a special market in which they were sold. The price varied from 20 Roman dinars to 4,000. The same is stated concerning other ancient empires. The Persians, e.g., were in the habit of making slaves of Turks taken in war, and presenting them to each other, not excepting Turkish princes. A case recorded is that of Parwiz, king of Persia, presenting the Greek emperor Maurice with 100 slaves, belonging to princely Turkish families, all of them of great beauty, with gold earrings in their ears, the earrings containing pearls or gems. The Greek emperor made a return gift of (among other things) 20 slave-girls, all daughters of princes of the Burgundians, Gallicians, Sclavs, Gascons, all neighbouring peoples. Each of the girls had on her head a crown of gold.[1]

§ 10. SLAVERY IN ARABIA.

The Arabs, like other people, made slaves of captives taken in war, or purchased them of people dwelling near Arabia, such as the Abyssinians and the barbarous nations around Abyssinia. Slave-dealers brought slaves, male and female, from those regions to the Arabian peninsula, and sold them in their markets at festival times. The Ḳuraish dealt in slaves as they did in other merchandise. A famous slave-dealer of pre-Islamic times was Abdallah son of Jud'án, of the tribe Taim, leader of the Ḳuraish in the Fijár war.[2] When a man purchased a slave he would put a cord round his neck, and so drag him to his dwelling as though he were a horse.[3] If the slave were a prisoner of war his forelock would be shorn off and deposited in a quiver till his ransom was paid. Slaves were given as presents, just as they were sold, and inherited among other property, unless the operation called *tadbír* were executed, which consisted in the master promising the slave liberty after the former's death. A slave might form part of a bride's nuptial gift. Such a case was that of the poet Basshár Ibn Burd, who, with his mother, was the slave of a man of the tribe Azd, who, when he married an 'Ukailite woman, gave Basshár with his mother to her as part of the nuptial gift.[4]

This indicates how many of them there were; in the courts of princes and kings there would be hundreds and thousands. When the prince of the Ḥimyar, Dhu'l-Kulá', visited Abú Bakr, he had with him, besides the members of his family, 1,000 slaves.[5] Every respectable Arab had in his house some slaves employed in domestic duties. Abdallah Ibn Abí Rabí'ah had a number

[1] Mas'údi, i, 119.
[2] Ibid., i, 282.
[3] Ḳutaibah, Ma'árif, 112.
[4] Agháni, iii, 20.
[5] Mas'údi, i, 287.

of Abyssinian slaves employed in all sorts of crafts. Some of them did military service, but their fidelity could not be relied on.[1] Still, cases of their employment in battle occurred after the rise of Islam also. A slave's punishment for legal offences was half the punishment of a free man;[2] but in the division of booty after a battle they had no share; their share went to their master.[3]

A special sort of slave was that kind called *ḳinn*, who tilled the soil and was sold with it, resembling the serfs of the Roman empire. Sometimes a man lost his liberty gambling; this happened when Abu Laḥab played for liberty with Al-'Ási Ibn Hisham, and won. He made a slave of the other, and set him to feed his camels.[4] They used also to make slaves of their debtors.

The Arabs married their slave-girls, and the children of these slave-girls were regarded as slaves, unless the child were specially gifted, in which case he would probably be adopted as a son. The most famous case of adoption of this style is that of 'Antarah of 'Abs by his father Shaddad. He was the son of a slave-girl Zabíbah; he was driven from his father's house till he made himself a name, when his father adopted him.[5] Prior to Islam the Arabs only manumitted their slaves for important reasons. If a slave desired manumission he would demand to be sold, and if the master consented he would sell him to another master. After the rise of Islam manumission became frequent for religious and political reasons which shall be stated.

§ 11. Clients in pre-Islamic times.

The client (*maula*) in Arabia occupied an intermediate position between a slave and a freeman; in most cases he was a slave who had obtained his freedom. He corresponded then with the *Libertinus* of ancient Rome. Any slave or prisoner who was manumitted by his owner became his

[1] Agháni, i, 32. [2] Ibid., xiv, 124. [3] Ḳutaibah, Ma'árif, 110.
[4] Agháni, iii, 100. [5] Ibid., vii, 148.

maula or client. He would then be regarded as related to his master or his master's tribe or family. A client, e.g., of 'Abbás was a client of the family Banu Hashim, the tribe Ḳuraish, and the nation Muḍar. At times the ascription was to the country of the former owner, the client being called client of the people of Meccah or Medinah. He counted then as a relative, only the relationship which in the case of a real descendant was said to be genuine (*ṣarîḥ*) was in his case said to be not genuine. The word client (maula) is, however, sometimes loosely applied to a friend, neighbour, cousin, relation, confederate, son, uncle, guest, lover, follower, ally by marriage, etc. In all these cases the term may be said to be employed metaphorically. When it is technically used it applies to three sorts of clients: client by manumission, client by treaty, and client by blood.

Clients by manumission.—A client of this sort is one who, having been a captive or slave, has been freed. Release of prisoners was sometimes executed as a reward for good conduct. So, too, a slave would often be promised his liberty on some condition. He would then become the client of the person who had manumitted him. This principle was of some importance at the commencement of Islam, the Moslems not unfrequently obtaining the help of slaves against their masters by the promise of manumission. Thus at the siege of Ṭá'if, in the year 8 A.H., when the city made a stubborn resistance, the Prophet ordered a herald to offer liberty to all slaves who deserted to him, such slaves to become the clients of God and His Apostle; and many did so.[1] There were also other reasons for manumitting them.

When a slave was a captive taken in war, on the occasion of his manumission his forelock was shorn; and though he was let go, he counted as the client of the person in whose possession that forelock was to be found. To this there is an allusion in the verses of Ḥassán Ibn Thábit, the prophet's court-poet, after

[1] 'Iḳd Farîd, ii, 3.

the battle of Uḥud, in reply to verses by Hubairah Ibn Abí Wahb:

> "Took ye no thought how Allah's forces slew
> Those foes whose corpses in the well they threw:
> While many a captive ransomed without pay
> Became our client, his forelock shorn away?"[1]

Manumission by contract.—At times the manumission was effected by a contract of sale between slave and owner, called *mukatabah.* This meant that the slave should give a bond for the payment of a certain sum, which when he had earned and paid, he should be manumitted. Payment was sometimes in these cases made by instalments. Abu Sa'íd al-Muḳri, one of the most distinguished of the Epigoni, or second generation of Moslems, was originally a slave of a member of the tribe Jundu'. He contracted for his manumission by payment of 40,000 dirhems, and a sheep yearly for sacrifice, and so obtained it.[2]

It has already been stated that a slave became the client of the person who manumitted him. He thereby was entitled to inherit him at his death. At times it was contracted that the slave should become the client of some person who paid his manumission contract, instead of his former master. At times, too, manumission was 'free,' i.e. without bringing the slave into the condition of client. The formula, "Thou art *sá'ibah*'," addressed to a slave, implied that the slave was not to become a client, but had the right of leaving his money as he chose. Among the most famous persons manumitted after this style was Salim, client of Abú Ḥudhaifah Ibn 'Utbah, who came originally from Istakhr, and was the slave of Buthainah, wife of Abu Ḥudhaifah.[3]

The Islamic code made it unlawful for the manumitted slave to become the client of any one but the former owner. Burairah, daughter of Sa'úd the Thaḳefite, came to 'Á'ishah to request the latter's aid in making up her manumission contract-money. She had undertaken to pay five ounces of gold in five years. 'Á'ishah offered to pay the whole sum at once on condition of becoming the woman's patroness, when manumitted. Her

[1] Hisham, ii, 105. [2] Ḳutaibah, Ma'árif, 154. [3] Ibid., 92.

owners, however, declined this proposal. 'Á'ishah consulted the Prophet on the subject. His advice was that she should buy the woman (as a slave), then manumit her, and so become her patroness, on the ground that the person who actually manumitted a slave was the patron.[1] It was, however, permissible to purchase the right of patronage; thus Abu Ma'shar (traditionalist) had obtained manumission by contract from a woman of the tribe Makhzúm; after he had obtained his liberty the right of patron over him was purchased by Umm Músá, daughter of Manṣúr the Ḥimyarite.[2]

Client by treaty.—Also called client by confederation, or benefaction. In this case one man is connected with another by some service or other, confederacy, association, or connection, going back for a series of generations; an example of such clients by confederation or association is to be found in the Jews of Yathrib, who, when the Prophet came thither, were reckoned among the clients of the Aus and Khazraj. This status of theirs had a lengthy history behind it, the substance of which is that the Jews took up their abode in Yathrib some generations before the Christian era, and had made their home tnere before the migration of the Aus and Khazraj from Yemen. Coming there they found the Jews in sole possession of the soil and the cattle, while they remained in poverty till one of their rulers named Malik Ibn 'Ajlán consulted the King of Ghassán in Syria on the subject of these Jews and requested his assistance against them. They agreed to get the better of them by treachery, and succeeded in their plot. The Jews were in consequence depressed, and after this time if a Jew met with any injury from a member of the Aus or the Khazraj, instead of calling in the assistance of his tribesmen, he would appeal to his Arabian neighbours; and each Jewish tribe put itself under the patronage of one or other of the Aus and Khazraj clans.[3] They thus became the clients of those tribes: in some cases the patronage belonging to a special family, e.g. the Banú'l-Najjár, the Prophet's uncles on the mother's side.

[1] Bokhárí, ii, 20. [2] Ma'árif, 172. [3] Agháni, xix, 97.

The nature of the clientship which existed after Islam is in most cases of the sort that has been last described; the Arabs being the powerful lords, to whom the peoples of the conquered countries attached themselves as servants, friends, or associates: the resulting relation received the name patronage (or clientship). Where it was formally instituted the following formulæ were employed: one person says to another, "Will you be my patron on condition of inheriting me at my death, and paying blood-money in my place during my life?" The other says, "I accept."

Each class of the Arabs had a corresponding class of clients; so the Barmecides were clients of Al-Rashíd; Persians below them in rank were similarly clients of persons less exalted than the Caliph.

A client in pre-Islamic times might perhaps be a Jew, Christian, or Magian; this fact made no difference in his status. So of the clients of the Prophet one was originally an Abyssinian, another a Greek, another a Copt, another a Persian.[1] 'Adas, client of 'Utbah Ibn Abí Rabí'ah, was from Nineveh, and was killed at Badr, still being a Christian.[2]

After the rise of Islam the clients had in all cases to be Moslems, since a text of the Koran prohibited the bestowal of this relation on Jews or Christians. Members of these sects were therefore reckoned among the *dhimmis* (or tolerated sects).

Uterine Clientship.—Clientship of this style was acquired by marriage with the client of a tribe. The patronage in such a case would belong to the tribe whose client was the wife. Such a case is that of the poet Sudaif, who had been a client of the Khuzá'ah; presently he married a client of Abû Lahab, and claimed the patronage of the Banu Háshim.[3]

There were various rules, both special and general, affecting clients in Arabia. A general rule was that a client was lower in rank than a free man, but higher than a slave. He might not be sold like a slave; but in respect of marriage and inheritance he had not the rights of a free man. He might not marry a free woman, and the blood-money paid for him was

[1] Athír, ii, 151. [2] Mas'údi, i, 31. [3] Aghání, xiv, 162.

only half what was paid for a free man.[1] (The same was what was paid for a slave.) Similarly, if he incurred a legal penalty, only half was exacted from him of what was exacted from a free man.

The special rules varied with the various sorts of clientship. A client by manumission was inherited by his patron, but did not inherit him; a uterine client inherited, but was not inherited;[2] a client by treaty neither inherited nor was inherited. If a man manumitted his slave, he became his patron, and had a right to his inheritance; he was called 'benefactor.' The ancient Roman law gave a third of the freedman's estate, however acquired, to the master, who, if the freedman died without offspring, inherited the whole.[3]

The clients counted as a factor of importance in the 'clan-feeling' of the Arabs, and under Islam their influence became considerable; they even caused the transference of empire and the change of dynasties.

§ 12. SETTLEMENT OF ALIENS IN ARABIA.

The bulk of the population of the Arabian peninsula consisted of 'Adnánite and Ḳaḥṭánite tribes, with their slaves, clients, and allies; but there were also large numbers of settlers from Abyssinia, Syria, 'Irák, Egypt, Persia, and India Some of these alien immigrants intermarried with the people of the country and presently lost their nationality, as was the case with the Syrians, Chaldæans, and others. Some entered the relation of allies or clients, e.g. the Jews and Christians. Some, e.g. the Abyssinians, Persians, and Indians, were lost among the slaves and clients. Hence at the rise of Islam the population of Arabia consisted of Arabs who counted as pure, with the exception of certain Jewish tribes, such as the Ḳainuḳá' and Naḍír, a few Christians, and a few free Persians, known as 'the Sons.'

[1] Aghani, ii, 176. [2] 'Iḳd Faríd, ii, 262.
[3] Gibbon, "Decline and Fall," ii, 197

These last were a Persian community resident in Yemen, and known as the Free Sons of the Persians, or more briefly the Sons, to distinguish them from the Persians who were clients. They were the descendants of that Persian army that came to the assistance of Saif Ibn Dhí Yazan the Ḥimyarite against the Abyssinians, who had conquered the country. Saif fled to the King of Persia, who (after a series of negotiations) despatched with him some thousand Persian soldiers under a commander named Wahriz; in a battle fought after the arrival of the Persians in Yemen the latter were victorious, and the government was taken over by Saif with Wahriz for four years; he made slaves of the Abyssinians, who, however, one day slew him in the chase, and fled to the mountain-tops. They were sought and killed, but the Yemenites were depressed by the death of Saif, and did not appoint a ruler from among themselves, and remained under the government of the Persians until the rise of Islam. The two Persian governors at that time were named Fairúz the Dailemite, and Radhúyah: both adopted Islam.

When the Persian army had obtained possession of Yemen, they married Arab women, and the offspring of these marriages got the title 'Sons.' Distinguished persons who thus originated were Ṭá'ús Ibn Kaisan and Wahb Ibn Munabbih, who lived early in Islam. The former was prominent in the generation that followed the Companions, the latter was eminent as a traditionalist and romancer. Another was the poet Waḍḍah al-Yaman.

Persons of similar origin were also to be found in Syria, 'Irák, and Mesopotamia. Their names, however, varied in different countries. In Yemen, as we have seen, they were called the 'Sons.' In San'a in particular they were known as the 'Sons of the Free.' In Kufah they were called *Aḥámirah*, in Baṣrah *Asáwirah* (the chevaliers), in Mesopotamia *Ḥaḍárimah*, in Syria *Jarájimah*.[1] They were of some importance at the commencement of Islam, as they formed corps for the assistance of the

[1] Agháni, xvi, 76.

Moslems, in consequence whereof they continued to be distinguished from other non-Arabian Moslems as not being clients.

§ 13. GOVERNMENT IN PRE-ISLAMIC TIMES.

The Arabs had no dynasty in pre-Islamic times, with the exception of that of the Tubba's in South Arabia, which does not come within the scope of our present inquiry. In place of government, then, they had a system of principles which served as the pivot of their judgments and transactions for the preservation of their political relations and social ethics: a system serving as a substitute for the Administrative and Political Codes of civilized nations.

The chieftainship or headship could only be given to persons commended by the clan-feeling, and otherwise of eminence. If the claims of several from the point of view of the clan were equal, the eldest was preferred. Thence it comes that the word *sheikh* means both old man and chieftain. If for any reason it was not easy to choose, they had recourse to drawing lots. Similarly, when there was a confederacy of tribes for the purpose of fighting, and they wanted a chief, lots would be drawn between the several chieftains; he on whom the lot fell became captain of the confederacy. This was the case with the Bedouin Arabs who formed the bulk of the population of Arabia; as for Meccah, the chieftainship there belonged to the keeper of the Ka'bah: in the first part of this work an account has been given of their administrative system.

In every tribe in pre-Islamic times certain houses were renowned for holding the chieftainship and for nobility; in such houses, then, the right to the chieftaincy would inhere. Such houses were that of Háshim Ibn 'Abd Manáf among the Ḳuraish, that of Ḥudhaifah Ibn Badr al-Fazari in Ḳais, that of Zurárah Ibn 'Adí in Tamím, that of Dhu'l-Jaddain Ibn Abdallah Ibn Ḥammám in Shaibán, that of the Banú Rayyan of the Banú'l-Ḥárith Ibn Ka'b in Yemen. These houses acquired a superior degree of nobility by the fact of the chieftancy having been held for three successive generations in them at the least. Members of such families were more influential than other members of the same tribe. The Islamic rulers used to take account of this fact in their appointments to office. Ibn 'Abbás in his counsels to Al-Ḥasan son of 'Alí said, "Give the offices to the people of the ruling families, as thereby their tribes will be conciliated."

Though the Bedouin chief was an absolute monarch, he would not ordinarily give judgment entirely on his own responsibility, but would in most cases consult his friends and the members of his family. Still, he would be ready to give audience to any member of the tribe, and have no bodyguard. He would be ready to sit and talk with humble and exalted alike. Titles of honour and respectful modes of address were unknown to the Bedouins. When they addressed their ruler they called him by his name. In demanding his right the Bedouin would employ language which reflected his nobility of soul and detestation of injury, or Bedouin pride. Terms denoting various relationships according to age, such as father, uncle, son, brother, were, however, employed by the chieftain in addressing his subjects. Something of the same was kept up after the commencement of Islam, when the Caliph was addressed by his ordinary name, and openly contradicted. At a later period the customs of a court were introduced; the sovereign was isolated, and the distance between governor and governed increased.

§ 14. Virtues of the Arabs in pre-Islamic times.

Fidelity.—The Arabs, it must be observed, rarely required any judge to settle their disputes, owing to those natural virtues which served as a substitute for judge and jury, and kept them from committing any base act. The chief of these virtues is fidelity, for that when it takes root in any nation renders the law court unnecessary for it. For the judicial authority only has to decide where one party or the other is not faithful. This quality was deeply rooted in the Arab character, the more deeply the further the Arab was from the towns, the more he was in the heart of the desert. Perfidy and deceit only live in tall castles where they are shaded by luxurious gardens.

Fidelity is printed in the sayings of the people of the desert, in their songs and their proverbs, and is revealed in their customs and characteristics, and indeed in all their works: with them it is instinctive, with others artificial and factitious. The story of Ḥanẓalah of Ṭay and Al-Nu'mán Ibn al-Mundhir gives an excellent illustration of this quality. Ḥanẓalah promised Al-Nu'mán that he would come back after a year to meet his death. Al-Nu'mán demanded a warranty. Suraik son of 'Adí offered himself, doubtless trusting in Bedouin fidelity, which was maintained by Ḥanẓalah, who returned at the appointed time, without having to be fetched by soldiers or policemen. This induced Al-Nu'mán to pardon him.[1]

A still more signal instance of fidelity is that recorded of Samau'al Ibn 'Adiyá. Imru'ul-Kais the Kindite had deposited with him some valuable armour and furniture, and after doing so had migrated to the Byzantine empire, where he died before he could return. The King of Kindah sent to demand the arms and furniture deposited with Samau'al, who refused to deliver them. His reply, when pressed, was that he would not betray a trust, nor fail in the fidelity which was his duty. The king sent an army against him, and besieged him in his fortress; and Samau'al's son was taken prisoner by the besiegers. The king thereupon threatened Samau'al that he would slay this son, unless the deposit were delivered to him; but Samau'al still refused, declaring that he would be faithful to his trust whatever the king might do. The son was presently slaughtered before the father's eyes. Still the fortress held out, and the king was compelled to raise the siege. Samau'al endured the pain of bereavement, and only delivered the arms to Imru'ul-Ḳais's heirs.

[1] Mustaṭraf, i, 161.

Men of this character required no system of laws, and could dispense with armies and police. Especially if we add to this their loftiness of soul, their high spirits, their dislike of baseness, their liberality, and similar qualities, all characteristic of the Bedouin Arabs.

§ 15. NEIGHBOURHOOD.

The right based on vicinity is of the same class as that which is observed when the Bedouin is faithful to his engagements and defends those who are committed to his care. The Bedouin will defend his neighbour as he defends himself. This notion of vicinity originally means defence of a near neighbour, which indeed is a natural form of mutual assistance. A proverb says, "Rather a neighbour near than a brother far away." The word, however, came to be used rather more loosely, and derivatives of it mean only protection, and to implore protection. It is curious that the root of these words appears to signify almost the opposite of these ideas, viz. 'to wrong.' When a man was afraid of suffering any wrong, he would go to one who was capable of protecting him, and say to him, "Make me a neighbour," in which case the man so appealed to would defend him to the best of his power; and, indeed, such a neighbour would receive more attention than the protector's own family.

An illustration of this process is to be found in the story of the poet Al-A'sha. This person composed an encomium on Al-Aswad al-'Ansí, and received in return a present of robes and ambergris. He had to pass on his way home through the territory of the Banú 'Ámir, and he feared they might rob him of his goods. So he went to 'Alkamah Ibn 'Uláthah, and used the formula which has been mentioned. 'Alḳamah made him 'his neighbour'; the poet then asked if this implied protection from mankind and Jinn. He was told that it did. "And from death?" he went on to ask. The answer to this was in the negative. So the poet left 'Alḳamah and went to 'Ámir Ibn Ṭufail. This person answered both questions in the affirmative.

The poet asked him what he meant by guaranteeing him against death; the other answered that in the event of the poet being slain, he would send blood-money for him to his relations. With this the poet expressed himself satisfied.[1]

If a man came seeking "to be made a neighbour," and found his protector away from home, it was considered sufficient for him to tie the end of his robe to a tent-rope. By this act he became the neighbour of the owner of the tent, who was bound to defend him, and seek satisfaction for any wrong done him.[2]

It is stated that when 'Ámir Ibn Ṭufail died his sons erected stones enclosing the space of a square mile round his grave, in which space neither cattle were to feed nor was anyone to tread or ride. This signified symbolically the care with which 'Ámir observed the rights of 'neighbours' in his lifetime.[3]

This right continued to be observed after the introduction of Islam by the Arabs, except perhaps such as had intermixed with foreign nations in conquered countries. The limits within which it could be exercised were narrowed by political necessity, for important persons became government functionaries, and protection when demanded was against a governor who was searching for a man. When such a person demanded 'neighbourhood,' he would be told that a man could protect another against his tribe, but not against his sovereign. This was because they were afraid of losing their posts. Such a case was that of the poet Ibn Mufarrigh. Having satirized the Banu Ziyád, he requested the protection of Al-Aḥnaf Ibn Ḳais against 'Ubaidallah son of Ziyád, who was at that time governor of Baṣrah. Al-Aḥnaf refused, fearing lest he might lose his place. At the same time he offered to protect the poet against the Banú Sa'd, his own tribe. The poet went to other distinguished Arabs, but they all refused to take up his cause for the same ground.[4]

[1] Aghání, viii, 83. [2] Ibid., ii, 184. [3] Ibid., xv, 139. [4] Ibid., xvii, 56.

§ 16. CHIVALRY.

Another quality natural to the Arabs and enabling them to dispense with police and judicial authority was one that belongs to the age of Bedouin Paganism, and corresponds with the European chivalry. It is a combination of courage, generosity, and courtesy. This quality played a great part in pagan days, owing to the sensibility of the Arabs, whose feelings could be roused or allayed by a verse of poetry, and whom a single word could fire with enthusiasm. Oftentimes an Arab would sacrifice his life to the utterance of a single word, or to escape hearing one. Hence different forms of boasting-matches were common at the Arabic fairs and meetings, such matches having the effect of encouraging the pursuit of virtue, and rendering judicial administration unnecessary.

Other Arabic virtues, such as hospitality, munificence, high-mindedness, scarcely belong to our present subject.

CHAPTER I.

Arabian Polity in the time of the Pious Caliphs. From the years 11–41 A.H.

§ 1. ISLAMIC SOCIETY.

We have seen that the rivalries and contentions of the Arabs had for their subjects clan-feeling and pedigree. Among the alterations introduced by Islam was this, that the Arabs became united and formed one society, however different their pedigrees or their homes. Before Islam, Yemenite would contend with Ḥijázite, Muḍarite with Ḥimyarite, etc. Similar rivalry was to be found between the various clans, tribes, and families; but when Islam came they were all united under one banner, with one title, Islam. "Moslems are brethren," said the Prophet; and in his discourse on the day of the taking of Meccah he informed the Ḳuraish that God had abolished the pride of pagan days and contentions concerning nobility of pedigree: all men were of Adam, and Adam himself of the dust.[1] Similarly, in the Sermon at the Farewell Pilgrimage he told his audience that God was one, and their father one; all were sons of Adam, and Adam was taken out of the dust; the most honourable in God's eyes was the most pious; only piety gave the Arab any advantage over the non-Arab.[2]

The first Caliphs followed the Prophet's example in this matter, especially Omar I. The story of Jibilah Ibn al-Aiham illustrates this. After his conversion to Islam this man, who had been king of Ghassán, was making the circuit of the Ka'bah, when the end of his tunic was trodden on by a member of the

[1] Hisham, ii, 219. [2] Jáḥiẓ, Bayán, i, 164.

tribe Fazárah, the tunic becoming undone in consequence. Jibilah raised his hand and hit the Fazarite a blow that broke his nose. Omar, on being appealed to by the wounded man, desired to break Jibilah's nose in retaliation. How so, asked Jibilah, am I not a king and this man a plebeian? Omar replied that Islam had made the two equal, and that Jibilah had no advantage over the Fazarite except in piety and health. Jibilah was so displeased with this ruling that he determined to desert.[1]

Clearly, then, the great bond of union was Islam. Nevertheless some superiority was assigned to the Arabs as being the mainstay of Islam. Omar in his will left instructions that the Bedouins should be treated well, as being the stock of Arabia, and the substance of Islam.[2] He warned against foreign ways; and indeed Islam was an Arabian movement which united the Arabs against non-Arabs. Omar was the first sovereign who assigned the Arabs their privileges, making it unlawful for them to be made captive. A maxim of his was that it was a disgrace for an Arab to possess the person of an Arab, since God had given them plenty of opportunities of making slaves, by enabling them to conquer foreign countries. All Arab women who had been enslaved, whether before or after the beginning of Islam, were redeemed by him,[3] in virtue of a tradition "No captives in Islam."

Omar would permit no foreigner to enter Medinah;[4] he also divided Khaibar among the Moslems and drove the Jews out. Similarly, he divided the Wádi al-Ḳura and drove the Christians of Najrán to Kúfah,[5] in order that the Arabian peninsula might be free from non-Moslems. He was greatly anxious concerning the Arabian union, and encouraged the Arabs to guard their pedigrees, lest their clan-feeling should be lost. A maxim ascribed to him is, "Learn your pedigrees, and be not like the Nabatæan, who when asked about his origin says from such and such a village."[6]

[1] Agháni, xiv, 4. [2] Athír, iii, 25. [3] Id., ii, 186.
[4] Mas'údi, i, 29. [5] Athír, ii, 280. [6] Khaldún, i, 109.

§ 2. ARABIAN UNION.

Still, anxious as was Omar to keep the Arabs together, he nevertheless urged them to make homes in 'Irak and Syria, one of his maxims being, "The Ḥijáz is no home for you except as a forage-ground; traverse the land which God has promised in His book that you are to inherit."[1] He was aware that there were to be found in Syria and 'Irák Arabs who would associate themselves with the Arabs of Arabia and assist them to victory. The Arabs of 'Irák bore a grudge against the Persians for persecutions that they had been forced to undergo at their hands. It is true the religion of the Persian and Syrian Arabs was Christianity, but in spite of this they welcomed the Moslems and helped them, their patriotism being a more powerful motive than religion. Specially great was the help given by the Arabs of 'Irák, who fought side by side with the Moslems and indicated to them the weak spots in the enemy. So Zubaid of the tribe Ṭay fought on the Moslem side in the Battle of the Bridge, and was killed there, he being a Christian, his motive being Arab patriotism. Similarly, on the day of Buwaib, Anas Ibn Hilál al-Namirí joined the Moslem ranks, bringing with him a great force of his tribesmen, who were Christians, but they wished to take the side of their countrymen.[2] Many of the Taghlibites, who also were Christians, acted in the same way.

Similarly, cases can be cited as illustrating the conduct of the Arabs of 'Irák and Syria who, even when they did not actually join the Moslem ranks as fighters, nevertheless assisted them by counsel or as spies. When Khálid Ibn 'Ukbah went to raid the Byzantine territory, he was met by a Christian Arab, who told the general that, though not of his religion, he would as a countryman give him good advice. So he told him that the Byzantines would fight till midday: if they found the enemy weak, they would annihilate them; but if the enemy made

[1] Khaldún, i, 122. [2] Athír, ii, 215.

a stubborn resistance, the Byzantines would leave them and fly. This observation was of assistance to the Moslem general.[1]

Omar was well aware of the tie that bound the Arabs together, when he urged his followers to conquer Syria and 'Irák. And when he saw how the Arabs of 'Irák had helped the Moslems, he had before him the following problem. The Moslems when conquerors thought of laying the burden of the capitation-tax on the members of tolerated cults, who included the Christian Arab tribes Taghlib, Iyád, and Namir. These tribes objected to such a tax. Omar consulted his colleagues. They pointed out that as Arabs they would never be content to pay the tax, and that having it in their power to do the Moslems damage, they ought not to be tempted to help the foe. This agreed with Omar's own opinion, who made them pay alms like the other Moslems, only stipulating that they should not Christianize their children.[2]

His purpose herein was to maintain the Arabic union, which he regarded as of first importance; and when Al-Walíd Ibn 'Ukbah started to conquer 'Irák and Mesopotamia, he was joined by the Christian Arabs in that country with the exception of the tribe Iyád; this tribe migrated into Byzantine territory. Information of this was sent by Al-Walíd to Omar, who wrote to the Byzantine emperor as follows: "Know that an Arab tribe has left our country and entered yours: either send them back to us, or we will send all the Christians in our country to you." The Byzantine emperor accordingly commanded the tribe to return.[3]

Expansion.—Omar urged the Arabs to conquer Syria and 'Irák, in order to extend the Arabic community, and to employ its aid in fighting Greeks and Persians. He would not permit his forces to venture into the countries beyond these before the year 17 or 18 A.H., this extended sphere of operations being termed by them 'expansion.' So when 'Amr Ibn al-'Áṣ asked for leave to conquer Egypt, a country with which he was acquainted from Pagan days, saying that if Egypt were taken

[1] Agháni, iv, 187. [2] Ma'árif, 193. [3] Athír, ii, 262.

it would be a source of strength to the Moslems, as being the richest, and at the same time the least warlike of lands, Omar would not at first grant permission. Even when after 'Amr's urgent entreaty he had yielded, he still hesitated, and said to 'Amr: "Go, I pray God's blessing on thy expedition, and despatches will reach thee from me: should one reach thee commanding to retreat, before thou hast entered Egypt or set foot upon its soil, then retreat; but if thou have entered it before the despatch reaches thee, then go on thy way, relying on God's aid." 'Amr set out hastily with his army, fearing the arrival of a despatch ordering him to retreat; and, indeed, a letter did reach him at a spot near Al-'Arísh, outside the boundaries of Egypt; so he would not open the letter till he had got to Al-'Arísh, which is within Egyptian territory. The text of the letter was found to be as follows: "In the name of God, etc. From the Caliph Omar Ibn al-Khaṭṭáb to 'Amr Ibn al-'Áṣ, on whom be God's peace and blessings. If this my letter reach thee before thou hast entered Egypt, return; but if thou hast already set foot on Egyptian soil, go on, and know that I will reinforce thee." So he went on and conquered the country.

When the Moslems conquered Ahwáz, Omar said he wished there were a mountain of fire between the Moslems and Fars, so that neither the Persians nor the Moslems could get at each other. In a similar strain he forbade the Moslems to cross the sea. When a Moslem force thought of settling in any place or forming a camp in a conquered district, he always commanded them to erect their dwellings nowhere where they would be separated by water from the capital (Medinah). It must be somewhere where he would be able to come to them on his camel. He was clearly herein adhering to his Arabic patriotism, and anxious that the centre of Islam should continue to be in Arabia. Even when he was compelled by circumstances to assent to expansion, he maintained his former opinion with regard to the Ḳuraish, whom he confined to Medinah, and would not permit to go away. The worst thing he feared for the nation, he used to say, was dispersion in foreign countries. If ever a man came and asked for leave to join a foray, Omar would reply, "Thou hast raided sufficiently with the Prophet of God; rather than thou shouldst go raiding to-day it were better for thee to quit the world." This of course was meant only for the Kurashite refugees. When 'Uthmán came to the throne he relaxed the rule, and most of them joined Mu'áwiyah in Syria, or spread over various countries.[1]

The policy of Omar then aimed at restricting the Arabs to the Arabian peninsula, Syria, and 'Irák, while the Kuraish were to remain in Medinah, as the centre of Islam, of which they were the source and the foundation. He was, however, unable to arrest the wave of conquest, and had finally to countenance the expansion.

That patriotism which Islam maintained was equivalent to the bond of Arabic union, whence the two terms (Islamic union and Arabian union) were synonymous at this time, especially among the nations that were subject to the domination of the Caliphs. So with the Syrians the word Ṭayyáyúthá means both 'Moslems' and 'Arabs.'[2] The difference introduced by Islam was that in pagan days the Arabs formed a variety of nationalities according to their different pedigrees, whereas in Islamic days they became a single nationality, thinking of themselves as Arabs, and forgetting the founders of the individual tribes, in accordance with the spirit of Islam. For pride of pedigree, pride in piety was substituted; and within Islam itself fresh bonds of a subsidiary sort were started such as had been unknown before.

§ 3. Classes of Arabs within Islam.

When the Prophet started his mission he required listeners and helpers. There gathered round him many of his tribe, who believed his assertions and gave him their aid; some of them migrated to Abyssinia, and all migrated to Medinah with him,

[1] Athír, iii, 90. [2] Hilál, xiii, pt. 2.

and took the name Emigrants. They were the earliest class of Moslem. When he came to Medinah the people of that city believed him and helped him, and these received the name Helpers. These formed another class. The two together were called Companions of the Prophet. These were afterwards further subdivided into a number of companies, united by some special bond, consisting in some special circumstance common to them all, connected in some way with the furtherance of Islam. Thus the battle of Badr being of great consequence for the support of the new religion, those Companions who took part in that battle formed a special class, who received the name Badris. Another class was formed by those persons who took part in the battle of Kádisiyyah, which determined the fate of Persia: these were called the Ḳádisiyyah Veterans. Special privileges were assigned by the Moslems to the members of each of these classes; and the persons who had taken part in either of these fights were entitled to higher pay than the others.

Something of the same sort holds good of those who took part in the taking of Meccah, and the other battles that determined the fate of Islamic parties, such as the battle of the Camel and the battle of Ṣiffín. 'Alí's followers paid special honour to those who had fought in the former of these battles, since in it the partisans of 'Alí were victorious, whereas for a similar reason Mu'áwiyah's followers paid honour to those who had fought in the second. Mu'áwiyah gave such persons extra pay.

Another ground for distinction was priority in migrating to Medinah, or in swearing allegiance to the Prophet. So we get as special classes those who swore at 'Aḳabah and those who were in the Cave. Those who accompanied the Prophet before the Oath of Agreement (at Hudaibiah) were regarded as superior to those who joined the Prophet after that date. A further series of distinctions were such as were produced by religious or administrative circumstances, such as 'Those who knew the Koran by heart,' 'Readers of the Koran,' 'Those whose hearts were united' (i.e. persons bribed to accept Islam),

Governors, Judges, Epigoni (i.e. the second generation of Moslems), Successors of the Epigoni, etc.

Clan-feeling, or the patriotism of descent, did not entirely cease after the introduction of Islam, but it was turned into a religious direction. The noblest pedigree came to be that which was nearest to the Prophet's tribe, Ḳuraish; members of that tribe were not only regarded as exceeding others in nobility, but they had the priority for offices and commands, as well as pay, especially after the propagation of the tradition "The Sovereigns are of Ḳuraish."[1] Members of the tribe were supposed to possess various natural privileges over the rest of mankind, e.g., Ḳurashite women can (it was supposed) conceive after the age of 60, and Arab women after 50, whereas in the case of others the latter even is impossible.[2] No daughter of a Ḳurashite woman could become a slave-girl;[3] no Ḳurashite could possibly be a free-thinker;[4] no Ḳurashite should study deeply anything but sacred history.[5] It was, indeed, very long before any disputed the right of the Ḳuraish to the sovereignty.

Each of the above-mentioned classes of the Companions of the Prophet, both Emigrants and Helpers, had special interests and special partisans, especially in the Umayyad period, when the awe inspired by the prophetic office had departed, and the spirit of pagan times had returned. The Refugees and Helpers began to remember the old disputes between the 'Adnán and Ḳaḥṭán, the former being of the first nationality (Muḍar), whereas the latter (Aus and Khazraj) were of the second. These two parties were apt to range themselves on opposite sides in the disputes that broke out, e.g., the Helpers ranged themselves with 'Alí and the bulk of the Refugees with Mu'áwiyah. As of old, their disputes took the form of mutual satire and boasting-matches.

The Helpers—the people of Medinah—were among the bravest of mankind, and formed an elective council, who were authorized to select a sovereign, and whose ruling bound the

[1] 'Iḳd Faríd, ii, 40. [2] Aghání, xiv, 88. [3] Ibid., xiv, 110.
[4] Ibid., xiv, 60. [5] Jáḥiẓ, Bayán, i, 151.

rest of the community: they formed the party of 'Alí and the rest of his house. When Mu'áwiyah endeavoured to possess himself of the sovereignty, the people of Medinah were his most vehement opponents, and thereby incurred the detestation of his partisans, who tried by all means to humiliate them; they would even try to deprive them of the title Helper. A certain Helper, it is said, asked to be introduced to Mu'áwiyah's presence. The chamberlain proceeded to announce some Helpers. 'Amr Ibn al-'Áṣ, who was present, asked the Caliph what that title meant, and requested that their original tribal names should be brought into use again.

§ 4. Policy of the Pious Caliphs.

During the time of the Pious Caliphs Islam had no political sovereignty, the Caliphate being a religious office, with rules based on piety, mercy, justice, etc., in a style to which no age can show any parallel. The hero of this age, indeed we may say the hero of Islam, was Omar Ibn al-Khaṭṭáb, whose acts and judgments were of a sort rarely united in an individual. His virtues are well known and are recorded in many books. Abu Bakr would not have been inferior to him, had it not been for the short duration of his rule. His services to Islam are sufficiently characterized by his defeat of the Apostates, i.e., the Arabs who revolted from Islam after the Prophet's death, when the Moslems were afraid that their empire would melt away, it being still in its infancy. Abu Bakr fought strenuously with the Apostates, and saved the religion. The same is also true of 'Alí and 'Uthmán.

(*a*) *Abu Bakr.*—The age of the Pious Caliphs is the real golden age of Islam. The Caliphs of this period are celebrated for temperance, piety, and justice. When Abu Bakr was converted he was in possession of 40,000 dirhems, an enormous fortune at that time, and he spent the whole of it in furthering Islam, as well as what he made in trade. When Caliph he kept a treasury, but expended all its contents on the Moslems, and at his death nothing was found remaining therein save one dinar. He would ordinarily walk on foot to his house at Sunkh, on the outskirts of Medinah, and scarcely ever rode his horse. When he came to Medinah he would conduct public prayer, and return in the evening to Sunkh. Each day he would go early to market, and buy and sell ; he had also a small flock, which he would at times lead to pasture himself. Before he became Caliph he was in the habit of milking the sheep for his tribe, and when he had attained that dignity, hearing a slave-girl regret that she and her household would not get sheep milked for them gratis, he assured her that he would not get sheep milked for them gratis, he assured her that he would continue to do the milking, and that he hoped his new dignity would cause no change in his conduct. Six months after he became Caliph he came to live in Medinah, and asserted that it was impossible while driving a trade to look after the concerns of the Moslems, since the latter required undivided attention. He therefore gave up his business, and lived on the 6,000 dirhems which was allowed him yearly as stipend. At his death he ordered that a small estate which belonged to him should be sold, and the proceeds returned to the Moslem community as a set-off for the sums which he had taken from them.

(b) Omar Ibn al-Khattab. -- In his time various countries were conquered, spoil multiplied, the treasures of the Persian King and the Roman Emperor were poured in streams before his troops, nevertheless he himself manifested a degree of abstemiousness and moderation at no other time attained. Thus it is stated that he would address the people clad in a garment patched with leather. When he had spent his allowance, and required more money, he would go to the keeper of the treasury and borrow some, promising to pay it back out of the next instalment of his stipend. He was a severe guardian of the property of the Moslems, which he would expend on objects of public utility, He managed both religious and political matters himself; he occupied himself personally with spreading the faith, with teaching the Arabs the articles of religion, and going from street to street to read the Koran and exhort his hearers to

piety. He was himself the first to practise what he preached. He assigned a penalty of 80 stripes for the drinking of wine. He would send Readers of the Koran to the Bedouins to instruct them in the sacred book, and presently send examiners to test their knowledge; if a man were found to know nothing of the Koran he would be beaten, sometimes to death.[1] He kept sharp scrutiny of his governors and generals, and inquired strictly into their conduct. If any of them showed a tendency to deviate from the straight path he would bring them back into it, without respect of persons; even the famous General Khálid Ibn al-Walíd was not spared. On one occasion, when he was supposed to have been guilty of some improper act, he was summoned to appear before Omar, who rebuked him and threatened him as if he had been a slave, and Khálid did not reply.[2] He at times chastised governors of provinces with the rod, or rated them, and not one of them would venture to offer any opposition. He used to punish with special severity those who drank wine or coveted the property of the Moslems. Nevertheless, he treated the Moslems in a fatherly way, and would often entertain them at tables in parties of ten. When he despatched his generals on expeditions, he would visit their houses and see that their families wanted for nothing. He was just to all mankind and kindly even to non-Moslems. Discipline was maintained everywhere during his reign, and all who either entered the Moslem community or abode under the Moslem flag were content and satisfied. He kept an iron hand on the reins of government; when he was assassinated it was shaken, and revolts broke out everywhere, especially in Khorasan, Sijistan,[3] and other distant regions.

(*c*) *'Uthmán Ibn 'Affán.*—This Caliph resembled the other Pious Caliphs, except for his weakness and subservience to some of his Umayyad relatives, which provoked resentment on the part of the other Moslems, and especially the people of Medinah, for causes that have already been explained. His murder was presently used by the Umayyads as an excuse for appropriating

[1] Agháni, xvi, 58. [2] Athir, ii, 174. [3] Ibid., iii, 60.

the Caliphate to themselves. 'Uthmán, it should be observed, was the first Caliph who amassed wealth for himself: on the day of his death, it is stated, his steward had in his hands 15,000 dinars and a million dirhems on 'Uthmán's account; he was also in possession of estates at Wádi al-Ḳurá, Ḥunain, and elsewhere, valued at 100,000 dinars, to which must be added great herds of camels and horses. In his days the Companions of the Prophet began to amass estates and to build themselves residences, as well as to store up money.[1] Thus they accustomed themselves to comfort and luxury. When he was followed by 'Alí, who reintroduced Omar's asceticism, they disliked the change, and were encouraged to resist by the enterprise of Mu'áwiyah, who dangled before their eyes hopes of gain.

(*d*) *'Alí son of Abú Ṭálib.*—Numerous anecdotes are on record illustrating the asceticism and piety of the fourth Caliph. He was a fervent Moslem, free both in speech and in action, unacquainted with crooked ways, and unable to employ ruses. His sole concern was religion, and the basis of all his actions was the truth. As an illustration of his plainness of living, it is recorded that when he married Fáṭimah, the Prophet's daughter, they had no bed save a ram's skin to lie on at night, and to feed their camel from in the daytime. They had no servant. When he was Caliph some money came to him from Ispahan; this he divided into seven portions, and, as a loaf of bread remained over, he divided that also into seven portions. He wore a tunic too thin to protect him from the cold. Once when he was seen carrying a dirhem's worth of dates that he had bought in a wrapper, some of his subjects offered to carry them for him; he replied that this was the duty of the paterfamilias. Once when asked to describe the proper condition of a Moslem, he replied, "Pinched with famine, dry with thirst, blear-eyed with tears."[2] An anecdote illustrating his justice is that, seeing a cuirass belonging to himself in another man's possession, he brought the man up before the

[1] Mas'udi, i, 301. [2] Athír, iii, 204.

judge Shuraiḥ, yet acted as the other's advocate. When he sent soldiers on expeditions he urged them to deal gently with the enemy, and particularly to see that no harm befell the women.

He held severe scrutinies over his officials, out of his zeal for justice and truth; this was what Omar also had done. Had he come to the throne in Omar's time, when the Moslems were still under the awe inspired by the Prophet, and still zealous believers, he would probably have enjoyed a longer reign; but when he became sovereign, men's dispositions had already been spoiled, and political ambition was rife. The most ambitious and the most astute of all was Mu'awiyah son of Abú Sufyán, who got a party together by his liberality, his plotting, and his unscrupulousness; while 'Alí was alienating his own followers by his scrutiny of the conduct of his governors and generals, and his exactitude in religious matters and in all that could appertain to piety. Most of the Companions of the Prophet therefore abandoned his cause, including even his cousin 'Abdallah Ibn 'Abbás, his governor at Basrah. 'Alí was informed of this defection by Al-Aswad al-Du'alí, and wrote to 'Abdallah charging him with disloyalty, but without mentioning the name of his accuser. His reply was, "The information which has reached you is false; I am keeping a firm hand on my subjects." 'Alí replied, "Give me an account of the tribute which you have received, stating from whom you took it, and how you have disposed of it." Ibn 'Abbás wrote back, "I see that you rate at a high figure the losses which I have endured from the people of this place; you had better send there as governor whom you please, for I am about to leave." 'Abdallah thereupon called together his relations on the mother's side, the Banu Hilál Ibn 'Ámir, and the whole body of the Kaisites joined him; he then brought a great sum of money, and told them that this was their joint pay. The people of Baṣrah then followed him to Meccah,[1] and neither 'Alí nor his party got any profit from him. 'Alí's treatment

[1] Athír, iii, 196.

of his lieutenants was precisely similar to what Omar's had been, only the times had changed. So Mu'áwiyah proceeded to win partisans by gifts, and to gain over the Caliph's generals by ruses.

Further, it should be remembered that Omar's followers had been no less zealous and fervid than himself; there still remained with them the old Bedouin virtues of pride, chivalry, and loyalty, and to these Islam had been added, so as to culminate the forces leading to unity, vigour, and progress.

The policy of the Pious Caliphs was, notwithstanding all this, not of the sort which suits the needs of civilization, or is required by the theory of a monarchy. It was a religious sovereignty, suitable for a few rare individuals, and conditions such as have rarely occurred. Those conditions comprised the Islamic union, religious fervour, Bedouin pride, Arabian chivalry, all of which being united at one time, and harmonized with each other, produced a series of miracles. Thus Islam was propagated and the world conquered in little more than ten years. Those who are acquainted with political science are aware that the methods of the Pious Caliphs would only suit such unusual conditions, and that the change from a religious to a political sovereignty was a matter of natural necessity.

§ 5. Spread of the Arabs over the World.

We have seen how eager the Caliph Omar was to unite the Arabs and weld the various tribes together, and to strengthen the connections between their various habitations, and how he urged them to conquer Syria and 'Irák, because he was aware that those countries had Arabs among their inhabitants, and that if these were joined to the Arabs of the Ḥijaz and Yemen, Islam would thereby gain a great accession of strength. But the same Omar prohibited them from going beyond those countries, and gave orders that if any town were built in the conquered land the site must not be separated by any water from Medinah, he being afraid lest the edges of Islam should be extended too far, whence the fabric might be rent, and also anxious that the centre of the Caliphate should remain by the grave of the Prophet, and that the conquered countries should remain as a source of supplies and wealth to the Ḥijáz. For the same reasons he forbade the Moslems to till the soil, and indeed took pains to see that this prohibition was effective, relying on the tradition "Never has the ploughshare entered a house but humiliation has entered it also."[1] He was also afraid lest agricultural occupation should distract them from military service, it being his desire that they should remain as a standing army for the purpose of gathering land-tax and tribute and maintaining the supremacy. Such cities, then, as were built at the commencement of Islam, such as Baṣrah, Kúfah, and Fusṭáṭ, were merely forts or camps, in which the Moslem soldiery were to dwell, like garrisons or an army of occupation. With the same idea Omar banished from Arabia all the non-Moslem population, wherein he was supposed to be carrying out a dying injunction of the Prophet to the effect that not more than one religion was to be tolerated in the peninsula.[2] Similarly, he prohibited idolaters from taking part in the Pilgrimage,[3] and so freed himself from all anxiety on that account. Had any non-Moslems remained in the peninsula it is likely that they would have disturbed the tranquility of the Moslems, and also have given help to the enemy of the Moslems, as indeed the Christians of Syria and 'Iráḳ gave help to the Byzantine emperors, as we shall presently see.

The political principle at the commencement of Islam was, then, that the Arabs should remain in the countries which they already occupied and their immediate neighbourhood; but the generals who had conquered Syria and 'Iráḳ, having tasted the sweets of easy victory, would not leave Omar alone till he had granted them permission to make further conquests, as we have seen. Omar, remaining in Medinah, wished to keep in touch with the limits of his empire, and to restrain

[1] Khaldun, i, 119. [2] Hishám, ii, 195. [3] Id., iii, 50.

it within bounds, while his associates wished to extend it east and west, till at last he was compelled to assent, and to countenance expansion; and, indeed, the Arabs spread abroad and conquered Egypt, Persia, Africa, etc. When 'Uthmán came to the throne he gave the Ḳuraish leave to quit Medinah, of which they availed themselves. The Arabs dispersed over all the countries that have been mentioned, their numbers at that time not exceeding 200,000,[1] these being the Moslem army, the defenders of the new kingdom, who also had the right to enjoy its fruits, the population of that kingdom exceeding a hundred millions, and their power being menaced by the Byzantine empire.

§ 6. Growth of the Population by the increasing Birth Rate.

In pagan times the number of the Arabs was small as compared with what it grew to in Islamic times: the greatest army ever got together in pagan days is thought not to have exceeded 8,000 men, who formed the army on the day of Ṣafakah.[2] Those who formed the first Islamic armies and who won the first victories were few in number. Their wide empire presently needing great numbers of men, they endeavoured to meet the demand by raising large families; and that, indeed, was a principle of Arabic patriotism in pagan days. Thus, the Prophet's grandfather 'Abd al-Muṭṭalib, when outdone by other Ḳurashite tribes, vowed that if ten sons were born him and reached manhood, so as to be able to protect him, he would sacrifice one of them. Ten sons were born to him, and he became a mighty man.

The Moslems, then, being conscious of the paucity of their numbers, made concubines of their Greek, Persian, and Coptic captives, and so founded large families. Conduct of this sort is not a bad thing for the early period of an empire, which derives strength from the increasing birth rate. Men vied with

[1] Khaldun, i, 136. [2] 'Iḳd Farid, iii, 78.

each other in the acquisition of slave-girls, and some men had as many as 80 wives at once: thus Al-Mughírah Ibn Shu'bah shared his house with four legitimate wives and 76 concubines.[1] Hence we are not surprised at some of them being parents of 50 or 100 children. Three hundred, it is said, were born to Al-Muhallab.[2] 'Abd al-Raḥmán Ibn al-Ḥakam the Umayyad left 150 sons and 50 daughters.[3] Tamím Ibn al-Mu'izz the Fatimide left more than 100 sons and 50 daughters.[4] Omar Ibn al-Walíd had 90 sons, of whom 60 rode horses.[5] Ibn Sírín had 30 sons and 11 daughters by one wife. We shall presently see that many a dynasty was maintained by the family feeling of the members, sons, brothers, and uncles, e.g. the 'Abbásids and the Ayyúbids.

§ 7. Expansion of the Arabs by Conquest.

In pagan times the Arabs were confined to the Arabian peninsula, with the neighbouring parts of Mesopotamia and Syria. When Islam appeared the Arabs were united in its defence, and betook themselves to conquest; they went far into foreign lands, and stormed their capitals, nor could the prohibitions of Omar stem the tide. Indeed, so far did they travel that they planted their standards on the banks of the Ganges in the east and on the shores of the Atlantic Ocean in the west. Their victories filled the earth. They took the strong cities of the Persian and the Byzantine empires. Accustoming themselves to town life, they developed a taste for luxury, and in course of time their pedigrees became mixed with those of foreigners, whence the old Arabian patriotism began to cool, their vigour departed, and the tribes that had at the first won the battles of Islam and spread it abroad, also failed.

Note.—Names of the tribes which did most for the propagation of Islam at the commencement:—'Adnánite tribes—Muḍarite

[1] Agháni, xiv, 143; Ma'árif, 100. [2] Khillikán, ii, 147.
[3] Nafḥ al-ṭíb, i, 164. [4] Khillikan, i, 99. [5] 'Iḳd Faríd, ii, 258.

branch: Ḳuraish, Kinanah, Khuza'ạh, Asad, Hudhail, Tamím, Ghaṭafan, Sulaim, Hawázin, Thaḳíf, Sa'd Ibn Bakr, 'Ámir. Rabi'ah branch: Taghlib Ibn Wa'il, Bakr Ibn Wa'il, Shakr, Ḥanífah, 'Ijl, Dhuhl, Shaiban, Taimallah, Namir Ibn Ḳásiṭ, etc. Ḳaḥṭánite tribes—Kahlánite branch: Aus and Khazraj, Ghassán, Azd, Hamdán, Khath'am, Bajílah, Madhḥij, Murád, Zubaid and Nakh', Ash'ar, Lakhm and Kindah. Ḥimyarite branch: Ḳudá'ah and its subdivisions; Kalb, Salíḥ, Tanúkh, Bahrá, 'Udhrah, etc. These tribes, at the commencement of the Islamic conquests, did not make themselves homes in the villages or mix with others, but were continually under arms; presently, however, they became more sociable, spread over different lands, and were employed by the imperial government in distant wars and in the administration of remote regions. Thus their pedigrees gradually got lost in course of time, and presently the empire passed out of their hands.

§ 8. Expansion of the Arabs by Migration.

The Arabs spread over the world not only by process of conquest, but often by voluntary emigration, a householder taking his family, tents, and live-stock, and endeavouring to improve his condition by settling in one or other of the civilized countries which had become the possession of the Moslems. At the commencement of Islam various clans of the tribe Khuzá'ah migrated to Egypt and Syria, owing to their own land suffering from drought, whence they were forced to go somewhere to seek water and pasture.[1] Even before Islam this proceeding was known. In certain years, known as the years of Migration,[2] they used to migrate to Egypt or Syria. At times, too, when there was drought, they would direct themselves towards 'Iráḳ or Fars, and obtain dates and barley from the Persians. They made no prolonged stay, however, in those countries, but would return home,[3] fearing the humiliation of subjection to a foreign ruler. But in Islamic days this objection

[1] Agháni, xiii, 6. [2] Ibid., xi, 47. [3] Athír, ii, 228.

no longer held good, as they could very well remain in countries which had been conquered by their fathers or other relatives, in which they had planted their standards, and whose fruits they had appropriated.

Most frequently, however, the reason why the Arabs left the home of their tribes and migrated to some city or its neighbourhood, was an order given them by a Caliph or governor, especially after the old clan-rivalry between 'Adnán and Ḳaḥṭán or Muḍar and Ḳais had been revived—in Umayyad days. When a governor or a Caliph was installed in a country, and was in fear of some other prince, who was supported by a clan, the former would summon a number of members of his own clan, or of some clan confederate with his, and settle them in the neighbourhood of his residence, in order to be able to rely on their aid in emergencies. They would be given free grazing rights, and stipends were assigned them. A case of this sort happened during the Caliphate of Hishám Ibn 'Abd al-Malik, when Al-Walíd Ibn Rifá'ah was governor of Egypt. The Umayyad Hishám favoured the tribe of Ḳais of 'Adnán, because they had helped him to the throne. Only a few families of this tribe were in Egypt, whereas the tribe was a large one, with many subdivisions. One Ibn al-Ḥabḥáb suggested to Hishám to transfer this tribe to Egypt, and obtained leave to remove three thousand of them, and transfer their names to the Egyptian rolls, i.e. so that they were to receive their stipends from the Egyptian Government; they were not, however, to be settled in Fusṭáṭ. They were therefore settled in the Eastern Ḥauf, especially in Bilbis. They were told to cultivate the land,[1] and presently increased to a great multitude.

The Banú Sulaim and the Banú Hilál.—At times the ground for the migration was the desire of the prince or Caliph to get rid of a nuisance. This was the case in the affair between the Faṭimide Caliph Al-'Azíz bi amrillah and the Banú Hilál with the Banú Sulaim, two Muḍarite tribes which, up to the time of

[1] Maḳrízí, i, 80.

that Caliph in the fourth century A.H., had been in the nomad state, located east of Ḥijáz and towards Nejd, the Banú Sulaim near Medinah, and the Banú Hilál on Mount Ghazwán, near Ṭá'if. In summer and winter they used to wander about the outskirts of 'Irák̤ and Syria, and raid the suburbs of the towns, doing mischief to the passers-by; sometimes the Banú Sulaim attacked the pilgrim-caravans going to Meccah or Medinah; when the Carmathians arose, the Banú Sulaim joined them, and ravaged the country with them. The 'Abbásid Caliphs were quite unable to suppress them; and when the Fáṭimide sovereignty came into the hands of Al-'Azíz billah the whole of Syria was in Carmathian power. Al-'Azíz rescued the country from the Carmathians, whom he sent back to their villages in Baḥrain; whereas the two tribes, Banú Hilál and Banú Sulaim, were settled by him in Upper Egypt, on the eastern bank of the Nile: there they abode, but continued to do great damage to their neighbours, being gently treated by the Fáṭimide Caliphs, who searched long for some means of getting rid of them. It came to pass after some years that the Fátimide governor of Africa rebelled, and removed the name of the Fáṭimide Caliph from the public prayer, the robes of State, and the standards; the Fáṭimide Caliph of the time, Al-Mustanṣir, being greatly vexed thereby, was advised by his vizier, Al Ḥasan Ibn 'Alí, to conciliate the chieftains of the tribes Hilál and Sulaim, and commit to them the African provinces, and also send them to take possession. One good thing, the vizier said, must inevitably result: he would get rid of one or the other, the rebellious governor or the vexatious tribes. The vizier was accordingly sent by the Caliph to these tribes in the year 441, to urge them to go westward and take possession of the province: they gladly accepted, crossed the Nile, and went by land to Barkah, which they captured. Other tribes followed them, certain Diyáb and Zughb clans, out of greed: North Africa became the home of these tribes, and they divided up the land among them.[1]

[1] Khaldún, vi, 14.

Similar to the above was the series of events in the case of the migration of the Moslem Arabs to Spain after it had been fully conquered. Its fertility and the excellence of its climate induced many of the Syrian and other Arabs to settle there. Whole families of Arabs migrated to Spain, and left the land they occupied to their descendants. Both the great Arab families were represented.[1] Each tribe took up its abode in a place whose climate and products resembled those of the tribe's original home. To such settlers we must, of course, add such as had migrated thither in Umayyad times as soldiers either in the first expedition or as reinforcements.

§ 9. SLAVES AND FREEDMEN IN ISLAM.

Both slaves and freedmen play a considerable part in Islamic history, having left their mark on the political and military administration, as well as on science, manners, and law. We are therefore justified in devoting some chapters to them.

Servitude in Islam.—It has already been stated that in pagan times slaves were acquired by captivity and purchase. In Islamic times the former was the more common method, especially during the times of conquest, when numbers of captives were consequently constantly falling into their hands. When the Moslems defeated an army or stormed a city, they would make prisoners of both the men and the women with the children, all of which with the rest of the spoil were then divided up. Tens of thousands were often the produce of a single battlefield. A stamp would be put on their necks and they would be parcelled out into lots. Sometimes a single horse-soldier won off a single battlefield as many as a hundred male and a hundred female slaves; in course of time there might accumulate in the hands of a single owner a thousand slaves or more.[2] Naturally princes had more than other folk. Their numbers increased greatly after the time of Hárún

[1] Nafḥ al-ṭíb, i, 137. [2] Athír, i, 147.

al-Rashíd; still, even 'Uthmán (the third Caliph) possessed a thousand slaves.[1]

Ordinarily, however, when a great number of captives had been taken, they would be sold in a mass before distribution by lot, being offered at a hundred or a thousand dirhems a head, though of course the sum varied at different times. Sometimes the sale of the captives taken on a single field took a series of months. The campaigns that brought in the greatest amount of slaves and booty were those of Spain; six months were required for the sale of the booty acquired in one of the battles.[2] After the taking of Amorium the captives were so numerous that they had to be offered for ten or even five dirhems apiece.[3] Also at the field of Al-Ark in Spain so many were taken that a slave went for a dirhem, and a sword for a half-dirhem.[4]

They used, moreover, to regard a conquered country as the property of the conquerors with all that it contained, whether men, beasts, orchards, running waters, or trees. The Umayyads were very clear on this point and expressed it most distinctly. Sa'íd son of Al-'Áṣ called 'Irák the garden of the Kuraish; and 'Amr son of Al-'Áṣ told the owner of Kharibta that he and his people were the storehouse of the conquerors. He regarded Egypt as taken by force. A saying ascribed to the Umayyads is "Egypt was stormed, so its people are our slaves, of whom we can dispose as we will."[5]

The ordinary soldier would sell such captives as he had acquired and pocket the price, being unable to support a slave. Only princes would retain them in their service, until they were either ransomed by their relatives or manumitted for some reason or other.

One source of slaves in Islamic times that was distinct from capture in war was a tax paid in slaves instead of land-tax in parts of the empire, especially Africa, Turkestan, and Egypt.[6] Certain subject peoples (such as the Berbers) used to pay part

[1] Damírí, i, 49. [2] Nafḥ al-ṭíb, i, 213. [3] Athír, vi, 199.
[4] Nafḥ al-ṭíb, i, 209. [5] Athír, ii, 279. [6] Maḳrízí, i, 313.

of their poll-tax in children of their own whom they brought to be enslaved.[1]

The Islamic law with regard to captives gave the sovereign his choice between four ways of dealing with them; he might kill them, enslave them, let them be ransomed either with money or other prisoners, or finally bestow their liberty on them. If they adopted Islam, the first alternative ceased, and only three remained.[2] Which one was adopted depended on circumstances.

Whoever became possessed of slaves by capture or purchase, or otherwise, had the right to retain them, to sell them, or to bestow their liberty on them. A man who had manumitted a slave became his patron. Manumission was occasioned by various causes, foremost among which was the display of piety or zeal in the cause of religion. Hence, when a slave became a Moslem, and made show of sincerity, he was ordinarily manumitted. Abdallah son of Omar I manumitted 1,000 slaves for such grounds,[3] Mohammed Ibn Sulaimán as many as 70,000, male and female. Manumission was also at times an act performed in discharge of an oath, or in fulfilment of a vow, or with the view of obtaining future reward, or as a thanksgiving to Allah for some favour. Pious persons would at times purchase slaves with the view of manumitting them, as an act of devotion. Omar Ibn Abí Rabí'ah vowed in his old age that he would manumit a slave for every verse of poetry that he composed, and often had occasion to carry this undertaking out.[4] At times, too, slaves were manumitted in order to encourage them to fight, as was done by Junaid Ibn 'Abd al-Rahmán al-Murrí, governor of Khorasan, for Hishám Ibn 'Abd al-Malik, at the battle of Al-Shi'b. When the fight waxed hot, and Junaid feared his troops might slacken, he made a proclamation that any slave who fought should be manumitted: many of them, in consequence, fought so well as to arouse the admiration of those that saw them; and the

[1] Athír, iii, 13. [2] Máwerdí, 125. [3] Khillikán, i, 247.
[4] Aghání, i, 64.

enemy was vanquished.[1] Not unfrequently the slaves of a city that was besieged by Moslems were urged to desert and join Islam, with a promise of manumission: this was done by the Prophet himself at the siege of Ṭá'if.[2] At times the slaves came over with a view of returning to their former faith after the termination of the war; but such men were counted as renegades, and outlawed.

Nevertheless Islam came as a benefit to the slave-population, and the Prophet ordered that they should be treated kindly. He commanded that they should not be made to carry more than they could bear,[3] that they should be given to eat the same food as their masters, and that for the names slave and slave-girl there should be substituted when they were accosted the phrases 'my lad' and 'my girl.' The Koran, too, inculcates similar humanity. "Serve God, associating nothing with him; be kind to your parents and relatives, orphans and poor, neighbours near and far, companions near, beggars, and those that are possessed by your hands: verily God loves not him that is puffed up and proud." Islam, on the other hand, encourages slaves to be pious and to be faithful in their service;[4] it also excludes Arabian Moslems from servitude and captivity by the maxim "There is no captivity in Islam," and the maxim "No Arab is to be a slave in Islam." It is also a principle that a slave should be treated as the half of a free man; so when a slave commits an offence, he is to be beaten one-half the number of stripes that a free man would receive. If, however, he performs an act of virtue, his master will receive the reward. When foreign prisoners, Christians, Jews, Magians, Sabians, Samaritans, etc., fall by the fortune of war into the hands of Moslems, then either their relatives may redeem them, or the Moslems may sell them to slave-dealers, or retain them in their service, to perform household duties, to feed sheep or camels, to cut bows, shoot arrows, or pick up fallen arrows

[1] Athír, v, 78. [2] Ma'árif, 97. [3] Makrízí, i, 137. [4] Bokhárí, ii, 59.

in the battlefield, or to recite poetry, or to learn by heart the Koran or Tradition, or for other purposes.

The price of slaves varied with the nature of their acquirements. A slave who knew no trade was worth 100 dinars; if he was a skilled shepherd he would be rated at 200 dinars; a capable arrow-maker was valued at 400 dinars; one well versed in poetry at 600 dinars: these prices ruled in the middle of the Umayyad period.[1]

The serf—or slave attached to the soil—remained in Islam as he had been in pagan days. He was only to be found in the villages. If the land on which he was were given away in fief or sold, he went with it: he had himself no prospect of being sold or manumitted, nor was it in his master's power to do either. He remained a serf all his life, and his children were serfs after him; they became the slaves of the occupier of the soil.

§ 10. Clients in Islam.

Those who remained in captivity, if they embraced Islam, ordinarily escaped slavery. For usually they were manumitted in compensation for their change of religion. Such persons acquired the status of clients. Hence clients were ordinarily non-Arabs, since, as we have seen, Arabs might not be enslaved. The Umayyads, however, applied the term to all non-Arab Moslems, and called clients all Moslem Persians, etc., who having been Magians and members of a tolerated sect, had embraced Islam; as well as all such persons as had attached themselves to the Arabs, or taken refuge with them. They used to call them 'the Red party,' a word which the native lexicographers say is equivalent to non-Arab.

Under Islam the clients became a distinct order in the social system, of considerable historical importance. Since the Prophet said "the clients of a family belong to that family,"[2] they come into the Arabian clan system; and so in another

[1] Aghání, i, 133. [2] 'Iḳd Faríd, ii, 111.

saying of the Prophet a curse is invoked on any man who claims to be the son of any save his real father, or the client of any save his real patron.[1] A man's family, according to Arabian ideas, includes his descendants and his clients. A man puts no less confidence in his client than in his son; for manumission is an act inspired by affection, for which the client is bound to be grateful, whence he makes that new relationship serve as a substitute for parentage, and is called client of So-and-so, instead of son of So-and-so. Or he may keep his filiation to his father but take the title client of such and such a tribe: so Ibn Suraij, client of the Banú Naufal; Muḥriz, client of the 'Abd al-dár; Ḥakam al-Wádi, client of the Al-Walíd Ibn 'Abd al-Malik; Ibn 'Abbád, client of the Banú Makhzúm, etc. The relation was then one of great sanctity, especially where the client lived in the house of his patron: ordinarily, however, he would live away from it, owing to the business in which he was engaged, though in case of war he would range himself under the patron's standard.

Islam owes much to the clients, since the greater number of Ḥuffáẓ (persons who know the Koran by heart), commentators, lexicographers, poets, and scholars were of their number, for the Arabs were distracted from such pursuits by politics and political rivalry. The greater number of clients who served the Arabs in the early days of Islam were the remains of the spoil taken in Persia and elsewhere. Most of them were at that time of tender years, so that they were reared as Moslems and became prominent, they or their children; we may mention forty youths who were learning the Gospel at 'Ain Tamar when it was taken by Khálid Ibn al-Walíd; and being taken captive by Khálid, were sent by him to Abú Bakr, at Medinah, who distributed them among the great warriors, when all of them embraced Islam to be manumitted by their masters. Their children then became of great value to the Moslems as administrators, warriors, scholars, and divines. Among them was Músa Ibn Nuṣair, conqueror of the Maghrib and Spain;

[1] Hishám, iii, 77; Bayán, i, 164.

likewise Mohammed Ibn Sírín, a famous dream-interpreter; Ḥumrán, client of 'Uthmán Ibn 'Affán.[1] Mohammed Ibn Isḥáḳ, author of the Life of the Prophet, was also the grandson of one of these forty, named Yasár.[2] Other examples could be given.

Other examples of eminent men who sprang from clients: Abú Ṣafar, of the captives of Daba in the time of Abu Bakr;[2] Ḥammád, the reciter of poetry, whose father was a Dailemite by birth, of the captives taken by Muknif, son of Zaid of the Horses;[3] Sá'ib Kháthir, by origin of the captives taken when Persia was conquered; the poet Marwán, son of Abú Hafṣah, descended from a Jew taken captive at Istakhr;[4] the grammarian Al-Harawí, originally a prisoner who fell into the lot of some Bedouin Arabs;[5] Ibn al-A'rábi, originally of Scinde; Abu Dulámah, a black slave at Kúfah to an Arab of the Banú Asad,[6] who manumitted him; many other names of learned men might be added.

At times the client was of exalted ancestry, reduced to slavery by captivity, and unable to produce a ransom. So one of Al-Manṣúr's clients was a descendant of the Marzubáns,[7] and the traditionalist Abú 'Alí Ibn Badhímah, and Abú Zuhair, grandfather of Al-Muṭṭalib Ibn Ziyád, were of the blood of the Kisras, their ancestors having fallen into captivity on the day of Madá'in. They were presented by the victor Sa'd to the Companion of the Prophet, Samurah Ibn Junádah, whose son Jábir manumitted them.[8] Similarly, Abú Músa al-Ash'arí selected sixty lads of the families of the Dihḳáns out of the captives of Birudh in Persia, and distributed them among the Moslems, these being persons who had not been ransomed by their families.[9]

The Caliphs and governors of provinces had great confidence in their clients, to whom they entrusted all their business. Most of the chamberlains of the Pious Caliphs were clients,

[1] Athír, ii, 192. [2] Khillikán, i, 483; Ma'árif, 168. [3] Ma'arif, 183.
[4] Aghání, ix, 36. [5] Khillikán, i, 501. [6] Aghani, ix, 120.
[7] Ibid., xx, 82. [8] Ma'árif, 103. [9] Athír, iii, 23.

whether originally Persians, Dailemites, Abyssinians, or Greeks. The earliest client of Abu Bakr was Bilal Ibn Rabah, an Abyssinian slave owned by someone at Meccah, and purchased by Abu Bakr for 5 *ukiyahs,* who afterwards manumitted him. He was the first caller to prayer at Medinah, and was of importance in the history of Islam. Similar was the case of 'Amir Ibn Fuhairah, Murrah Ibn Abi 'Uthmans,[1] and others. The other Pious Caliphs and chief companions of the Prophet similarly manumitted many slaves. Such freedom were ready to sacrifice their lives for the sake of those who had manumitted them, acknowledging that they owed them a tremendous debt. History gives numerous examples of this. When the war broke out between Amin and Ma'mun, Mohammad Ibn Yazid al-Muhallabi was of the party of the former. He was anxious to guard Ahwaz against the followers of Tahir Ibn al-Husain, the general of Ma'mun's forces. Tahir, however, surprised him before he could fortify himself. Being in difficulty, Mohammed Ibn Yazid turned to his freedmen, and asked for their advice. "I," he said, "regard my people as already defeated, am not sure of their loyalty, and doubt whether they will rally : my own intention, therefore, is to defy the enemy by myself, leaving the issue to God. Any of you who cares to desert is at liberty to do so : and,, indeed, I had rather you survived than died." They replied that such conduct on their part would be rank ingratitude : "You have freed us from slavery, exalted us when we were humble, enriched us when we were poor, and are we going to desert you at such a time ? God's curse be on the world if we are to live therein after you !" They went to battle, disabled their horses, and fought to the death before him.[2]

Nevertheless the client remained in a humbler position than the Arab. At the commencement of Islam they had committed to them much business of a sort that required fidelity and loyalty as well as knowledge and piety; and for this they were given yearly stipends.[3] They were, however, excluded from

[1] Ma'arif, 58. [2] Athir, vi. 106. [3] Aghani, 103

those exalted stations which required noble blood and patriotic feeling, such as the Judgeship—that was regarded as above the status of a client. So, when Omar II wished to invest Makḥúl with that office, he refused, quoting a saying of the Prophet, "None shall utter judgment between the people save him that is of nobility in his people"; and acknowledging to being himself a client.[1]

[1] 'Iḳd Faríd, i, 8.

CHAPTER II.

Mode of Government during the Umayyad Period (41–132 A.H.).

§ 1. It has been seen that the fundamental principle of government during the period of the Pious Caliphs was the union of the Arabian race, whereas its mainstays were justice, mercy, and chivalry. Within a few years they founded the Islamic empire, subduing the greater part of the civilized world, their purpose being religious, their weapons piety, justice, and scrupulous observation of the Koran and the Tradition; their aim being the propagation of their religion, and their ultimate object the reward of the next world. Their appointment was by election and committees, whereas the methods of the Umayyads were the reverse of these in every respect.

§ 2. TRANSFERENCE OF THE CALIPHATE TO THE UMAYYADS.

When the Umayyads first began to aspire to the Caliphate, the throne had come to 'Alí son of Abú Ṭálib, the Prophet's cousin and son-in-law; the Moslems regarded him as the person with the greatest claim to the Caliphate on the ground of his near relation to the Prophet, his piety, courage, learning, the early date of his conversion, and his services in propagating it. A rival arose in the person of Mu'áwiyah son of Abú Sufyán, whose father and brethren had been the fiercest opponents of Islam at its rise, and who had only adopted it after the taking of Meccah in the year 8 A.H. They adopted it only because they were compelled, finding Islam already so firmly established in the Arabian Peninsula that there was no chance of resisting it.

Abu Sufyan, Mu'awiyah's father, had led the people of Meccah, had fought a number of pitched battles against the Prophet, had made no concealment of his animosity, and had assailed him in every way possible. When the Moslems had got sufficiently powerful to think of taking Meccah, and were started on their way, Abu Sufyan, with some of the magnates of the city, went out to spy the enemy's movements. They were met by 'Abbas, the Prophet's uncle, to whom Abu Sufyan, now repenting, made the observation that his nephew had grown very great; the uncle then advised him to capitulate, and this he felt compelled to do. Presently Meccah was taken ; Abu Sufyan and his family, including his son Mu'awiyyah, became Moslems, and received gifts from the Prophet to confirm them in their faith.

§ 3. Rivalry Between Umayyah and Hashim.

The reason that led Mu'awiyyah to seek the Caliphate goes back to pagan days. The Banu 'Abd Manaf were the most aristocratic clan Kuraish, the most numerous, and the most powerful. They were divided into two branches, the Umayyads and Hashimites, the former being the more numerous. Before Islam they were of recognized nobility, the last eminent man of the line being Harb Ibn Umayyah, leader of the Meccans in the Fijar wars. He was a man of power and influence in both clans. When Islam appeared, the fact that the Prophet was Hashimite was ungrateful to the Umayyads, and they, in consequence, headed the resistance to him, but without success. Still, they compelled the Prophet to migrate from Meccah to Medinah, where the Helpers--Kahtanites by race--aided him until his scheme was realized. Before his flight his uncle Abu Talib was dead, and his sons joined the Prophet's migration. Presently Mohammad was joined by his uncle Hamzah, then by his uncle 'Abbas and others of the sons of 'Abd al-Muttalib, and the field was left free for the Umayyads in Meccah ; their leadership over the tribe Kuraish was confirmed.

and became additionally strong after the battle of Badr, since in that battle the leading men of the other Kurashite clans perished. Abu Sufyán became the leader of the Ḳuraish, and acted as general in the battle of Uhud, and again in the battle of the Ditch, and afterwards; and when the Moslems became strong and took Meccah, and Abú Sufyan capitulated, the Prophet regarded it as sound policy to deal generously with the Meccans after he had taken their city by force; so he gave them all their liberty, saying, "Go free, ye are the released." Among these persons was Mu'áwiyah, who, like the rest, became a Moslem.

After the Prophet's death, when Abú Bakr was Caliph, the Ḳurashites, and especially the Umayyads, came and complained to him of their being regarded as inferior to the Helpers and Refugees, but were reminded by him that they had entered the fold late and that only by zeal in the Sacred War could they overtake their brethren. Hence they displayed great zeal in the war with the Renegade Arabs. When Omar I became Caliph he perceived the feeling that lay hid in their bosoms, and was anxious that they should not remain in Medinah, so he sent them against the Byzantines, and held out to them the prospects of settlements in Syria. Abú Sufyán's son Yazid was made by him governor of Syria, and with him the bulk of the Ḳuraish wandered thither, where the fruitfulness of the land pleased them; there, then, they remained till the death of Yazíd, when Omar appointed his brother Mu'áwiyah in his place. When 'Uthmán became Caliph in the year 23 he confirmed Mu'áwiyah in his appointment, whence the leadership of the Umayyads continued in Syria as it had been in pagan times in Meccah over the Ḳuraish, the Háshimites being occupied with Prophecy and having cast aside this present world.

§ 4. MU'ÁWIYAH AND 'ALÍ.

The Umayyads then kept their eyes fixed on the sovereignty and honour which the Háshimites had gained by the prophetic office, and were biding their opportunity to seize on the reins of monarchy. And when Omar was killed and a commission appointed to choose another Caliph, the Companions of the Prophet chose 'Uthmán son of 'Affán, who was himself an Umayyad, and doubtless his choice was due to some Umayyad plotting. He was a weak man who favoured his relatives in his administration, and the Umayyads taking advantage of his weakness possessed themselves of the governorships, and also obtained great wealth, to the vexation of the other Companions of the Prophet, who out of resentment killed the Caliph.

This murder was seized by the Umayyads as a means of obtaining the Caliphate, the chief of the Umayyads being Mu'áwiyah, who, as we have seen, held the governorship of Syria for the last two Caliphs. The people of Medinah had already chosen as Caliph 'Alí son of Abú Ṭalib, they being mostly Helpers. Thus the Moslems found themselves divided into two parties, recognizing each a different head—the Helpers, who claimed the right to appoint to the sovereignty a member of the Prophet's house, in virtue of their having aided him when he fled to them from Meccah, and the Kuraish in Syria, who claimed the right to bestow it on the head of the family which had been supreme in pagan days. The majority of the Companions of the Prophet acknowledged the claims of 'Alí, and Mu'áwiyah saw no way of gaining his end save by cunning and underhand dealing, and in these qualities he was the first man of his age. He proceeded therefore to compass the sovereignty, like the ambitious of every age, without any thought of religion. And his efforts were aided by the fact that his rival 'Alí thought of the Caliphate as a religious office, and was of an ascetic turn of mind, with no ambitions save for his reward in heaven. And a further aid was the circumstance that Mu'áwiyah's supporters had outgrown their awe of religion and the prophetic office, and had tasted the pleasure of wealth, had grown accustomed to the first place, and the sphere of their ambitions had been enlarged. Mu'áwiyah's efforts to gain adherents were rendered fruitful by his employment of a principle which he is supposed to have stated in a conversation with 'Amr Ibn al-'Áṣ: "Were there but a hair between me and my followers," said Mu'áwiyah, "it would not snap." When asked to explain, he went on to say that if they drew it tighter he would let it loose, whereas if they loosened he would tighten.

His first step was to press into his service three eminent members of the Companions, who were famed for their diplomatic ability—'Amr Ibn al-'As, Ziyád "his father's son," and Al-Mughírah Ibn Shu'bah. Without their aid he could scarcely have succeeded. At the battle of Ṣiffín, when things were going against Mu'áwiyah, 'Amr saved the day by suggesting that copies of the Koran should be lifted up with a view to stopping the war; he then advised arbitration, and as arbiter deceived 'Alí's representative, Abu Músá al-Ash'arí, and declared 'Alí's election void and Mu'áwiyah's valid—a service in return for which he obtained the governorship of Egypt for life.[1] Ziyád "his father's son" was a man of unknown parentage: when Mu'áwiyah was satisfied as to his talents, he made an adherent of him by declaring him to be his brother, and giving him a place in the pedigree of his own family as Ziyád son of Abú Sufyán (his own father); the narrative of this is lengthy, and a summary of it has been given above. This adoption of Ziyád was the first occasion on which an Islamic law was publicly abrogated.[2] Ziyád was of great help to Mu'áwiyah in governing 'Iráḳ and Fars. Al-Mughírah Ibn Shu'bah has the distinction of being the first Moslem forger of false coin, and the first who gave a bribe.[3] It was he who encouraged Mu'áwiyah to proclaim as his heir his son Yazíd, making the Caliphate a hereditary office.

The assistance of these and other eminent leaders was gained by Mu'áwiyah by diplomacy and by offering inducements: Egypt was given in fief to 'Amr, Fars to Mughírah, whereas of Ziyád he made a brother. He was easygoing in the scrutiny of

[1] Maḳrízí, i, 300. [2] Athír, iii, 225. [3] Ma'árif, 189.

his lieutenants, and winked at malversation,[1] while bestowing on them lavish honours. Had 'Alí displayed any similar qualities, the Moslems would have been on his side, but 'Alí was a sharp scrutinizer, obstinate in carrying out his own ideas, and unable to swerve from what his conscience dictated. Similar had been the character of the first two Caliphs, but in their days religious fanaticism and Arab patriotism were still in their bloom: a word from their Caliph was sufficient for them. 'Alí's conduct was regarded by his contemporaries as weakness, and his partisans gradually deserted him for Mu'áwiyah. Of these deserters the first was Al-Mughírah Ibn Shu'bah: he came to 'Alí the day on which the latter had been proclaimed Caliph, while Mu'áwiyah was watching for an opportunity of dethroning him, and advised 'Alí to deal gently with Mu'áwiyah and refrain from cashiering him till he ('Alí) was quite secure in his throne, when he might cashier Mu'áwiyah if he so pleased; 'Alí did not assent, so Al-Mughírah came again on the following day and treacherously advised him to cashier Mu'áwiyah, as he wished to do. Al-Mughírah thereupon deserted to Mu'áwiyah, and became one of his most zealous supporters.

Quite similar was 'Alí's treatment of his cousin Abdallah Ibn 'Abbás, whom, as we have seen, 'Alí by his conscientious scrutiny vexed and alienated from his cause; when 'Alí was assassinated, his son Al-Ḥasan regarded himself as unequal to the task of opposing Mu'áwiyah, and he, therefore, conceded the Caliphate to him, whence Mu'áwiyah's seat became firm. This happened in the year 41. In the sequel the fortunes of the 'Alids and Umayyads reproduced those of 'Alí and Mu'áwiyah: the unscrupulous side was always the winning side, and the 'Alids passed most of their time in fear and exile, and the majority of them died violent deaths, notwithstanding that they were persons of piety, worth, and probity. Whence we may infer that religion and politics do not go together, save in rare cases, and that their union in the days of the Pious Caliphs was

[1] Athír, iii, 260.

an accident such as is unlikely to recur. Still, the word political is scarcely applicable to the dynasty of the Pious Caliphs, whose sovereignty was religious in type.

§ 5. The Ambition of the Umayyads.

The pivot on which the policy of the Umayyads turned, and the object which they regularly held in view, was the recovery of the sovereignty which they had enjoyed in pagan days. They cared little for the difficulties that stood in the way of the realization of that end, and the ghastly character of the means to be employed in its accomplishment. Accomplish it they did; and in their days the Islamic Empire grew strong, stronger than ever it was in 'Abbásid times.[1] They wished to enjoy the sovereignty exclusively. The most autocratic of all was 'Abd al-Malik Ibn Marwán, whose motto was "There is not room for two stallions in one thicket."[2]

The Umayyad desire for exclusive sovereignty, while others existed who had a better right to it than they, led them to commit many acts which blacken their memories. The two instruments whereby they succeeded in acquiring autocracy in the face of all their rivals were the clan-feeling of the Ḳurashites, and pressing into their service the other clan-feelings. These lie at the base of all that is known of Umayyad politics.

§ 6. Arab Patriotism in Umayyad Days.

The Arabs and the Ḳuraish.—In the pagan period Arabic patriotism was confined to the tribes; when Islam arose, that form of patriotism was forgotten, and the Arabs were united under the name Islam, or the Islamic community. And during the period of the Pious Caliphs this name included all the Arabs with their different tribes and clans; and, indeed, when the Umayyads aspired to autocracy, and seized on the Caliphate,

[1] Fakhrí, 25. [2] Athír, vi, 91.

they displayed a sort of chauvinism in favour of the Arabs, maintained the obligations of Bedouin life, held firmly to Bedouin customs, and allowed Bedouin asperity to characterize their government and affect their policy, albeit the Bedouin virtues which have been mentioned had disappeared. Of all the principles of pagan days the only one which they maintained was patriotism towards their tribe, Ḳuraish, and preference for their family over others. This aroused much envy in the breasts of those other tribes that had been of importance in pagan days, and been deprived of it by Islam; especially was this the case with the people of Baṣrah and Kúfah, as well as Syria, most of the Arabs who settled in these places having been ill-disposed towards Islam and having associated but little with the Prophet, and so having scarcely experienced the refining influence of his character, while retaining the old wildness and clan-patriotism of pagan times. When the Umayyads became firmly seated, these tribes found themselves under the thumb of the 'Refugees' and 'Helpers,' members of the tribes Ḳuraish, Kinánah, Thaḳíf, Hudhail, the people of Ḥijáz, and the people of Yathrib: to this condition they strongly objected, remembering the nobility of their ancestry, the numbers of their families, and how they had borne the brunt of the Byzantine and Persian powers. The tribes of which we are speaking included Bakr Ibn Wá'il, 'Abd Ḳais Ibn Rabí'ah, Kindah, Azd, all Yemenite; with Tamím and Ḳais of Muḍar. They began to detract from the Ḳuraish, and to display open hostility towards them. Thus clan-patriotism, similar to what had existed in pagan times, was restored.

This renewed patriotism, then, began with the general aversion of the Arabs to the Ḳuraish, occasioned by envy of that tribe, as we have mentioned, and by the fact that the Kuraish assumed absolute sovereignty to the exclusion of the rest of the Companions of the Prophet and the succeeding generation, and that they claimed the whole of the booty for themselves and such members of the Yemenite or 'Adnánite tribes as Mu'áwiyah thought fit to conciliate. The first dispute of this sort that arose in Islam was in the time of 'Uthmán. When Sa'íd Ibn al-'Áṣ had been appointed by this Caliph governor of Kúfah, he selected the chief Kúfans, and the people who had fought at Ḳádisiyyah, and the Kúfan Koran-readers to keep him company. These persons would sit with him at night, having among them members of all the tribes. The Umayyads and other Companions of the Prophet had by this time commenced owning landed property and building mansions, the Umayyads being able to carry on these operations on a vaster scale than others owing to their relationship with the Caliph. It happened that at one of these entertainments one of those present made mention of the liberality of Ṭalḥah son of Ubaidallah, an eminent Companion of the Prophet. Sa'íd observed that "a man with an estate like Nishastaj may well be liberal; had I an estate of the sort, God would have bestowed abundance on you all out of it." The estate to which he referred was a vast one in Kúfah, producing a vast revenue, purchased by Ṭalḥah of some Kúfans who had taken up their residence in the Ḥijáz with some property of his own at Khaibar.[1] He had then cultivated the estate with care, and increased the revenue.

When Sa'íd said this, a young man who was present rose up and said, "I wish Milṭáṭ here were yours!" Miltáṭ was land belonging to the Persian kings in the neighbourhood of Kúfah on both banks of the Euphrates. Another of those present, not a member of the Kuraish, rose and rebuked the young man, for whom his father made excuse, saying, "He is a lad, don't be severe with him." "How dare he," said they, "want our *Sawád?*" Sa'íd replied that the *Sawád* was the Garden of the Kuraish. Al-Ashtar al-Nakha'í, a Yemenite, and a vehement partisan of 'Alí son of Abú Tálib, then said angrily to Sa'íd, "Do you aver that the Sawád which God has given us by our swords is your and your friends' garden?" Hereupon 'Abd al-Rahmán al-Asadí, of Sa'íd's bodyguard, said to him, "Do you bandy words with your commander?" and

[1] Yáḳút, iv, 783.

rebuked him coarsely. Thereupon Al-Ashtar made a sign to his friends, who leaped on 'Abd al-Rahmán, and trampled on him so violently that he fainted; they then dragged him by the feet and sprinkled water on him till he recovered, when he said to Sa'íd, "Your choice entertainers have killed me." Sa'íd determined to have no more nightly gatherings.[1]

From that time relations became strained between the Kuraish and the other tribes, especially between the former and the Yemenites, particularly the Yemenite Helpers. The Helpers remained constant in helping the people of the Prophet's House against the other Kurashites, as they had done at the beginning of Islam when the Prophet came to them as a refugee, flying from his relatives. The battle of Ṣiffín, fought in the year 37 between 'Alí and Mu'áwiyah, was regarded as a trial of forces between the Helpers and the Ḳuraish. When that battle was raging furiously a Yemenite Helper of 'Alí said, "Ye people, is there any among you that would find his way to God under the spears? By Him in whose hand is my soul, we shall fight you for its [the Koran's] interpretation, as we have fought you for its revelation." So he went forward to the fight, reciting:

> "We fought you for its revelation,
> Now fight you for its explanation;
> Our blows will cause decapitation,
> And interrupt all conversation,
> Till right return to its location."[2]

§ 7. YEMENITE AND MUḌARITE TRIBES.

The bulk of the Yemenites became partisans of 'Alí, excepting, however, those whom Mu'áwiyah conciliated with gifts, knowing that the favour of the Ḳuraish and his other adherents would not be sufficient. He therefore made overtures to the tribe of Kalb, and married one of their women, named Baḥdal, who became the mother of his son Yazíd. He easily

[1] Athír, iii, 72, 97. [2] Mas'údi, ii, 16.

obtained their help against the murderers of ' Uthman, because ' Uthman's wife was also one of their tribe ; but he also won them over with presents, so that they fought on his side. When he succeeded in his wars, and was firmly seated on the throne, many tribes, both Mudarite and Yemenite, joined his party, and Kalb remained faithful to his son Yazid after his death, Yazid being their nephew on the mother's side.

When Yazid died Ibn al-Zubair remained in Meccah, as a claimant of the Caliphate ; dissension arose among the Umyyads as to which they should choose--Khalid son of Yazid or Marwan Ibn al-Hakam, both of them Umayyads Ibn Zubair had no his side the Kaisites (a division of Mudar) whereas the Kalbites of Yemen were on the side of Khalid owing to his father's connexion with them. Certain Umayyad then came forward and brought objections against Khalid on the score of youth, so the Umayyads agreed on Marwan, who was of mature years. Khalid, however, was to succeed him. Then came the battle of Marj Rahit, between the followers of Ibn Zubair and Marwan, respectively Kais and Kalb. Marwan won the battle, and so his Chaliphate was secured. Then Marwan died without keeping his promise to Khalid, for he left the throne to his own son, 'Abd al-Malik, a powerful ruler. Kalb continued to favour him, whereas Kais were against him; so throughout the Islamic Empire the Arabs were split into these two parties, called variously Kais and Kalb, Mudar and Yemenite, Nizar and Kahtan. The dissension between them spread through Syria, 'Irak, Egypt, Fars, Khorasan, Africa Spain ; everywhere the two factions were represented, and each got the upper hand alternately, with the changes in Caliphs governors, and lieutenants. The Mudarite governor would promote Mudarites, the Yemenite Yemenites. The balance was perpetually shifting. This distinction was of great importance in every branch of the administration, and even affected the appointment and dismissal of Caliphs, governors, etc. The preponderance of one of the parties at the time would after decide the appointment.

Ḳais, as we have seen, was against 'Abd al-Malik son of Marwán; still, it constituted the main supporter of his son Hishám, who favoured the Ḳaisites accordingly, and introduced their names into the register, i.e., assigned them permanent salaries and stipends. In his days the Kaisites were the dominant party, and the Mudarites as a whole became partisans of the Umayyads, especially after the death of Al-Walíd Ibn Yazíd, whose mother was of the tribe Ḳais.[1] Marwán Ibn Mohammad, last of the Umayyad Caliphs, came forward to avenge his death, hoping to secure their support, in which he succeeded, for the Mudarites supported him unswervingly till his death, whereas the Yemenites favoured the 'Abbásids when they rose.

Within these two main factions there were a variety of other factions that quarrelled and fought: notwithstanding this, the dignity of the Kuraish continued to be maintained and their influence to exceed that of all other tribes. When there was any danger of a province rebelling against its governor, a Ḳurashite governor was ordinarily appointed, who would quickly succeed in restoring discipline.[2]

The Kuraish were also divided, the chief division being that between the Umayyad and Háshimite families. Other Moslems would take up the cause of one or other of these families, whose rival claims led to much brawling; men would spend their time in urging their respective claims till the dispute assumed formidable proportions, and resulted in civil war and bloodshed. The Háshimites were powerful in the Ḥijáz and 'Irák, whereas the headquarters of the Umayyads were in Syria. The spheres of influence varied at different times. Sometimes the dispute began between rival poets, some of whom became celebrated for their performances in this field. The most famous poetic match of the sort was that between Sudaif, client of the Háshimites, and a fanatic adherent of the family, and Sayyáb, an adherent of the Umayyads. These two poets used to go outside Meccah and satirize the rival families: the

[1] Athír, v, 159.
[2] Id., v, 178.

Meccans divided into two groups favouring the one or the other. Hence there were developed at Meccah two great parties, called Sudaifites and Sayyábites; they continued down to 'Abbásid days, when their names were changed into the 'embalmers' and the 'butchers.'[1] Sudaif was the author of a poem recited before Al-Saffáḥ, which caused the death of the Umayyad Sulaimán Ibn Hishám.

§ 8. CHAUVINISM OF THE ARABS AGAINST FOREIGNERS.

Just as in Umayyad times the Ḳuraish were supreme over the other Arab tribes, so were the Arabs generally supreme over the other nations that were subject to the Moslems. To this claim the latter made little objection, holding that the Arabs had the whole merit of establishing the new religion, and constituted its origin and chief part. They did not mind calling the Arabs their masters, and reckoning themselves clients; indeed, they deemed loyalty and affection towards the Arabs a duty incumbent on them, in accordance with the tradition of the Prophet, "God hates him who hates the Arabs."[2] Often, too, they would acknowledge the superiority of the Arabs to themselves in intellect, common-sense, and other good qualities. The following anecdote is told of Ibn al-Mukaffa':—This famous author, who was by origin a Persian, found himself in an assembly at the house of a distinguished Persian at Baṣrah. There were also some noble Arabs present. Ibn al-Muḳaffa' started speaking, and propounded the question: Which nation is the most intelligent? Supposing him to mean his own nation, the audience replied: The Persians. He said it was not so: the Persians were, indeed, at one time masters of the world, and possessors of a mighty empire, but they had discovered nothing by the light of their intellects. Next the Greeks were suggested: this also he denied. Other suggestions were then made till all known nations were exhausted, each being answered in a negative by the speaker. At last the audience grew tired, and told him to

[1] Aghání, xiv, 162. [2] 'Iḳd Faríd, ii, 42.

answer his own question, and he named the Arabs. "Though," he said, "I have the misfortune not to be descended from them, still I have the good fortune to know them. The Arabs have attained perfection without having before them any model or pattern. Owners of camels and sheep, and dwelling in tents of hair or skin, they share with each other their food and labour, and are partners in wealth and poverty. An Arab describes a thing intuitively, and it becomes a model; he executes it, and it becomes a pattern; when he would make a thing appear fair, it appears fair; when he would make it seem foul, it seems foul. The Arabs have been taught by themselves, exalted by their own minds, raised by their hearts and tongues. There have continued with them God's gifts and their gifts to each other, till their glory has been exalted, and brought them the fairest fame, and as a crowning prize given them the empire of the world for ever. God's religion commenced with them, as also his vicegerency, and will last till the last day, with blessings for them and among them."

§ 9. THE ARABS AND THE CLIENTS.

Such language as this naturally increased the boastfulness of the Arabs, and their claim to be superior to other nations, and especially to the Moslems of other nations. We have already seen that the Arabs did this, and, indeed, called the Moslems of other nations their clients. Language of the following sort was employed by the Arab chauvinists in reference to foreign Moslems: "Had we no other claim to the gratitude of these clients beyond having rescued them from unbelief, and brought them out of the house of paganism to the house of faith, as in the Tradition 'There shall be men dragged to their fortunes with collars of iron,' and 'God marvels at men that are dragged to Paradise with chains,' it would be sufficient: now we have yet further exposed ourselves to death for their sakes; and who can have conferred a greater favour upon you than one who let himself be slain in order that thou mightest live? Now, God commanded us to fight you, and made it a sacred duty to go to war with you, and after all we preferred to let you contract for your manumission."

They used to dislike praying behind a 'client,' and when they did so declared that it was a special act of self-abasement. The famous Moslem of the second generation, Náfi' Ibn Jubair, when a funeral passed by would ask whose it was: if he was told a Kurashite he would lament for his family; if an Arab, he would lament for his town[1]; if a client, he would say, "God's property: He takes and leaves what He will." A maxim was "Three things only stop prayer: the passing of a client, an ass, or a dog." It was not customary to call them by patronymics, but only by their actual names or sobriquets. A client was not allowed to walk in line with or in front of an Arab in a procession; if they were invited to a feast the Arab would take precedence, and if on any occasion a meal was offered to a client owing to his age, merits, or knowledge, he would be set in the passage which the bread-bringing servant used, that the spectator might not think he was an Arab. Nor would they let a client pray over a corpse if an Arab was present. We shall presently give further details concerning the treatment of clients at this time.

The Arabs, as we have seen, believed themselves at this time to be superior to all other nations, whether clients or members of tolerated creeds, in natural endowment; the others, as has been said, were called by them "the Red," a term often used, especially of clients. In his own opinion the Arab was born to rule, and everyone else to serve; whence, at the commencement of Islam the Arabs occupied themselves only with governing and politics; all other occupations, especially arts and crafts, were relinquished by them to non-Arabs. One of their proverbs places folly with weavers, spinners, and teachers, these being trades pursued by members of tolerated creeds.[2] An Arab and a client had a dispute in the presence of 'Abdallah Ibn 'Ámir, governor of 'Irák, when the client said to the Arab:

[1] 'Iḳd, ii, 73.

[2] Bayán, i, 100.

"God give us few like thee!" The Arab retorted: "God give us many like thee!" Being asked why he blessed in answer to the other's curse, he replied: "Do not these people sweep our streets, patch our shoes, and weave our garments?"[1]

The Arabs took no interest in any form of learning except poetry and history, this last being requisite for government and conquest; calculation and clerical work were left to the members of tolerated creeds and clients; hence, in Umayyad days, Arabs were rarely employed in the public offices, in spite of the Umayyad chauvinism, the Arabs being rarely able to count[2] or to write.

In the time of Mu'awiyah the Umayyads regarded the clients as mere satellites and slaves: when they became numerous Mu'awiyah took fright, and bethought him of massacring them all or partially. Before actually resorting to this measure he asked the advice of some of the chief statesmen who were also his intimate associates, such as Al-Ahnaf Ibn Ḳais and Samurah Ibn Jundub: he told them that he found this "red race," i.e. the clients, were ousting the earlier Moslems, and he was in hourly dread of an assault by them on the Arabs and the supreme power. "I suggest, then," he said, "that I should kill a large portion of them, leaving the remainder to maintain the market, and keep up the roads. What do you think?" Al-Aḥnaf replied that he could not acquiesce in such a plan; his brother on the mother's side, his maternal uncle, and other near relations were clients: they were closely akin to many clients. Samurah, however, desired that there should be a massacre, and offered to undertake it himself. Mu'awiyah thought Al-Aḥnaf's counsel the better, and desisted. This story illustrates the contempt in which the clients were held by the Arabs, else how should it have occurred to a Caliph to massacre a number of them without offence committed, as though they were so many sheep?

The Arabs were apparently intoxicated with sovereignty and victory, having been raised in little more than ten years from

[1] 'Iḳd, ii, 73 [2] Mas'údi, ii, 114.

camel-herding to the administration of empires ; whence they began to suppose themselves possessed of talents which nature had denied all others save them--a fancy that the ancient Romans had held before them, and one that is held at this day concerning some of the sovereign nations, who are supposed to be privileged by certain natural endowments above their fellows. Thus did the Arabs imagine not only their souls but even their bodies to be possessed of special qualifications : only a Kurashite woman, they said, could conceive after sixty, and only Arab women after fifty ; then the palsy could not strike their bodies, nor any of their offspring, unless the mother were a Greek or Slav,[1] in which case the children might get the liability to it from their mothers. For this reason in Umayyad times they were careful to guard their pedigrees from foreign taint, and all non-Arabs were excluded from all important religious posts such as the Judgeship ; a maxim was that only Arabs were qualified to be judges.[2] The office of Caliph was further closed to the son of a slave-girl, even though his father was a Kurashite. This rule was used as a plea by Hisham against Yazid son of 'Ali son of Husain when the latter was candidate for the Caliphate. "I am told," said Hisham Ibn 'Abd al-Malik to him, "that you are a candidate for the Caliphate, though not properly qualified, being the son of a slave-girl."[3] Nevertheless, his mother was descended from the ancient Persian kings. The first Caliph who was the son of a slave-girl was the Umayyad Yazid son of Al-Walid, who ascended the throne in the year 101. The son of an Arab father and a foreign mother was called *Hajin*, 'hybird.' An Arab girl was not given in marriage to a foreigner, even though he were a prince and she of the humblest clan. Thus a Persian dihkan wished to marry a girl of the tribe Bahilah, dwelling in a Turkish fortress : she refused the offer, although Bahilah was one of the humblest clans. Nothing provoked so much indignation as that an Arab should be made a slave.[4]

[1] Usaibi'ah, i, 150 ; Aghani, xv, 88.

[2] Khillikan, 1, 205.

[3] Siraj al-Muluk (margin of Khaldun's Proll.), 288.

[4] Athir, v. 44 and 131.

At the commencement of Islam the theory of the superiority of the Arabs was an acknowledged principle, only when the Umayyads carried the principle of contempt for foreigners beyond all bounds, and the awe inspired by the prophetic office had calmed down, the spirit of the foreigners began to assert itself, and they gave assistance to the 'Alids, the Khawarij, and every other enemy of the Umayyads. They also thought nothing of replying to the Arab boasts of superiority, and there arose a party known as the Shu'ubiyyah, who refused to acknowledge Arab superiority. They made a point of refuting the arguments adduced by those who maintained the excellence of the Arabs over other nations *(shu'ub)*. In Umayyad days this party was unable to gain the upper hand,[1] but when the Caliphate came into 'Abbasid hands, and when the Arab prestige was destroyed by the result of the war between Amin and Ma'mum, they became prominent and composed works dealing with the censure of the Arabs, as shall be seen.

§ 10. Influencee of the Umayyads of Islam.

The Umayyad dynasty was jealous of the dignity of the Arabs, and careful to maintain the pedigrees. In every government office there was a register for the insertion of the names of all Arab children born in the conquered countries of Arab parents.[2] The Umayyad made of Islam and empire, whereas in the days of the Pious Caliphs it had been a religion. It took the form under their early rule of chauvinism and militarism ; presently it took the form of an empire, which was strengthened by the spread of the Arabic language wherever the Moslems had control; this was done by translating the public deeds from Coptic, Greek, or Persian into Arabic. So Egypt, after being Coptic, Syria Greek, and 'Irak Chaldaean or Nabatean, became Arabic as generation succeeded generation ; the original languages were forgotten, and in these

[1] Aghani, iv, 125. [2] Makrizi, i. 94.

days they are thought of as Arabic countries. A Turk or European who settles in one of them and founds a family, founds an Arabian family.

During the days of the Umayyads the people of Arabia remained Bedouins and half-savages ; the Caliphs would send their children to the desert to learn correct Arabic and to acquire the ways[1] and moral principles of the Arabs ; many of the old fashions of pagan days remained in vogue in Umayyad times, such as the boasting-match, the execration-match, and the recitation-matches at public meetings. Thus the nobility of Kufah were accustomed to go outside the city and recite poems in competition, as also tell stories and recount battles of old time ;[2] outside Basrah, too, there was a valley called Mirbad, where the people of Basrah used to collect, as also other persons for similar purposes, whence the scene resembled the market of 'Ukaz. Rings were formed there also by teachers or poets, round whom pupils gathered, or admires; so the 'Camel-herd,' Farazdak, and their colleagues had a circle at the top of Mirbad.[3] Matches of various sorts took place there, reproducing the clan-patriotism of pre-Islamic times. Never did the Arabs acquire such power and glory as they had in the days of the Umayyads. Their numbers multiplied greatly, and they spread over the kingdoms of the earth.

§ 11. Home Patriotism in Umayyad Times.

Before Islam the Arabs had no national hearth whereto they could gather and which they could defend, since they had no fixed home, being nomads by nature, always raiding and changing their location. When Islam came, and they conquered countries and built cities, and took up fixed abodes in them, they became townsmen, and zeal to guard their homes sprang up in them, and this is what we have termed home-patriotism.

[1] 'Ikd, ii, 258. [2] Aghani, xix, 153. [3] Aghani, xx, 169.

§ 12. GROWTH OF TOWN LIFE AMONG THE ARABS AFTER THE CONQUEST.

The Arabs adopted town-life quite gradually, and, indeed, this had not been intended at the first; they were dragged into it by the current of civilization, since at the beginning of Islam they still retained Bedouin institutions; so when they went out to conquer a country they took with them their wives, children, flocks and herds, as they had done in the raids of pagan days. When they took a city they would erect their tents in its suburbs on the side facing Medinah, the seat of the Caliphate. As we have seen, Omar forbade them to till the soil, and wished to prevent their adopting the town-life, with the view of retaining them as soldiers: men in active service, unhindered by lands or houses, and kept away from the battlefield neither by luxury nor by comfort. The Moslems, then, remained in their suburban camps, just as armies of occupation remain in these days, and they would call themselves garrisons or permanent forces. The whole body of Moslems in the days of the Pious Caliphs was broken up into regiments, each of which was stationed in the neighbourhood of one of the great cities. They were called *Jund* (army). The armies of Syria were four, being stationed in the suburbs of Damascus and Emesa, and by the Jordan and in Palestine, whence these provinces were habitually called 'Armies.' The armies of 'Irák were stationed on the bank of the Euphrates nearest the Arabian peninsula, in two divisions, which afterwards became the two cities of Basrah and Kufah. The army of Egypt was stationed in a camp on the bank of the Nile at the foot of Mount Mukattam, facing the Arabian peninsula, where in after time the city of Fustat was built.

The Arabs—or, rather, the Moslems—abode in these camps, having with them their wives and children, and not mixing with the people of the villages; in the spring they would send their horses out to graze in the villages, accompanied by slaves or servants, yet with some of the masters. When their horses had grazed sufficiently they would return to their encampments, being still Bedouins and raiders, having the centre of their government in Medinah, which was the dwelling-place of the Caliph, and the general rendezvous of Moslems when anything was wanted.

After long residence in these encampments, when the Caliphate came into the hands of the Umayyads, and they preferred Damascus to the Ḥijaz, the Moslems found no difficulty in assigning a second place to Medinah, with the rest of the Ḥijáz, and were quite content to abide in Damascus and the other capitals. Neglecting the injunctions of Omar, they began to acquire land and estates and to plant orchards; and so, in course of time, the encampments turned into populous cities, of which the most famous were Baṣrah and Kufah, Fusṭáṭ and Ḳairawan, among the cities which were actually built by Moslems, unlike the ancient cities which they appropriated in Syria, Egypt, 'Iráḳ, Fars, etc. And so they continued planting and building, and acquiring land and pursuing agriculture, and learning the arts of the townsfolk, such as trade and handicraft.

This took a long time to develop, since at first they did not require any improvement in their material condition, owing to their all sharing in the plunder that was brought to the public treasury from 'Iráḳ and other conquered countries. Wherever a Moslem was to be found he had a right to his share. The plunder of 'Iráḳ, for example, was enjoyed by the people of Medinah and also by those of Damascus. When, however, they began to regard the places of their sojourn as their homes, at the end of the time of the Pious Caliphs, and the persons settled at each capital wished to be independent, this principle injured the people of Medinah, who were accustomed to live by the spoil of the conquered countries. They complained to the Caliph, at that time 'Uthman Ibn 'Affán; they demanded of him their share of the plunder of the land of 'Iráḳ; he gave them in lieu thereof some land in the Ḥijáz or Yemen, or elsewhere in Arabia, that had belonged to the residents in 'Iraḳ.[1]

§ 13. CHAUVINISM OF THE CAPITALS AS AGAINST EACH OTHER.

The home-patriotism of the Arabs at this time was increased by the division of the political parties according to cities. The first dispute that rose between two Islamic cities was that between Kúfah and Damascus, in the days of 'Uthmán son of 'Affán[2]; then came the civil war after his death, the cause of which was the personal inclination in favour of one or other of the candidates for the Caliphate, who at that time were 'Alí, Mu'awiyah, Ṭalḥah, and Zubair. The people of Damascus were on the side of Mu'áwiyah, he being their governor, and most of the population were Ḳurashite. The people of Medinah, the Helpers, were on the side of 'Alí; they were followed by the Moslems of Egypt; Kufah was on the side of Zubair, and Baṣrah on the side of Ṭalḥah. When the battle of the Camel was fought in 36 A.H., and Ṭalḥah and Zubair were killed, the people of 'Iráḳ all went over to 'Alí's side, in addition to the people of Medinah and Egypt. The people of Damascus remained on the side of Mu'áwiyah. When the battle of Ṣiffín was fought and the affair of the arbitration took place, in the year 37, and 'Amr Ibn al-'Áṣ won by a trick, so that Mu'áwiyah was proclaimed, and Egypt was assigned to 'Amr, Egypt became part of Mu'awiyah's domain. When 'Alí was killed in the year 40, and Ḥasan was dead, after the death of Mu'áwiyah and the succession of Yazíd, Ḥusain became a candidate for the Caliphate, and relied on the people of 'Iráḳ, to whom he went; meanwhile the people of the Ḥijaz proclaimed Ibn Zubair. So the Ḥijaz was with Ibn Zubair, 'Iraḳ with Ḥusain, and Syria with Egypt for the family of Mu'awiyah.

In the same way, as the generations succeeded each other, different countries took up with different claimants to the

[1] Athír, iii, 52; Yáḳút, iv, 783. [2] Athír, iii, 65.

Caliphate. Each thereby, in course of time, came to possess a sort of independence, and some special customs distinguishing it from other countries; though it is to be observed that as early as the days of Mu'áwiyah they were so distinguished. Mu'áwiyah is said to have asked Ibn al-Kawwá about the inhabitants of the different capitals, and to have obtained the following reply:—"The Medinese are most anxious to do mischief, and most incompetent therein; the Kúfans start together and return divided; the Egyptians are the readiest to do mischief, but also the readiest to repent; the Damascenes are the readiest to obey a good guide and to disobey a bad one."

The inhabitants of each place had some special political object which we express by the term 'home-patriotism,' as opposed to patriotism of descent, since it might often occur that the people of one place shared a common object, and recognized one common bond of union, e.g., the Baṣrans, Kúfans, or Damascenes, or people of Fusṭáṭ, whilst being in each case a mixed population, made up of a number of tribes. In Umayyad times, however, each formed a single community, with a common cause for which they could fight, yet each town was composed of tribes of varying origin, each with a clan-feeling of its own. Yemen, Muḍar, Rabí'ah, and others were represented, and each of them had a separate and tribal existence. So Baṣrah, e.g., was made up of five divisions, known as the fifths, each of which was constituted by a single tribe (Azd, Tamím, Bakr, 'Abd Ḳais, the people of the Upper Country). The last name included clans of Ḳuraish, Kinánah, Azd, Bajílah, Khath'am, Ḳais 'Ailán, and Muzainah.[1] The case was similar in other cities.

When two places were at war with each other, the members of a tribe who were resident in one place fought their fellow-tribesmen of the other place. So, in the battle of the Camel, fought between the people of Basrah and the people of Kúfah, the tribes of Yemen who were at Basrah attacked the Kúfan members of the same tribe; similarly with the members of

[1] Athír, v, 34.

Mudar and Rabí'ah. Likewise at the battle of Ṣiffín, between the Syrians, under Mu'áwiyah, and the 'Irákites, under 'Alí, when the parties joined battle, 'Alí made inquiries as to the location of the tribes in the Syrian army, and began to urge their brethren in his own army against them; so he bade the Azdites answer for the Azdites in the rival force, the Khath'amites for the Khath'amites, and so with the rest. Where a tribe in his host was unrepresented in the other, he made them fight similarly unrepresented tribes.[1] Thus, home-patriotism got the victory over tribe-patriotism, yet only gained that victory because circumstances compelled it, and this arrangement suited men's interests.

Still, as we have seen, the population of each place varied in number and descent according to the personal circumstances of the governor or Caliph; and the aims of different cities varied similarly, in ways that cannot be enumerated, and wars would break out between cities as they did between tribes. The most famous case of an inter-city war at the beginning of Islam was that between the cities of Baṣrah and Kúfah; in the days of 'Alí and the Khawárij, Baṣrah was on the side of 'Uthman, and Kúfah for 'Alí, while Syria was Umayyad, Al-Jazírah Khárijite, and Ḥijáz Sunnite.[2] These attachments varied at different times and with different dynasties. Further, with successive political convulsions fresh unions arose: the first, as we have seen, was the bond of descent between Muḍar and Yemen respectively; the second, that of country, between the inhabitants of 'Irák, Egypt, Syria, etc.; the third, that of religion, as between members of the various Islamic sects, Sunnites, Shí'ites, Mu'tazils. At times a couple of individuals would represent all these antitheses.[3]

A fact that aided the growth of home-patriotism was that the people of the Ḥijáz had a common centre in the two sanctuaries, and could claim superiority over the other Moslems in virtue of these possessions, with which Islam could not dispense. It is true that the sanctuaries, and especially Medinah, contained

[1] Athír, iii, 121, 149, 171. [2] 'Iḳd, iii, 277. [3] Khillikán, ii, 100.

the followers of 'Alí. The Umayyads, much as they hated the 'Alids, could not avoid visiting the sanctuaries and paying court to their inhabitants, and this set a stumbling-block in the way of their supremacy, especially after Ibn al-Zubair had entrenched himself in the Ka'bah and had banished the Umayyads and their partisans from the Ḥijáz, so that the Umayyads were unable to subdue him, except by storming the Ka'bah with engines. For this reason the idea occurred to the Umayyads of transferring the Prophet's pulpit from Medinah to Damascus, in order that the centre of both religion and politics might be there; and some similar object may have been in the mind of Ḥajjáj when he built the green Cupola at Wásiṭ, just as afterwards Manṣúr built one at Baghdad in order to reduce the importance of the Ka'bah[1]; the political object in all cases being to divert people's affections from the Ḥijáz, and to lessen the importance of the descendants of 'Alí. These devices were, however, useless.

§ 14. Acquisition of Partisans in Umayyad Times.

In the course of conquest the Umayyads, desiring to possess themselves of the Caliphate, found it necessary to conciliate people and to form a party. This had already been done by Mu'áwiyah when he acquired the support of 'Amr Ibn al-'Áṣ, Ziyád, 'his father's son,' and Al-Mughírah Ibn Shu'bah. This support he had acquired by skill and bribes, and this became a principle adopted by the Umayyads as a means of staying the pillars of their rule, which was contested by the 'Alids, descendants of the Prophet by his daughter. Still, no-one rose among the Umayyads comparable with Mu'áwiyah for political ability, as understood by our age; for Mu'áwiyah, if compared with the most famous statesmen evolved by Mohammedan or other civilization, will be found to surpass most of them in sagacity, wisdom, astuteness, especially if we

[1] Mas'údi, ii, 166.

think of him side by side with the other claimants for the Caliphate among the Prophet's uncles, cousins, and grandsons, whose claims were generally recognized by the Moslems, whereas they supposed Mu'áwiyah to be an outcast,[1] who had no right to be Caliph, and who had only adopted Islam of necessity. Nevertheless he gained the upper hand over them all, seized the reins of empire, made the Caliphate hereditary in his house, and to accomplish all this shed very little blood, his chief instruments being tolerance, craft, and liberality.

With regard to the first of these qualities it may be observed that he paid no attention to the accusations launched against him by members of the Prophet's family, even when this took place in his presence; instead of resenting such conduct, he would bestow rewards and distinctions on those who were guilty of it. It would even occur that in his Court and in the presence of his ministers charges would be levelled against him, and he might be accused of having obtained the sovereignty by violence, and 'Alí would be declared his superior. Mu'áwiyah would give a mild answer, and a reward in money, till the speaker joined his party, even though he were a relative of 'Alí. 'Alí's brother 'Uḳail paid him a visit while 'Alí was alive; he was welcomed by Mu'áwiyah, who was delighted to see him, and overjoyed at his preferring him (Mu'áwiyah) to his own brother. He therefore treated him with great kindness and consideration; asking him how he had left 'Alí, he received for reply, "I have left him as God and His Apostle would wish, and find you as God and His Apostle disapprove." Mu'áwiyah's reply was that had not 'Uḳail come as a visitor and suppliant, he would have given him a rejoinder that would have caused him pain. Mu'áwiyah then stopped the conversation, for fear of saying something that would vex 'Ukail, and, leaving his audience-room, he ordered that his visitor should be hospitably entertained, and that a large sum of money should be given him. At next day's audience Mu'áwiyah sent for 'Uḳail and again asked him how he had left 'Alí; the answer this time

[1] Mas'údi, ii, 12.

was, "I left him better to himself than you are, whereas you are better for me than he."[1]

Many stories are told of interviews between Mu'áwiyan and Ṣa'ṣa'ah Ibn Súhán the 'Abdite, as well as others of 'Alí's followers, which give proof of Mu'áwiyah's forbearance; where forbearance would not suffice, Mu'áwiyah resorted to deceit or bribery; nor did there come in his way any person whose enmity he feared, but that person went away satisfied. At times persons came to him to beg, with intent also to deceive. Mu'áwiyah would pretend to be deceived, grant the man's request and a largess as well. So there is a story that before Ibn Zubair became a claimant for the Caliphate himself, he fled to Mu'áwiyah from 'Abd al-Raḥmán Ibn Umm al-Hakam, who had burned his house in Kúfah; coming to Mu'áwiyah to complain, he was asked how much his house had been worth. He replied 100,000 dirhems, and when a witness was demanded he produced a friend who attested his statement. Mu'áwiyah then ordered that the sum should be given him. When the two men had left his presence, he asked his courtiers which of the two was, in their opinion, the greater liar. "I," he said, "know the house, which was a structure of reeds; however, it is my principle, when I hear a falsehood of the sort, to pretend to believe it."[2] Dealings of this sort served to prevent Ibn Zubair and others from making pretensions to the Caliphate in Mu'áwiyaḥ's time.

Very different was the conduct of 'Alí, who scrutinized the accounts of his lieutenants so as to anger them in most cases, and lose the benefit of their assistance; this happened to him in the case of his cousin Abdallah Ibn al-'Abbás, whom he irritated on account of a trifling slander, as we have seen; and while this was going on, Mu'áwiyah was meanwhile bestowing whole provinces in fief on his lieutenants, and, when any one of them came to him on a visit, he would bestow on him endless honours and rewards. So when Mu'áwiyah Ibn Ḥudaij visited his namesake at Damascus, he found the streets

[1] Mas'údi, ii, 54. [2] Agháni, xiii, 48.

decorated with arches containing fragrant scents to do him honour.[1]

Mu'áwiyah was ready to put up with fault-finding and criticism, especially from heads of tribes, chieftains, and representatives of parties, even when their language was unrestrained. Al-Aḥnaf Ibn Ḳais of the tribe Tamím, one of the chief Epigoni and a man of influence, was a follower of 'Alí, and had helped him on the field of Ṣiffín. After Mu'áwiyah's position as Caliph had become secure, he was visited by this person; and Mu'áwiyah told him that whenever he (Mu'áwiyah) recollected the day of Ṣiffín his heart was pierced, and would be till the Day of Judgment Al-Aḥnaf replied: "Mu'áwiyah, the hearts wherewith we hated thee are still in our breasts; the swords wherewith we fought thee are still in our sheaths; advance an inch towards war and we shall advance a foot; walk towards it and we shall rush towards it." Mu'áwiyah's sister was listening behind the curtain, and asked the Caliph who it was that was threatening him; he replied, "One whose anger stirs the anger of 100,000 Tamimites, without their knowing what he is angry about."[2]

Moreover, whenever Mu'áwiyah was unable to overcome an enemy in battle or to win him over by bribes, he was accustomed to resort to poison. Thus he got out of the way 'Abd al-Raḥmán Ibn Khálid Ibn al-Wálid, who was a man of great influence with the people of Damascus, who were attracted towards him by the recollection of his father's exploits, by his own in the Byzantine wars, and by his great courage. Mu'áwiyah, being afraid of him, ordered Ibn al-Uthál the physician to try to murder him, promising, if he succeeded, to release him from tribute for the rest of his life, and also to put in his charge the tribute of Emesa; Ibn al-Uthál got one of the man's slaves to convey to him some poisoned honey, whereof the man partook and died.[3] Thus Mu'áwiyah got him out of his way. A similar expedient removed from his path Al-Ashtar al-Nakha'í (Málik Ibn al-Ḥárith), one of, if not

[1] Athír, ii, 357. [2] Khillikán, i, 230. [3] Athír, iii, 329.

the most powerful of 'Alí's adherents, who had fought bravely on his side at Ṣiffín. When, owing to the intrigues of Mu'áwiyah, the affairs of Egypt were in confusion, but it still remained within 'Alí's jurisdiction, the latter sent this Al-Ashtar as governor. Mu'áwiyah, thinking that if Al-Ashtar were there it would hold out against himself, sent a message to the agent for the land-tax at Kulzum (Klysma), which lay on Al-Ashtar's route, and by which, on his journey to Egypt, he would necessarily have to pass, informing him that if he (the agent) could get rid of Al-Ashtar, who had been appointed governor of Egypt, he would have to furnish no more land-tax so long as both he and Mu'áwiyah were alive. The man accordingly went and waited at Klysma till Al-Ashtar came, when the agent came out to meet him and offered him lodging, which he accepted. Dinner was then produced, and when it was over a draught of honey was brought into which poison had been put; of this Al-Ashtar drank, and died in consequence. Meanwhile Mu'áwiyah had informed the Damascenes how 'Alí had sent Al-Ashtar to Egypt, and requested them to invoke God's curse on him; this they continued to do every day, till Mu'áwiyah was visited by the agent who had poisoned Al-Ashtar. Mu'áwiyah thereupon ascended the pulpit, and told his hearers that 'Alí had had two right hands, one of which had been cut off at Ṣiffín (meaning 'Ammár Ibn Yásir), whereas the other had been cut off just before he spoke, meaning Al-Ashtar.[1] When 'Amr Ibn al-'Áṣ heard the news he exclaimed, "God Almighty has armies of honey." [2]

§ 15. 'Amr Ibn al-'Áṣ.

Mu'awiyah and his associates never neglected an opportunity, and never minded committing murder or any other atrocity with the view of effecting their objects. 'Alí and his adherents, on the other hand, never ventured away from the path of justice and the dictates of honour, which sense of honour on

[1] Athír, ii, 179. [2] Makrízí, i, 300.

their part aided Mu'áwiyah very considerably in overcoming them. At the battle of Ṣiffín the scales were swaying on 'Alí's side, and had this been permitted to go on Mu'áwiyah and his plans would have been done for, and with his ruin the ruin of the Umayyads would have been accomplished. 'Alí and his house would in that case have won a complete victory. 'Alí was kept from victory only by the astuteness of 'Amr Ibn al-'Áṣ, with whom Mu'áwiyah had taken refuge when the battle waxed fierce, and Mu'áwiyah perceived that his side was giving way, and expected defeat. 'Amr was then fighting on Mu'áwiyah's side. The latter bade 'Amr bring out his mysteries, recognising that destruction faced them, and to recollect the government of Egypt. 'Amr advised him to raise aloft the Korans and make proclamation: "Let the Book of God judge between you and us. Who will be left to defend the Syrian frontier if the people of Syria be destroyed? Who to defend the frontier of 'Irák if the people of 'Irák perish? Who will be left to fight the Byzantines, the Turks, and the idolators?" This ruse took in the followers of 'Alí, who stopped the battle and agreed to appoint arbiters. Then 'Amr was able to finish his stratagem, to declare 'Alí's appointment void, and to invest Mu'áwiyah. Had it not been then for 'Amr, Mu'áwiyah's cause would have been lost; and had it not been for the generosity of 'Alí, 'Amr would have been slain in the battle before he could contrive his plot. For the story is that 'Amr had accepted single combat with 'Alí, and when they met 'Alí raised his sword to smite him, and 'Amr, feeling certain that he would be slain if the fight continued, uncovered himself, saying, "Your brother is forced to fight, but is no fighting man." 'Alí, overcome by generosity, turned away his face, saying "How horrid!" And by this device 'Amr escaped.[1] This expedient of 'Amr became a proverb, and is alluded to in the following verse:—

> "Permit not by baseness thy life to be saved,
> Though that was the way in which 'Amr behaved."

[1] Mas'údi, ii, 19.

Nor were 'Alí's adherents inferior to their chief in generosity, piety, and veracity. Such was the character of the Moslems in that golden age, save when men's covetousness led them to espouse the cause of Mu'áwiyah. In 'Alí these virtues reached their summit, and had he only adopted a slightly lower standard he might have escaped from many troubles. Hence the Ḳuraish used to say of him that he was a brave man, but of no counsel in war.[1]

By astuteness, then, and similar qualities Mu'áwiyah succeeded in acquiring the Caliphate and handing it down as an heirloom to his son, after whom it fell to the Marwanides, who were also of Umayyad stock. He was not able, however, completely to cut off the other claimants, of whom the most important were the family of 'Alí. Still, he could quiet them by a peaceful demeanour and by lavish gifts, and they, fearing him, would acquiesce in his rule, while on the other hand they expected that the sovereignty would return to them after his death; when it was found that it had been transmitted to his son Yazíd, the various claimants in Ḥijáz, 'Iráḳ, etc., created disturbances, each one regarding himself as the best qualified. In the year 68 there were collected at 'Arafat four standards, each of them belonging to a pretender to the Caliphate; these being respectively the Umayyad prince, the 'Alid Muḥammad Ibn al-Hanafiyyah, Abdallah Ibn al-Zubair, with as a fourth Najdah the Ḥarúrí representing the sectarians called Khawárij. After them there arose others, yet none but the Umayyads were able to secure possession of the throne, and they succeeded in virtue of Arabian clan-patriotism, and also the trouble they had taken to form a party. The causes which helped them to form a party in addition to what has already been mentioned (Mu'áwiyah's astuteness and 'Alí's feeble counsel) must now be given.

[1] Aghání, xv, 15.

§ 16. LARGESSES IN UMAYYAD TIMES.

Stipends paid out of the Treasury.—The stipend was one of the most powerful agents which assisted the Umayyads to conciliate followers and to break the force of their enemies. By stipends we mean the pay of the soldiers, or the pay of the Moslems, who at the commencement of Islam were all of them soldiers. To each a stipend was assigned, which varied according to the nearness of his connection with the Prophet or the date at which he had embraced Islam, or some other cause out of those specified in our account of the Registers in the days of Omar. It will there be found that even women and children had stipends which varied according to class. The basis of these stipends was the spoil taken from the conquered countries. There was, however, another class of poor Moslems, unable to take part in the wars, who received their stipends out of the Alms-fund, and the Stipend and Alms each had a separate bureau.

The control of the Moslem community was assured by the control over the public treasury; whoever had control of it could count on their attachment. When the treasury was controlled by a sagacious man such as Mu'áwiyah, knowing how to give and to whom, this power would render all others unnecessary, and indeed Mu'áwiyah would increase, diminish, or entirely withdraw stipends in accordance with political expediency; ordinarily he would bestow largesses or redouble stipends where he perceived that some advantage would accrue to him from so doing. His chief fear being that the 'Alids or other members of the Prophet's house might dispute the sovereignty with him, he gave them all most liberal allowances. Omar e.g. had assessed the stipends of Ḥasan and Ḥusain at 5,000 dirhems annually; Mu'awiyah assessed them at a million. In other words he multiplied them by 200. Similar stipends were assigned by him to 'Abdallah Ibn al-'Abbás, as the Prophet's cousin and a formidable personage; to 'Abdallah son of Ja'far Ibn Abi Ṭálib, and eminent and influential sons of Companions of the Prophet, who remained in Medinah. So, while on the one hand he conciliated them by gifts, on the other he diverted and distracted them by luxury from contesting the sovereignty. And in the third place he conciliated thereby the people of Medinah, since the money lavished on these persons was spent in Medinah in procuring various pleasures. Some, for example, would spend their stipends on poets and singers. The most liberal in this respect was 'Abdallah Ibn Ja'far, cousin of Ḥasan and Ḥusain; he used to visit Mu'áwiyah in Syria, who would bestow on him his stipend, after receiving which he would return to Medinah and expend it on the people of the place. Mu'áwiyah, hearing of this, used to favour him and treat him with special liberality, hoping thereby to conciliate the Medinese.

He is said to have paid a visit to Yazíd, Mu'áwiyah's son, after the latter had become Caliph, when he was asked how much his stipend had been. He replied a million dirhems. Yazíd offered to double it. 'Abdallah then informed the Caliph that he had never told anyone how much his stipend had been before Yazíd. Yazíd, hearing this, doubled it yet again. Being remonstrated with for giving a single individual a stipend of four million dirhems, Yazíd observed that it was given to the whole population of Medinah, since 'Abdallah regarded it as a loan for distribution.[1]

This is an example of the lavish liberality of Mu'áwiyah, when he wished to conciliate the tribes; if a tribe fought on his side, he would bestow money on it, though it might be far removed from him genealogically. So he would bestow largesses on the people of Yemen, whose power he feared; whereas he made no distribution to Ḳais, though more closely related to him, because he was not afraid of their power. He even refused members of the tribe who came to him to ask for a subvention. Such a case was that of Miskín al-Dárimí, who asked for a stipend from Mu'áwiyah, but met with a refusal.

[1] 'Iḳd Faríd, i, 110.

Miskín thereupon composed a poem, in which he complaine of this, reminding the Caliph of their mutual kinship :—

"Your brother, stand by him ; the brotherless wight
Is as one who advances unarmed to the fight.
Like wings to a brave man are those of his race ;
A falcon that 's wingless can't go to the chase.
Now risks must be run if you aim at good things ;
And nought can be aimed at that 's better than wings."

Mu'awiyah paid no attention to the verses, because his liberality was always done in his own personal interest. Now the tribes of Yemen had become powerful and warlike, and were formidable to the empire, whereas Ḳais and all 'Adnán were depressed. Mu'áwiyah heard that a Yemenite one day threatened to leave no Muḍarite in Syria—indeed, to drive every Nizárite thence before he loosed his garment. This alarmed the Caliph, who thought he must make the Muḍarites a counterpoise to them. He immediately ordered stipends to be assigned to 4,000 members of the latter community and of other 'Adnánite tribes, and sent a message to Miskín, telling him that his stipend would be sent him if he returned to his own country, but that if he preferred to remain in Syria it would be sent him none the less. Mu'áwiyah also employed the Yemenites on sea and Ḳais on land expeditions.[1] Without such astuteness and tact he could never have kept the two parties at peace.

Something of the same style is recounted with regard to the increase of the stipends of those who took part in important battles, such as that of Ṣiffín,[2] and so gave effective help to the Umayyad cause. Mu'áwiyah increased the stipends of those who had taken part in Ṣiffín, just as Omar did to those who had taken part in the battle of Ḳádisiyyah. The succeeding Umayyad Caliphs followed in the footsteps of Mu'áwiyah, and bestowed stipends on their partisans They even bestowed them on poets, either for the purpose of "cutting out their tongues" (i.e. preventing their satirizing them) or to obtain their aid in conciliating their subjects. Pious persons regarded

[1] Agháni, xviii, 69. [2] Mas'údi, ii, 157.

this as malversation of the public treasury; the money there was, they held, the property of God or the Moslems, and ought not to be given away to any individual. This proceeding was one of those with which 'Alí's partisans reproached Mu'áwiyah on the day of Ṣiffín.[1] When Omar II became sovereign, in imitation of the ways of the Pious Caliphs, he took away the poets' stipends; but after his death the custom was resumed.

Distribution was made to any visitor at the seat of government, even to Bedouins, whence many of them sold their camels and came to one or other of the great cities in order to demand a stipend. It is true the nobler sort could see through the Umayyad liberality, and perceive that its purpose was to obtain a hold over the consciences of the subjects, and indeed for an object which these persons regarded as unjust, and from which they shrank, viz., the maintenance of their own government against the claims of the Prophet's family. There is a story that the wife of one Jabhá, an Ashja'ite Bedouin, urged her husband to go to Medinah, to sell his camels, and obtain a government stipend. The man consented. He drove his camels till near Medinah; here he took them down to a drinking-place. One camel (a female) then shrieked, got loose, and ran in the direction of home, and she was followed by the rest of the drove. The Bedouin pursued them, but failed to catch them. He said to his wife, "These dumb brutes, then, yearn after their home," and he composed the following ode:—

> "Said my consort, 'Abandon your country, and come
> To the forts of Medinah to find a new home;
> Get on the stipendiary register too,
> For that is what men of intelligence do.'"[2] Etc.

(The rest of the verses celebrate the delights of country life.) A saying of 'Abd al-Malik Ibn Marwán is, "The happiest of men is he who has money sufficient for his wants and an agreeable wife, and who has no acquaintance with our nasty courts."[3]

[1] Athír, iii, 150. [2] Aghání, xvi, 147. [3] Athír, x, 183.

The Umayyads paid great attention to the people of Medinah, because they were 'Alí's partisans, and also comprised the Helpers and the pick of the Ḳuraish. When the Umayyad governor of Medinah got the alms collected from different regions, he would give loans out of it to any Ḳurashites who desired such accommodation, who had, however, to give bonds for the money lent them. By this means the Umayyad governor got them into his power, and compelled them to visit him and pay him court. If any Ḳurashite gave offence, the money would be demanded of him. This system remained till the days of Hárún al-Rashíd, when 'Abdallah Ibn Mus'ab informed him about the bonds that were still overdue, and he ordered them to be torn up.[1]

If any Moslem displayed insubordination his stipend could be stopped, and this might be done to a whole city. Thus when Zaid Ibn 'Alí revolted the Caliph Yazíd stopped the stipends of both the Sanctuaries[2]; likewise Al-Walíd deprived of their stipends the family of Ḥazm, because the murderers of 'Uthmán used his house at Medinah as their headquarters; Al-Walíd seized their goods and estates, and they remained deprived of them till the days of Al-Manṣúr, who removed the ban.[3] Many times the Helpers had to go without their stipends, for no other offence than that their sympathies were on the side of the Prophet's family.[4] The Caliph 'Abd al-Malik Ibn Marwán stopped the stipends of the descendants of Abú Sufyán, albeit they were Umayyads like himself; his motive was offence given him by Khálid son of Yazíd son of Mu'áwiyah.[5]

People in consequence felt compelled to gratify and flatter them, although aware that they were opposing what was just by such conduct. In private they would even acknowledge that such was the case. This happened when Mu'áwiyah appointed his son Yazíd as his successor, and made him sit in a red tent, whither the Moslems came to salute Mu'áwiyah

[1] Aghání, xiii, 105. [2] Aghání, vi, 111. [3] 'Iḳd, iii, 41.
[4] Aghání, x, 62. [5] 'Iḳd, i, 132.

as Caliph and his son as Heir Apparent. A Moslem came, and, after saluting them both, returned to Mu'áwiyah, and said: "Commander of the Faithful, if you had not appointed Yazíd your successor, you would have ruined Islam." Al-Aḥnaf Ibn Ḳais the Tamímite was present, and Mu'áwiyah asked him why he was silent. He replied, "I fear God in case I lie, and I fear you in case I speak the truth." Mu'áwiyah said he hoped God would reward him for his piety, and ordered a sum of money to be given him. When he left the Caliph's presence he was met by the other Moslem, who told Al-Aḥnaf that he regarded Mu'áwiyah and his son as the worst villains in existence, only they had got the whole wealth of Islam under lock and key, and only such phrases as he had used could extract any of it.[1]

§ 17. THE SCRUPULOUSNESS OF 'ALÍ AND THE AVARICE OF IBN ZUBAIR.

The Umayyads were assisted in their endeavour to win the affection of the Moslems by bribes from the fact that their rivals, the Prophet's family and Ibn Zubair, were disinclined to give, whether from avarice or from conscientious scruples. The stinginess of both was proverbial.[2] This stinginess often led to their cause suffering and to people going over to the other side. The following is a typical case. Maskalah son of Hubairah, of the tribe Shaibán, was 'Alí's governor over Ardashir-khurah. Finding some prisoners who had been taken by 'Alí's soldiers, and pitying them, he purchased them and gave them their freedom. They were 500 in number, and their price half a million dirhems. 'Alí demanded the money, and Maskalah produced about half the sum. 'Alí, however, demanded the remainder, and his officers pressed Maṣḳalah for it. Maskalah said that if it had been Hind's ~~son~~ (Mu'áwiyah), he would not have demanded payment, and if it had been 'Uthmán Ibn 'Affán, he would have presented him (Maṣḳalah) with the

[1] Khillikán, i, 230 [2] Aghání, xiii, 105.

whole sum. He was assured that 'Alí would not relax, so he fled the same night and took refuge with Mu'áwiyah.[1]

The following illustrates the avarice whereby Ibn Zubair ruined his chances. When his brother Mus'ab had killed Mukhtár Ibn Abí 'Ubaid in 'Irák, and brought the country into subjection to his brother, he came to Meccah with leading men of 'Irák, who had assisted him in achieving this result. Ibn Zubair was taking refuge at the Ka'bah. His brother stated that he brought the chief men of 'Irák, the like of whom remained not in the country, and hoped that Ibn Zubair would give them presents of the treasury money. Ibn Zubair's reply was: "You have brought the slaves of the people of 'Irák, and want me to give them the wealth of God? By Allah, I shall do nothing of the kind." When they heard of this reply, they were very angry, and wrote to his rival, 'Abd al-Malik Ibn Marwán, and betrayed Mus'ab.[2] This refusal, then, was one of the causes of the ruin of Ibn Zubair's government.

The 'Alids were similarly stingy with stipends, except in the case of persons of notable piety, at the very time when the Umayyads were assigning stipends, not only to the men, but to their wives and children. So 'Abd al-Malik Ibn Marwán assigned a stipend of two thousand dirhems to 'Ámir al-Sha'bí, who was not a warrior, and also two thousand apiece to twenty of his sons and relatives, on account of a single tradition which the man had recited to him.[3] Similarly, in addition to their gratuities to poets, they assigned them fixed stipends to be paid at regular periods. Some got 2,000 dirhems, some more, some less. After an encomium they often increased the poet's salary, in order to encourage them to compose verses in their patrons' praise. The governors in every part of the Umayyad empire did the like. The virtuous Caliphs, however, thought a poet had no claim on the treasury[4]; Omar II, if driven into a corner by a poet, would give him a largess out of his privy purse.[5]

[1] Athír, iii, 188. [2] 'Iḳd, i, 119. [3] Aghání, ix, 171.
[4] Aghání, x, 99. [5] Ibid., xvii, 118.

However, even those who were not specially virtuous stopped the poet's salary when he failed to carry out their wishes. 'Abd al-Malik Ibn Marwán was eulogized by the poet Ḳais al-Ruḳayyat, who had already eulogized Mus'ab Ibn al-Zubair in a yet more extravagant strain. The Caliph deprived him of his stipend.[1] Omar I used to urge on the Koran-readers to get their own living and not be a burden on the others,[2] and such advice naturally applied with still greater force to poets.

§ 18. Means of obtaining Supplies in Umayyad days.

The plan of gaining partisans by money presents led the Umayyads to violate many of the principles which had been enforced by the Pious Caliphs with regard to the demanding and expenditure of money. Their theory was that the moneys paid into the treasury were the common property of the Moslems, and that the Caliph or his governor was only in the position of treasurer, whose duty it was to expend them on the common concerns of the Moslem world, while himself retaining a fixed stipend accorded to him as to the other Moslems. As we saw, when Abú Bakr died, his private treasury contained one single dinar; when Omar I wanted money over and above his stipend, he would borrow from the treasury and repay the loan out of the next instalment of his stipend. Omar's theory was that no money should be left in the public treasury, and so he forbade the amassing of wealth, the strangeness of which doctrine has been pointed out in Part II of this work. Omar also forbade agriculture, and declared it unlawful for a Moslem to acquire an estate, since their requirements and the requirements of their families should be paid out of the treasury; his intention being that the Moslems should remain constantly equipped for active service in the field, and that the conquered countries should remain under the public control, supplying land-tax and poll-tax for the support of the Moslems. And for both these

[1] Faraj, ii, 123; Aghani, iv, 159. [2] 'Iḳd, i, 236

taxes he arranged a strict set of rules both for collection and expenditure.

§ 19. The Umayyad Governors.

The Umayyads, being compelled to conciliate their subjects and acquire partisans, and put the tribes in good humour, as well as to build cities, neglected the greater number of Omar's rules, and secured a set of strong-willed lieutenants, being persons who thought nothing of religion nor of rules when intent on their objects; such persons were Ziyád "son of his father," lieutenant for Mu'awiyah, Ziyád's son 'Ubaidallah, lieutenant for Yazíd, Ḥajjáj Ibn Yúsuf, lieutenant for 'Abd al-Malik Ibn Marwán, Khálid al-Kasrí, lieutenant for Hishám Ibn 'Abd al-Malik, and others. The Caliph would write to his lieutenant, bidding him collect money, and the lieutenant would not care how he carried out the order. So Mu'áwiyah wrote to Ziyad, saying, "Appropriate to my use the white and the yellow." Ziyad wrote to the same effect to his lieutenants, bidding them bring all the money they collected to him, and to distribute neither gold nor silver among the Moslems.[1] On the other hand, the governors would reserve some part of what they collected for themselves, and there was no one to scrutinize them, for the Caliphs gave them a free hand in their provinces in order to keep them faithful to their cause. These governors used to amass enormous sums; one of them secured an annual revenue of 10,000,000 dirhems, with a capital of ten times that amount.[2] Their expenses also used to increase disgracefully, and the actual governor's stipend was of no account to them. One governor, Umayyah Ibn 'Abdallah, wrote to 'Abd al-Malik Ibn Marwán, stating that the whole land-tax of Khorasan was not sufficient to keep up his kitchen.[3] When the Caliphs perceived that malversation of this sort was occurring on the part of their lieutenants, they would fine them; and if they learned that any lieutenant had amassed money, they would

[1] 'Iḳd, i, 18. [2] Aghâni, xix, 62; Khillikán, ii, 361. [3] Aghâni, xiii, 56

send some one to seize it, and take his place in the government of the province. Personal greed was the motive in every case.

The governors felt no conscientious scruples in the matter of plundering the property of the natives of the conquered countries, believing this wealth to be their spoil, as we have already seen. This was the principle expressed by the Umayyad governor in 'Irák· "'Irák is the domain of the Kurashites; we may take or leave whatever is to be found there." The native chief of Ikhna in Egypt asked 'Amr Ibn al-'Ás to inform him what was the tax he had to pay. 'Amr replied that he would not tell him, even if he were to give him his house full of gold from floor to roof. "You," he said, "are our store. If great demands are made on us, we make great demands on you; if we are lightened, we lighten your burden."[1] This implied the belief that Egypt had been taken by force. Another said that Sughd was the domain of the Caliph.

§ 20. Islam and the Poll-tax.

The provincial governors did their utmost to collect money by any means in their power. The four sources they had were the Poll-tax, the Land-tax, the Alms, and the Tithes. The most important of these sources at the commencement of Islam was the poll-tax, owing to the number of the members of tolerated cults. The Umayyad governors exacted it mercilessly, and in consequence great numbers of these people adopted Islam. This expedient was ineffective, for the governors regarded their conversion as a device for escaping the poll-tax, and not as dictated by honourable motives; they therefore proceeded to exact the poll-tax from them even after conversion. Ḥajjáj Ibn Yúsuf was the first person who introduced this plan, and he was followed by other Umayyad governors in Africa, Khorasan, and Transoxania; in consequence many of these converts apostatized back, though quite willing to remain Moslems, especially the inhabitants of

[1] Maḳrízí, i, 77.

the last two countries, who down to the end of the Umayyad period were only kept from embracing Islam by the iniquity of the governors who demanded poll-tax from converts. When Ashras was made governor of Khorasan in the year 110, the people of Samarcand had apostatized. He sent to them a man named Abú'l-Ṣaida, who stipulated that any person there who returned to Islam should be relieved of poll-tax. The man accordingly went to Samarcand and invited the inhabitants to return to Islam on that condition. Numbers accepted it, and in consequence the proceeds of the poll-tax were greatly diminished. The governor of Samarcand wrote to Ashras to say that the poll-tax was spoiled. Ashras's answer was as follows: "The poll-tax is a source of strength to the Moslems, and I am informed that the people of Sughd and other places have adopted Islam, not out of conviction, but only in order to escape the poll-tax; find out, therefore, which of them have been circumcised, pray the proper number of times, and read a Surah of the Koran, and only in such cases relieve them of poll-tax." The people, however, proceeded to carry out the ordinances of Islam, and build mosques. When the governors reported this to Ashras his rescript was, "Exact the poll-tax of the persons from whom you previously took it." The poll-tax was therefore re-enforced on the converts to Islam, who refused payment, and seceded to the number of 7,000 to a distance of many leagues from Samarcand. The proceeding gave rise to a sedition, in the course of which the people of Sughd and Bokhara apostatized from Islam and the Turks took up arms. This state of things went on until Khorasan was placed under Naṣr Ibn Sayyár, who perceiving the error that had been committed issued an edict in the year 121 to the effect that all Moslems were to be relieved of poll-tax, which was to be imposed instead on those non-Moslems who had previously been relieved of it. Before a week was over there came to him 30,000 Moslems who had been paying poll-tax.[1]

[1] Athír, iv, 216; v, 68, 111.

We need barely allude to the arbitrary manner in which the Umayyad princes increased the poll-tax and imposed fresh taxes, and appropriated the whole of the booty. The only sovereign of the dynasty who forbade these practices was Omar II, who refused to spend money from the treasury on himself, or even take any of it;[1] and who also endeavoured to enforce similar abstinence on his relations, yet could not get them to obey. When he succeeded to the Caliphate he wrote to his governors, "Relieve all Moslems of the poll-tax; for God sent Mohammed as a guide, not as a tax-collector."[2] His reign, however, lasted only a short time. Yazid Ibn al-Walíd wished to imitate him, and had no better fate. One of their extortions was that the Caliph should appropriate one-half of the blood-money paid for the murder of a member of a tolerated religion. Omar II abolished this.[3]

§ 21. Alms and Bribes.

The Umayyads' need for fresh sources of wealth forced them to lay hands on the alms, or money taken from the wealthier Moslems to be expended on the poorer members of the community. This was a different destination from that of the rest of the public money—spoil, booty, poll-tax—all of which were to be distributed among the fighting-men. The Umayyads often gave douceurs to poets, etc., out of the alms.[4] Properly they should have been given out of the private estate of the Caliph or else out of the booty, on the supposition that such douceurs helped to maintain the Moslem empire. Perhaps, however, the Caliph regarded the poets as indigent Moslems, and gave them alms as such; but such a supposition would contradict known facts, since the douceur was remuneration for eulogizing the Caliph, and for this the Caliph should have paid out of his own means. Not unfrequently, also, the stipends of the fighting-men were paid out of the alms, a proceeding

[1] 'Ikd, ii, 262. [2] Makrízí, i, 75. [3] Aghani, xv, 13.
[4] Ibid., xi, 156.

which the soldiers disliked, and regarded as an indignity. Thus, once when the Caliph 'Abd al-Malik came to Medinah on a pilgrimage, and ordered that the people should be given their pay, when this was produced in the form of bags of money inscribed "Alms" the Medinese refused to take it; for they regarded such treatment as an affront bestowed on them by the Caliph on the ground that they were adherents of the Prophet's family. "Our pay comes from the booty," they cried. 'Abd al-Malik replied with an apologue, wherein he made no secret of the mutual antagonism that had existed between the Medinese and the Umayyads since the murder of 'Uthmán and the battle of the Ḥarrah.

Very often, when other sources of money failed them, they would sell governorships for sums paid down, especially during the decline of their dynasty. When Al-Walíd Ibn Yazíd became Caliph, he increased the stipends with the view of acquiring popularity; but he had not in his treasury money sufficient for this purpose, nor had he any unscrupulous lieutenant ready to furnish him with supplies immediately. He resorted, therefore, to the plan of selling the governorship of Khorasan and the subordinate states to Yusuf Ibn Omar; and during his reign any governorship might be had for a bribe paid to the Caliph or one of his favourites.[1] In the times of his predecessors they were ordinarily given by way of remuneration for a service rendered; as Mu'áwiyah had given the governorship of Egypt to 'Amr Ibn al-'Áṣ as a reward for the service rendered him in defeating 'Alí; an example followed by Mu'áwiyah's successors. When a Caliph wished to gain over some party he would lure its chiefs with the offer of a governorship. This became so common a practice that, whenever a leader was invited to assist a Caliph, he would stipulate for a fixed sum of money or a special governorship. Thus we read that when 'Abd al-Malik Ibn Marwan was warring with Mus'ab Ibn Zubair in 'Iraḳ he sent to the people of Kúfah and Baṣrah, soliciting their services with offers of reward. These overtures

[1] Athír, v, 125, 126, 132.

they accepted, but on conditions, and demanding governorships. It was remarkable that as many as forty persons demanded the governorship of Ispahan; so that 'Abd al-Malik asked his courtiers what this Ispahan could be?[1]

§ 22. Contempt for Religion and the Religious.

When the Umayyads desired to possess themselves of the Caliphate, well knowing that the Prophet's family had a better right to it than themselves, and that the claims of that family were based on a sound foundation, most of the lawyers, scholars, and other representatives of religion were on the side of the Prophet's family, and ready to maintain their claim; only the clan-patriotism of the Ḳuraish was on the side of the Umayyads, and force carried the day. The lawyers, etc., lost no opportunity of asserting the superiority of the Prophet's family, and reminding the Umayyads of the wrong, iniquity, and wickedness that they were committing in their usurpation; this formed the subject of many a sermon and exhortation addressed to them. Mu'áwiyah, mild-tempered and sagacious, would take no notice of this language, and "cut out their tongues" by gifts, kindly treatment, and gentleness; this procedure was maintained with excess by his followers, until the time of 'Abd al-Malik Ibn Marwán, who substituted for it severity and violence. When he went on pilgrimage in the year 75 A.H., after the death of Ibn Zubair, he came to Medinah, where were the adherents of the Prophet's family, and delivered the following address:—"Please to remember that I am not the weak Caliph ('Uthmán), nor the flattering Caliph (Mu'áwiyah), nor the stupid Caliph (Yazíd), and that I shall not cajole this nation except with the sword, until you come into line. You know by heart the acts of the original Refugees, but you do no such acts yourselves; you enjoin piety on others, but neglect it yourselves. No person after to-day shall enjoin piety on me but I strike off his head." 'Abd al-Malik was the first

[1] Aghání, xvii, 162.

Caliph who forbade the "enjoyining of right,"[1] and his language annoyed the enemies of the Umayyads so much that they sighed for the days of Mu'awiyah, saying over him what Ibn Zubair said when the news of his death came: "God have mercy on him! We used to deceive him, and he let himself be deceived."

§ 23. Contempt for the Koran and the Sancturies.

'Abd al-Malik was all for violence, and acknowledged openly that his policy was usurpation by force, even though he violated the principles of religion. It might be fancied that herein he was imitating his lieutenant and assistant and the helper of his dynasty, Hajjaj Ibn Yusuf. Yet it is not probable that he was imitating anyone else in these sentiments, for from the time of his accession he made no secret of his contempt of religion; before his accession, indeed, he made great show of piety; when seated on the throne fortune spoiled him. There is a story that when the news of his appointment reached him he was seated with the Koran on his lap; he closed it, saying "This is our final paring."[2] It is not therefore surprising that he should have permitted his lieutenant Hajjaj Ibn Yusuf to direct catapults against the Ka'bah, and cut off the head of Ibn Zubair within the Ka'bah Mosque;[3] the law being that there should be no fighting in the Ka'bah or in its vicinity. This rule was broken by Hajjaj, whose troops continued the work of slaughter there for three successive days. They also pulled down the Ka'bah, though regarded by them as the House of God, and kindled fire between its precincts and its curtains,[4] an atrocity the like of which never occurred at any other time in Islam. They entered the other sanctuary, Medinah, fought with the inhabitants, and shed their blood. If any house was locked against them they burned it with all it contained. Copts and Nabataeans were permitted to enter

1. Athir, iv, 190, 251.
2. Abu'l-Fida, i, 205; Siraj, 96.
3. 'Ikd, ii 256.
4. Athir, v, 39.

the chambers of Korashite women, tear the veils from their heads and the anklets from their feet, with swords on their shoulders, and trampling on copies of the Koran.[1]

Numerous Companions of the Prophet Epigoni, and devotees were killed by them in cold blood. Their purpose was to bring contempt on the cause of 'Ali and his party, and thereby to confirm their own pretensions to the throne. for this reason, too, they started the practice of cursing 'Ali from the pulpit, and issued orders that every person on pain of death should curse him. The first person who was executed for failing to comply with this order was Hujr Ibn 'Adi the Kindite in the time of Mu'awiyah.[2] The practice was continued to the days of Omar II, who abolished it.

§ 24. The Caliphate and the Prophetic Office.

The Umayyads procured the aid of certain unscrupulous lieutenants, who increased their arbitrariness by flattery and by violation in their cause of the principles of religion. 'Abd al-Malik's governor Hajjaj Ibn Yusuf was the first who ventured on such courses; he termed the Caliph 'God's vicegerent,' thereby setting the office of Caliph above that the Prophet; and he declared that the order of heaven and earth was maintained by the Caliphate, the Caliph being in God's eyes a greater personage than angels of the first rank or prophets. "God," he said, "created Adam with His hands, made the angles bow down before him, set him in Paradise, and then sent him down to earth, where He made him Caliph (vicegerent), whereas He made the angles messengers." When this was disputed, he used to ask the disputant whether a man's lieutant (or representative) at home was not more honourable than a messenger sent for a particular errand. When 'Abd al-Malik heard this doctrine he was elated by it;[3] and it was taken up by the unscrupulous ministers who succeeded Hajjaj,

[1] Khillikan, ii, 274. [2] Mas'udi, ii, 39.

[3] 'Ikd, iii, 18; Mas'udi, ii, 104.

such as Khálid al-Kasrí, minister to Hisham Ibn 'Abd al-Malik, who once addressed the people of Meccah in the following strain: "Ye Moslems, which is the more honourable, a man's representative in his household or his messenger unto them?" His meaning was that Hisham was superior to the Prophet.[1] The same view was adopted by other courtiers and sycophants, many of whom had only adopted Islam out of interested motives, and this made the mischief worse. Flattery of a similar sort used to be bestowed on the lieutenants themselves, who used to be encouraged to violate the ordinances of religion Khálid al-Ḳasrí, who has been mentioned, took little trouble to commit the Koran to memory, and when he had to recite a verse ordinarily made some mistake both in the wording and in the grammar. Once when he had to preach in the mosque he made a mistake of the sort, and lost countenance. A Taghlibite friend rose and said to him, "Do not take this to heart, prince: I never knew a wise man who knew the Koran by heart; they are all fools who do." Khalid told him that he was right.[2]

We are not surprised to learn that the 'Umayyad Drunkard,' Al-Walid Ibn Yazid, when mad with drink, shot arrows at the Koran. There is a story that one night he looked for a *sors* in the Koran, and opened the book at the words "They asked for a decision. And disappointment shall overtake every rebellious tyrant, behind whom is Hell, where he shall be given to drink of pus." He ordered the Koran to be hung up, and took a bow and arrows and began to shoot at it, till it was all torn to pieces. He then composed the following epigram :—

"Thou tauntest the rebel and tyrant? Ah, well!
A tyrant am I and prepared to rebel.
When thou meetest thy Lord on the last judgment morn,
Then cry unto God 'By Walid I was torn.'"[3]

[1] Athír, iv, 257; v, 130; Aghání, xix, 20.
[2] Aghání, xix, 63.
[3] Aghání, vi, 125; Mas'udi, ii, 134.

The propagation of Islam was no concern of the Umayyads: their only aims were conquest, usurpation, and the amassing of wealth. Hence in their time the spread of Islam made no progress in the remote regions of Scinde and Turkestan, though the inhabitants were ready to embrace it; the greed and tyranny of the Umayyads restrained them. They embraced Islam and apostatized alternately according to the manner in which they were treated. When the pious Omar II ascended the throne, and followed the footsteps of his namesake Omar I, he wrote to the princes of Scinde and elsewhere, inviting them to embrace Islam on the condition that they should retain possession of their country, and should have the same rights and burdens as the other Moslems; having already learned about his character, they accepted his proposal and took Arabic names. At his death in 101, when the Umayyads resumed their old policy, these princes apostatized.[1]

To the class of facts with which we are dealing we must reckon the massacres with crucifixion and mutilation of 'Alí's descendants by the Umayyads, with similar treatment of Epigoni and devotees, the chief offender in this respect being their minister, Ḥajjáj Ibn Yusuf.

§ 25. VIOLENCE AND CRUELTY IN UMAYYAD TIMES.

In the days of the Pious Caliphs obedience to the sovereign was regarded by the Moslems as a duty incumbent on them, whence the policy of the empire required neither astuteness nor violence. They never swerved from justice in either what they said or what they did. If anyone of them committed an offence he confessed and submitted to whatever punishment the Caliph imposed. The decisions required no investigation, rejoinders, or acuteness, nor was any violence required in order to carry them into effect. The punishment was often limited to censure or rebuke, and when the Caliph himself committed an offence he judged himself as he judged his subjects. There

[1] Athír, iv, 273; v, 26.

was no prison in their time; the first Caliph who built a prison was Mu'awiyah, who also started a bodyguard,[1] which had been unnecessary in the days of the Pious Caliphs. The chief captain in Omar's time would come humbly when the Caliph summoned him, though he well knew that if he refused to appear the Caliph had no power to make him come. The Caliph would order a Moslem to be beaten, and the Moslem would submit cheerfully. Omar would not wink at a light offence, for fear of such leading to grave offences, and he was ruined by his uncompromising firmness.

When Mu'áwiyah became Caliph, and set his shrewd agents over the provinces, 'Irak, Fars, Egypt, etc., the Moslems still maintained their old pride and their lofty spirit; and Mu'awiyah by his clemency and forbearance had given their tongues free rein. The governors, fearing this might lead to great disorders, began to employ severity. The first of them who ruled by terrorism was Ziyad, 'his father's son,' Mu'awiyah's governor over 'Irak. He professed to be merely imitating the firmness of Omar I, but in fact he transgressed all bounds. He first enforced the Caliph's authority by intimidation, and punished on suspicion and surmise.[2] After him his son 'Ubaidallah succeeded to the government of 'Irak as lieutenant to Mu'awiyah's son Yazíd. In his days 'Alí's son Husain came forward as a pretender to the Caliphate, declared the oath of allegiance to Yazid void, and advanced against 'Irak. Yazid wrote to 'Ubaidallah, bidding him imprison people on suspicion and arrest them on surmise, but kill only open enemies.[3]

When the government of 'Irák came into the hands of Hajjaj Ibn Yúsuf in the reign of 'Abd al-Malik Ibn Marwan (65–86 A.H.), there being now many claimants to the Caliphate, Hajjáj wished to imitate the firmness and severity of Ziyád and his son, and he did it to excess, bringing ruin and desolation on his province.[4] He was not really a stronger

[1] Makrizí, ii, 187. [2] Athír, iii, 228. [3] Athír, iv, 18.
[4] Khillikán, i, 124; Bayán, i, 175; 'Ikd, iii, 3.

ruler than either Ziyád or his son, but Ziyád was kept within limits by the clemency of Mu'áwiyah, and his son was also restrained by the order of Yazíd only to fight with open enemies. Ḥajjaj was encouraged by the ruthlessness of 'Abd al-Malik to go to extremes, at which the Moslems were indignant, who remembered it as a grievance against the dynasty. Great numbers of rebels arose, who charged the Caliphs with heresy. A saying current among the rebels was, "The Umayyads are a set of tyrants, who arrest on surmise and judge according to their caprice, and kill to gratify their anger."[1]

§ 26. Busr Ibn Artat and the Slaughter of the Infants.

It should be observed that the policy of the Umayyads was from the first based on the ruthless severity which characterized the governments of those days. They, however, exceeded all limits, and thought nothing of violence and assassination in order to confirm their sovereignty and get the better over their enemies. They gave their viceroys a free hand, permitting them to slay or crucify at their pleasure without consulting the Caliph, a proceeding which was not permitted in the days of the Pious Caliphs, for in their time the Caliph, while remaining in Medinah, administered the affairs of his subjects all over the empire. To this principle Omar II wished to return in his reign, but the short duration of it gave him no opportunity of carrying out his design.[2] After his death his successor, Yazíd Ibn 'Abd al-Malik, wrote to his viceroys bidding them return to the same ruthless methods that had been in vogue before.[3]

The Umayyad Caliphs thought that by giving their viceroys and generals a free hand they would thereby encourage them and carry out their own purposes. There were times when the Caliph himself encouraged some atrocity. So even

[1] Bayán, i, 195. [2] Athír, v, 29. [3] 'Iḳd, ii, 260.

Mu'awiyah sent Busr Ibn Arṭat after the decision of the arbiters, while 'Ali was alive, with an army, and orders to march over the country and slay all the partisans of 'Alí whom they found, not sparing women or children. Busr went on his way till he came to Medinah, where he put to death many of 'Alí's adherents, and destroyed their houses; he then proceeded to Meccah and other places, doing the same, till he got to Yemen, where 'Ubaidallah Ibn 'Abbas was governor for 'Ali, whose cousin he was; this man had fled in order to escape slaughter. Busr, finding two young sons of his, 'Abd al-Raḥman and Ḳutham, slew them both, cutting their throats with a knife that he had in his hand.[1] The lads, it is said, were in the desert in charge of a Kinanite, who, when Busr revealed his intention, asked why innocent children should be killed, and desired Busr to kill him (the guardian) with them. Busr complied with this request. A Kinanite woman then cried out, "Kill men, if you like, but why need you kill these children? Such a thing was never done either in pagan days or in Islam. O son of Arṭát, he must be a bad sovereign who cannot maintain himself except by the slaughter of small children and feeble old men, by mercilessness and violation of natural feelings." The mother of the lads composed a dirge over them which she used to recite at public gatherings, of which the opening verse was—

> "Oh, who has seen my boys that were
> Like new-found pearls, a lovely pair?"

Still, we are inclined to think that Mu'awiyah by no means approved of this action, which is so unlike his astuteness and clemency: probably he had given Busr a free hand, without assigning any limits to his action, and this Busr was a heartless monster who spared neither old nor young. This is supported by the action of Busr after the death of 'Alí, when Mu'awiyah was afraid of Ziyád, 'his father's son,' his governor over Fars. Mu'áwiyah told Busr to produce Ziyád.

[1] Aghani, xv, 44.

Busr seized Ziyád's children, and wrote to him to appear on pain of those children being slain. When Mu'áwiyah heard of this he forbade Busr to kill them.[1]

If such excesses by the governors were permitted in the time of the gentle and forbearing Mu'áwiyah, what must have occurred in the reign of the violent and bloodthirsty 'Abd al-Malik? We can scarcely feel astonished at the excesses ascribed to Ḥajjáj, and the numbers of the persons whom he is said to have slain in cold blood. The number of these is put at 120,000; and still less astonishment need be felt at the statement that there were in his prisons 50,000 men and 30,000 women.[2] 'Abd al-Malik was even more ruthless than his viceroy, and even more ready to break faith and violate amnesties. He is said, indeed, to have been the first ruler in Islam who did this. 'Amr Ibn Sa'íd al-Ashdal, one of his governors, desired the sovereignty for himself, and took advantage of 'Abd al-Malik's quitting Damascus to fight Ibn Zubair in 'Irák (in the year 69 A.H.), came to Syria, and took possession of the country. 'Abd al-Malik, who was on his way, hearing of this returned immediately to Damascus, and fought with 'Amr, the battle lasting several days without a decisive result. Fearing for his sovereignty, 'Abd al-Malik sought to make peace, to which proposal 'Amr assented; a treaty was drawn up, in which amnesty was promised to 'Amr. 'Amr was sufficiently assured by this promise to ride into 'Abd al-Malik's tent, where there was a meeting between the two, after which 'Abd al-Malik entered Damascus.

Four days after 'Abd al-Malik's entry he summoned 'Amr, who appeared, the following evening, bringing with him a hundred clients, who remained outside, while 'Amr went in to 'Abd al-Malik, with whom were many of his relations. 'Abd al-Malik came forward to receive him, made him sit on the divan with himself, and began to converse. Presently he ordered a slave to remove 'Amr's sword, asking him whether he expected to be allowed to sit with the Caliph with his sword

[1] Athír, iii, 195, 211. [2] Mas'údi, ii, 113; Kashkúl, 32.

girt on him? 'Amr let the sword be removed. 'Abd al-Malik then told 'Amr, calling him by the *kunyah* "Abu Umayyah," that when the latter had rebelled he, the Caliph, had vowed, if ever he obtained satisfaction and got him into his power, he would put him in a cage. Those who were present said, "and afterwards let him go?" To which he replied, "Certainly, for what else do you expect me to do to Abu Umayyah?" The persons present (relations of the Caliph) then requested 'Amr to let the Caliph fulfil his oath. 'Amr assented. A cage was then produced from under 'Abd al-Malik's divan, and a slave was ordered to rise and force 'Amr into it. 'Amr bade the Caliph remember his oath by God and exhibit him publicly in the cage. "What!" said the Caliph, "devising stratagems when you are face to face with death? We shall do nothing of the sort." The Caliph then pulled him so that he fell, and broke a tooth, owing to his mouth falling against the divan. 'Amr bade him in God's name break one of his ribs if he liked, but venture no further. 'Abd al-Malik then said: "If I thought you would spare me if I spared you, and reconcile the Ḳuraish to me, I should let you go. But no two men can ever come together on the terms whereon we are in a city, but the one drives out the other." When 'Amr saw what he meant he cried out, "What, treachery!" calling the Caliph by an insulting name. 'Abd al-Malik then killed him.[1]

This story shows that what induced 'Abd al-Malik to commit such treachery was the number of pretenders to the Caliphate, who had no internal monitor to restrain them, as was the case with the contemporaries of the Pious Caliphs. So the strong were devouring the weak, and the power was his who could first kill his rival. This might be called the policy of violence. It helped the Umayyads to consolidate their empire, and it presently became the law of their successors, the 'Abbasids. etc. The last coup of the sort

[1] Athir, iv, 146.

was the massacre of the Mamluks by Mohammed 'Alí Pasha. The Umayyads adopted it in order to hasten victory, and to free themselves from possible disputants. Whenever, therefore, a rebel arose, they tried to murder him, supposing that on the death of the leader the followers would necessarily disperse: if they failed to disperse, they could be conciliated by money or otherwise.

§ 27. THE STOREHOUSE OF SKULLS.

It was their custom to kill rebels, and mutilate their bodies, in order to intimidate their partisans. The ringleader's head would be cut off and carried from place to place, or the trunk would be crucified in crowded thoroughfares; this was done with the leaders of parties generally, and especially with leaders of the 'Alids: the Umayyad viceroy would execute such a person, and send his skull to the Caliph in Damascus that it might be paraded in the streets. The first skull taken from place to place was that of Omar Ibn Ḥumḳ al-Khuzá'i,[1] one of the murderers of 'Uthmán. The first paraded in the streets was that of Mohammed Ibn Abí Bakr;[2] the first brought to the Caliph were those of Háni' and Ibn 'Uḳail, partisans of Ḥusain in Kúfah; presently that of Ḥusain himself was sent by the son of Ziyád from Kúfah to Yazíd Ibn Mu'áwiyah in Syria. The same was done with the skulls of Ḥusain's murderers by Mukhtár, who sent them to Mohammed Ibn al-Ḥanafiyyah.[3] Similarly, Ḥajjáj sent the skull of Abdallah Ibn Zubair and those of his friends from Meccah to 'Abd al-Malik in Syria. 'Abd al-Malik himself sent the skull of Mus'ab Ibn Zubair from Kúfah to Syria, where it was stuck on a pole.[4]

There is a curious story that when the skull of Mus'ab Ibn Zubair was brought to 'Abd al-Malik he was sitting in a balcony at Kúfah, with Ibn 'Umair the Lakhmite for his

[1] Ma'arif, 187. [2] 'Iḳd, i, 39. [3] Athír, iv, 119. [4] Athír, iv, 162.

companion. When this man saw the skull before the Caliph he trembled. Asked what was the matter, he replied as follows: "God save us! I was on this balcony at this spot with 'Ubaidallah Ibn Ziyád, and saw the head of Ḥusain Ibn 'Alí set before him: then I was with Mukhtár Ibn Abí 'Ubaid the Thaḳafite, and saw the head of 'Ubaidallah Ibn Ziyád set before him: then I was with Mus'ab Ibn Zubair here, and saw the head of Mukhtár set before him: and now here is the head of Mus'ab Ibn Zubair set before you." 'Abd al-Malik took alarm, and when he rose ordered the balcony to be pulled down.[1]

Head-cutting after this fashion became an ordinance in the time of the Umayyads and their successors the 'Abbásids; and there was a storehouse made for them in the royal palace, where the skulls where kept, each in a separate basket:[2] it became also the custom to crucify the trunks or to impale the heads. The latter, however, was only practised in the case of the schismatics (*khawárij*), whose heads were stuck on lances and paraded.[3] The Umayyads reckoned the followers of 'Alí in this class, and crucified all whom they executed.

To the same class of institutions belongs the employment of torture before execution; this may, indeed, have been an invention of Ḥajjáj for the purpose of intimidating his enemies and breaking their spirit. The following is one mode of torture that was employed. *Arundo donax* was split and placed on the naked body, then withdrawn reed by reed, till the flesh was all lacerated, after which vinegar and salt were poured on the wounds till death ensued.[4] This was done by Ḥajjáj to some of those who fought against him with Ibn al-Ash'ath as an example to others. The 'schismatics' used to do the like to enemies whom they caught, placing children in boiling caldrons, whether to gratify their revenge or to intimidate.[5]

[1] Khillikán, i, 286. [2] Fakhrí, ii, 248. [3] 'Iḳd, ii, 272.
[4] Ma'árif, 115. [5] Mas'údi, ii, 123.

§ 28. Clients and their Treatment in the Umayyad Period.

When the Umayyads succeeded to the Caliphate in the middle of the first century of the Hijrah, the number of clients was steadily increasing, owing to the succession of conquests and the number of slaves either taken as prisoners or given, since the governors used to send hundreds and thousands of white and black slaves as presents to the Caliph's palace, or at times in lieu of land-tax,[1] etc. The Caliph would then distribute them among his private friends, or captains, who again would distribute them among their friends or else sell them, so that in these ways the slaves came to be lodged with people of very different social ranks. Any one of these slaves who distinguished himself in any way or was manumitted for any cause became a client, and this was regular and ordinary at that time. Besides these, others entered into the condition of clients by some sort of contract. In Umayyad times the number of the clients increased enormously, and they endeavoured to conciliate their patrons by performing such services as the latter required. The Arabs often employed them in manufacture and agriculture as well as in religious and literary posts, while themselves remaining occupied with the affairs of government. Hence the greater number of Koran readers, poets, musicians, scribes, and janitors were clients.

Many a client became wealthy enough to buy slaves, who in turn became his clients, whence it could happen that a man was a client to the third, fourth, or fifth degree. So the famous Malikite lawyer, 'Abdallah Ibn Wahb, was client of Yazíd Ibn Rummánah, who was himself client of Yazíd Ibn Anas al-Fihrí. Similar was the case of Ḥammád Ibn Sámah, Laith Ibn Sa'd, Abú Usámah, etc.; the poet Ibn Munádhir was client of Sulaimán al-Ḳahramán, who was client of 'Ubaidallah Ibn Abí Bakrah, who was a client of the Prophet.[2] What is stranger

[1] Mas'údí, ii, 354.

[2] Agháni, xvii, 9.

still is that each of these persons claimed Arab descent, the first from Thaḳíf, the second from Tamím, the third from Jubair Ibn Yarbú'. Hence Ibn Munádhir was not only a client to the third degree but also supposititious to the third degree. There are cases in which the clientship went to the fifth degree. The Traditionalists Dáwúd Ibn Khálid Ibn Dínár and his brothers were all clients of the family of Ḥunain, themselves clients of Muthaḳḳib, himself a client of Misḥal, himself a client of Shammás, himself a client of 'Abbas Ibn 'Abd al-Muṭṭalib.[1] We see therefrom how numerous were the clients in that time—Persians, Farghanians, Turks, Dailemites, Greeks, Berbers, Scindians, etc. All were engaged in those arts, trades, and pursuits which supplied the needs of the Arabs.

Besides these there were fighting clients. To each Arab tribe there were attached a number of these, often more numerous than the tribe itself. When the tribe went fighting they went out with it and helped. The proportion between clients and patrons varied at different times. In 'Alí's time the number of clients who went to war was to the number of citizens as one to five;[2] in the Umayyad period, owing to the steady growth of the numbers of the clients, they became more numerous than the others. Notwithstanding this the Umayyads despised and persecuted them, and they had to remain patient under this persecution or else flee to the extremities of the empire. Among those who fled from the oppression of the Umayyads we read the name of Ma'mún, grandfather of the famous musician Ibráhím of Mausil.[3]

§ 29. Resentment of Clients against Arabs.

When the numbers of the clients increased, and they saw the Umayyad partiality for the Arabs to the detriment of everyone else, especially the clients, which went so far that though they employed them as infantry in their wars they gave them neither stipend nor any part of the spoil or conquered land, this rankled

[1] Ma'árif, 197. [2] Athír, iii, 173. [3] Aghání, v, 2.

in their breasts, and finding themselves possessed of sufficient strength they became a prop for anyone who threw off his allegiance and pretended to the Caliphate, whether 'Alid or Schismatic; all such pretenders relied on the aid of the oppressed faction—the clients and slaves. The most famous insurgents who employed these forces was Mukhtár Ibn Abí 'Ubaid, who in the year 66 rose and demanded vengeance for the blood of Ḥusain, and further demanded the Caliphate for Mohammed Ibn al-Ḥanafiyyah. This person offered the booty as a reward to such clients as joined him, and mounted them on horses, and they, resenting the ill-treatment they had received from their masters and patrons, flocked to his standard, and were joined by a great number of runaway slaves, among them persons who out of hatred to the Umayyads had abandoned Islam. The numbers of the clients in Mukhtár's army were twice the numbers of the free citizens,[1] and they fought better than the free citizens owing to their detestation of the Umayyads Hence the slain on the battlefields of this war were mostly clients; in the battle fought in the year 67, out of 6,000 dead only 700 were free.[2] Mukhtár succeeded well in avenging the death of Husain, and slew all his murderers; but when the chief people of Kúfah saw that Mukhtar had gained his victory by employing their clients and slaves, they wrote to remonstrate, complaining that he had injured them by mounting their clients on horses and giving them the booty. He replied by asking whether if he rejected the aid of the clients and gave the booty they had acquired to the Kufans, the latter would fight with him against the Umayyads and Ibn Zubair, and would give him satisfactory oaths and assurances to that effect? This, however, they refused to do. Mukhtár was the first who formed corps of clients, and led them to victory. His success encouraged them to flout the Umayyad dynasty, which they ever after despised, and whose enemies they always aided. The wiser of the Caliphs endeavoured to conciliate them by stipends and the like. Mu'áwiyah himself assigned stipends in some cases to clients—

[1] Athír, iv, 121. [2] Id., iv, 136.

15 dirhems a head; 'Abd al-Malik increased this to 20; Sulaimán to 25, Hishám to 30.[1] It was not often that the intentions of these Caliphs in this matter were carried out; the governors used ordinarily to employ them without stipend or even provision.[2]

When a client was well treated and believed in his patron's benevolence, he became a devoted servant, and his patron could thoroughly rely on him. Even the Umayyad Caliphs used to employ clients in intimate capacities, and entrust important commissions to them. They would at times bestow on them high rank, and ask their advice on their affairs. These clients showed themselves faithful advisers, and willing to die in their defence. The same is true of the clients of the Abbásids. Boasting matches were instituted between the two orders, the most famous being that between Sudaif and Sayyáb, that has already been described.

A client might be of exalted rank, or rise to the highest posts even in Umayyad times, in spite of the Umayyad persecution of the clients as a whole, and the animus which the Caliphs of that line displayed against them. The most eminent and famous client in 'Irák̦ was Fairúz, client of the family of Khashkhásh, who held governorships, and rebelled with Ibn al-Ash'ath against Ḥajjáj. Ḥajjáj offered a reward of 10,000 dirhems for Fairúz's head; Fairuz one of 100,000 dirhems for that of Ḥajjáj. When Ibn al-Ash'ath was defeated, Fairúz fled to Khorasan, where he was arrested by Ibn al-Muhallab, who sent him to Ḥajjáj. Ḥajjaj had him executed after torturing him with reeds in the way described.[3]

§ 30. Marriages between Clients and Arab Women.

In general the clients in Umayyad times were enemies of the ruling dynasty, ready to join any insurgent, out of resentment at the indignities and injustices which they were compelled to undergo, owing to the chauvinism of the Arabs against the

[1] 'Ik̦d, ii, 249. [2] Athír, v, 24. [3] Ma'árif, 115.

foreigner; and the Umayyad contempt for them continued to increase. Although then the Prophet had declared that men's clients were of themselves, the Umayyads forbade marriages between them and Arab women, just as the Persians had forbidden marriages between Arabs and Persian women before Islam.[1] If a client ventured to marry an Arab woman, and the ruler heard of it, he would compel the man to divorce her. This happened to the Arabs of the Banú Sulaim at Rauhá. Coming thither, they were asked to give one of their daughters to a client, and married her to him; the matter was told the governor of Medinah, who separated the parties, and administered to the client a beating of two hundred stripes. He also shaved the man's head, beard, and eyebrows. Mohammed Ibn Bashír the Khárijite praised the governor for this action in the following verses:—

"Abu'l-Walíd would the honour save
Of maids whose fathers are in the grave;
And the freedman has got a lesson clear
In his ten score stripes and shaven hair.
If treated as peer of his own princess,
Why claims the freedman yet more redress?
What greater justice could freedman have
Than that slave, like him, should wed with slave?"

Abu'l-Walíd was the name of the governor of Medinah.[2]

The same was often done to clients who had attained high rank, or were renowned for piety or learning. Thus 'Abdallah Ibn 'Aun was famous among the Epigoni, but being a client he was beaten with scourges by Bilál Ibn Abí Burdah for marrying an Arab woman.[3]

The prohibition seems, indeed, to have been current before Islam, and the Arabs continued to maintain it in spite of the tradition that has been cited, and others. Salmán the Persian aided the Moslems in their wars in the time of the Prophet, and was a great benefactor to Islam. He asked Omar for the hand of one of his daughters, and Omar was willing to grant

[1] Mas'údí, i, 196. [2] Agháni, xiv, 150. [3] Ma'árif, 167.

it, not seeing any objection to such a marriage. His son 'Abdallah however, was very angry when he heard of it, and complained to 'Amr Ibn al-'Aṣ. Amr promised to help. Meeting Salmán, whose arrogance he knew, he congratulated him on the fact that the Commander of the Faithful condescended to give him his daughter, humiliating himself thereby before God. Salmán disliked this phrase so much that he withdrew his offer.[1]

The Umayyads, in accordance with their ordinary chauvinism, abhorred the marriage of a client with an Arab woman, even more than the marriage of an Arab with a non-Arab woman. There was, however, no religious objection, nor did pious people disapprove. 'Alí Ibn Ḥusain son of 'Alí, known as Zain al-'Ábidín (the ornament of the worshippers), who was one of the twelve Imams and the most eminent of the Epigoni, had for mother Salamah daughter of Yezdejird, the last of the Persian kings: when his father died, he gave her in marriage to Tharíd his father's client; he himself manumitted one of his slave-girls and married her. 'Abd al-Malik Ibn Marwán wrote to rebuke him for this. Zain al-'Ábidín wrote back, "'Ye have in the Prophet of God a good example': he manumitted Safiyyah daughter of Huyayy Ibn Akhtab and married her, and manumitted Zaid Ibn Ḥárithah, and gave him in marriage his cousin Zainab daughter of Jaḥsh."

Islam should have raised the status of the client, but the Umayyads thought fit to treat him with contempt on the ground of non-Arab descent. This theory became prevalent in their days, and men would taunt others with being allied to clients by marriage. There is a long poem of Abu Bujair declaiming against a member of the tribe 'Abd Ḳais in Baḥrain for marrying his daughter to a client. The whole tribe are taunted with allying themselves with tradesmen and cultivators.[2]

This doctrine took such deep root in men's minds that the

[1] 'Ikd, iii, 132. [2] 'Iḳd, iii, 232.

clients themselves began to disapprove of the marriage of one of themselves with an Arab woman ; the following story is told of the famous poet Nuṣaib. He was a client, and his son fell in love with the daughter of his patron, who was already dead. Nuṣaib's son asked his brother for the girl's hand ; the request was granted. When Nuṣaib heard of this he assembled the heads of the tribe, and said to the girl's uncle, "Do I rightly understand that you are prepared to give your niece to my son?" The answer was in the affirmative. Nuṣaib thereupon commanded some black slaves to drag his son by the feet and give him a sound thrashing. Then, turning to his patron's brother, he said, "Were it not that I am unwilling to hurt you, I should have done the like by you." He thereupon cast his eye on a youth who was a free member of the tribe, gave the girl to him, and paid the expenses of the contract out of his own purse.[1]

Nevertheless, a client might not woo a woman nor give his daughter in marriage without consulting his patron, and if a man desired to ask for the hand of a client's daughter he did not address himself to her father, nor her brother, but her patrons, and only if they consented did the marriage take place. If the marriage took place without this consent, it could be annulled ; and cohabitation under these circumstances was considered illicit.[2]

To sum up: the chauvinism of the Umayyads led them to hold in contempt all non-Arabs, and especially the clients. The latter resented this treatment, and became a powerful factor in the expulsion of the Umayyads.

§ 31. The Tolerated Sects and their Treatment under the Umayyads.

Treaties were made with tolerated communities at the beginning of Islam. These communities were called the people of the *Dhimmah*, a word which signifies 'covenant, amnesty, or

[1] Aghâni, i, 136. [2] 'Iḳd, ii, 73.

guarantee.' That name was given them because by paying poll-tax they obtained security for their lives, their honour, and their property. They consisted mainly of Christians and Jews, and are called in the Koran "people of the Book," i.e. of the Law or the Gospel, and the Koran recommends that they be well treated. The Tradition also contains many precepts recommending kindly treatment of them, and especially of the Copts in Egypt. There is a tradition that the Prophet said: "When ye conquer Egypt, then deal kindly with the Copts, for they have amnesty and the rights of kin," referring to the belief that Hagar (Abraham's concubine and Ishmael's mother) was one of them. Another tradition is worded thus: "For God's sake deal kindly with the people of the covenant, the black soil, the thick-haired, the swarthy. For they are of our blood and allied to us by marriage."

When the Pious Caliphs sent out expeditions they would always instruct the leaders to deal gently with the 'people of the Covenant.' Especially would they urge this in the case of the Christians and their monks. If the people of the cities came to them to offer terms of capitulation, these would be accepted, and a contract made whereby the Moslems undertook to provide for their protection against the payment of the poll-tax. The amount of that tax varied with the circumstances and the nature of the contract made between the parties. Each capitulation contained special stipulations, according to the country; but every one involved the protection of the 'people of the Covenant' by the Moslems. When anything prevented the Moslems from carrying out that obligation the poll-tax could be remitted.

The histories contain many examples of such contracts, guaranteeing the protection of the conquered nation and facilities for its business in return for the poll-tax. One of these is the letter of the Prophet to the Governor of Ailah in the Gulf of 'Aḳabah and that to the people of Adhruḥ, written during the Tabúk campaign, in the year 9 A.H. The former of these was worded as follows:—

> "In the name of God, etc. This is a certificate of safety from God and His Prophet Mohammed to Yaḥyá Ibn Ru'bah and the people of Aila, their ships and caravans on sea and land. They have a guarantee from God and His Prophet as well as the Syrians, Yemenites, and mariners that are with them. If any of them shall innovate, his wealth shall not avail him, and shall be lawful for him that shall seize it. Nor shall they fortify any places whither they alight nor any paths which they traverse by sea or land."[1]

The following is the letter to the people of Adhruḥ and the people of Maḳná.

> "In the name of God, etc. From Mohammed the Prophet of God to the Banú Habíbah and the people of Maḳná: peace be with you. It has been told me from above that ye are to return to your village; and when this letter comes to you, ye shall be safe and ye shall have the guarantee of God and the guarantee of His Prophet: for the Prophet of God has forgiven you your sin and any blood for which you might be pursued. You are to have no patron over you in your village except the Prophet of God; nor shall any do you wrong nor harm you, because the Prophet of God will defend you even as he defends himself: only to the Prophet of God shall belong your spoil and your slaves and your camp-followers and your cuirasses, save what the Prophet of God or his messenger shall exempt. And thereafter there shall be upon you a fourth of the product of your palms, and a fourth of the product of your nets, and a fourth of what is spun by your women, but all else shall be your own, and God's Prophet has exempted you from all further poll-tax or forced labour. And if ye hear and obey, then it will be for the Prophet of God to do honour to the honourable that are among you, and to pardon those of you that do wrong. Whosoever of the Banú Ḥabíbah and the people of Makná bethinks him to do well to the Moslems, it shall be well for him; and whosoever means mischief for them, mischief shall befall him. Ye are to have no rulers save of yourselves, or of the family of the Prophet. Written by 'Alí in the ninth year."[2]

The Prophet's example was imitated by the Islamic generals in the course of the conquests of Syria, Egypt, 'Iráḳ, and Fars.

[1] Hishám, iii, 40. [2] Baládhurí, 60.

Treaties were written for the 'people of the Covenant' in the style of those which have been quoted, in consideration of the poll-tax. The following is the text of the treaty given by Khálid Ibn al-Walíd to the people of Syria:—

> "In the name of God, etc. These are the terms granted by Khálid Ibn al-Walíd to the people of Damascus: If he be permitted to enter therein, he gives them security for their lives, goods, and churches. Their walls are not to be demolished, neither shall men be quartered in their houses. Thereunto we give the oath of God and the covenant of God's Prophet, and of the Caliphs and of the Believers. So long as they give the poll-tax nothing but good shall befall them."[1]

The following is the style of Abú 'Ubaidah's contract with the people of Baalbek:—

> "In the name of God, etc. This is the certificate of security to So-and-so son of So-and-so, and to the people of Baalbek, Greeks, Persians, and Arabs, for their lives, property, churches, and walls, to them that are inside and outside the city, and also for their mills. The Greeks shall be permitted to pasture their cattle within a space of fifteen miles, yet are they not to abide in any inhabited town. After Rabí' and Jumada i shall have passed, they shall go where they will; if any of them adopt Islam he shall have the same rights as we, and the same duties; and their merchants may travel whither they will in the countries which we have taken by capitulation, granting security to such as pay the poll-tax and the land-tax. God is witness, and His witness is sufficient."[2]

The same was the form of the treaties made by other conquerors, 'Amr Ibn al-'Áṣ, Sa'd Ibn Abi Waḳḳás, etc., when they took Egypt, Palestine, Fars, Africa, and Spain. They used, however, to stipulate that the people of the Covenant should pay the poll-tax with their own hands, "being humble." The conditions of capitulation varied with the countries and circumstances in respect of severity. Thus the terms on which Egypt was taken over differed from those which were enforced in the case of Syria, and those of Syria from those of 'Iráḳ.

[1] Baládhurí, 121. [2] Baládhurí, 130.

§ 32. THE 'PROPHET'S CHARTER.'

There are current copies of a contract supposed to have been made by the Prophet with the Christians and their monks, called the 'Prophet's Charter,' which agree in purport though they vary in wording. This Charter is supposed to have been written by the hand of 'Alí, and deposited in the Prophet's Mosque in the year 2 A.H. Different copies were made and transferred to various monasteries. One of these was guarded in the Monastery of Mt. Sinai, whence Sultan Selím the Conqueror removed it to Constantinople at the beginning of the sixteenth century A.D., after having exhibited it to an assembly of lawyers, by whom it was translated into Turkish. A Turkish copy was then deposited in the Monastery of Mt. Sinai, with charters confirming the monks in the rights guaranteed them by the Prophet's Charter.[1] The following is the text of the Charter as given in the "Compositions of the Sultans," by Ferídún Bey.[2]

> "In the name, etc. This is the certificate written by Mohammed son of 'Abdallah, the Prophet of God, and His messenger unto all mankind, delivering both promises and threats, and having in his keeping the deposit of God unto His Creation, that men might have no plea after the coming of the Messengers. And God is mighty and wise. This he wrote unto the people of the Christian religion, and to such as profess the Christian religion in the East and West, near and far, clear-speaking and barbarous, known and unknown. He wrote it for them as a charter, and whosoever violates, alters, or transgresses the covenant that is therein, shall have violated the covenant of God, broken His promise, ridiculed his religion, and earned His curse, whether he be a sovereign or any other Moslem. If any monk or pilgrim entrench himself in mountain, valley, cave, township, level, sand, or church, I shall be behind them defending them from any that shall envy them, by myself, my helpers, my people, my sect, and my followers, inasmuch as they are my subjects and the people of my covenant. And I exempt them from the vexation in victuals

[1] Hilál, vii, pts. 15 and 17.
[2] Dictionary of Administration, s.v. *Bitrikkhánah.*

which is endured by the people of the Covenant in that they have to pay the tax, save so far as they themselves of their free will offer it, and there is to be no compulsion nor force employed. No Bishop is to be removed from his diocese, nor monk from his monkdom, nor ascetic from his cell, nor pilgrim from his pilgrimage, neither is any of their assembling-places or churches to be pulled down, neither shall any of the wealth of their churches be employed for the building of mosques or houses for the Moslems; and whoever doeth this shall have violated the charter of God and the charter of His Prophet; neither shall there be taken from monks, bishops, or ministers any poll-tax or fine. I shall maintain their security wheresoever they be, whether on land or sea, east, west, north, or south. They shall at all times and in all places be under my protection and within my covenant and immunity from all mischief. Likewise the hermits in the mountains and blessed places shall not have to pay land-tax nor tithe on that which they sow, nor shall a portion be taken from them seeing that it is only enough for their own mouths, nor shall they have to render assistance at harvest-time, nor shall they be forced to go out on service in time of war, neither shall more be demanded of them that pay the land-tax and the owners of property and estates and those that engage in merchandise than twelve dirhems altogether once a year. None of them shall be made to pay more than is due, neither shall they be striven with save in kindly dealing. They shall guard them under the wing of mercy by keeping off them the vexation of all mischief wherever they be and wheresoever they dwell. And if Christians dwell among Moslems, the Moslems shall satisfy them, and suffer them to pray in their churches, and shall not interfere in any way with the practice of their religion. And whoso violates the charter of God, and does the contrary thereof, shall be counted a rebel against His covenant and against His Apostle; further, the Moslems shall aid in repairing the Christian churches and places, which shall remain in keeping of the Christians on condition that they abide in their religion and act according to the charter. None of them shall be compelled to bear arms, for the Moslems shall protect them. And none shall violate this charter for all time, even unto the Day of Judgment and the end of the world."

Our own opinion is that if the Prophet gave the Christians any general charter, it was different from this, or possibly he may have given an abstract of the charter which they filled up, or the original may have been lost or forgotten, and it was conjecturally reconstructed ; or possibly the Christians fabricated this charter for political ends, since none of the Mohammedan conquests or other early Mohammedan writers have mentioned this charter. Moreover, some of the expressions and provisions are such as are inconceivable at the commencement of Islam, especially in the year 2 A.H.

§ 33. THE CHARTER OF OMAR.

Mention is also made of a charter called the Charter of Omar I, and to this some of the Mohammedan chroniclers allude, and its text is given (among others) by Abú Bakr Mohammed Ibn Mohammed Ibn al-Walíd al-Fihrí (ob. 520 A.H.) in his work called "The Kings' Lamp," who professes to have got it from 'Abd al-Rahmán Ibn Ghanam al-Ash'ari (ob. 78). It runs as follows :—

> "We wrote to Omar Ibn al-Khaṭṭáb when he gave terms to the Christians of Syria, thus : In the name, etc. This is a letter addressed to Omar the Commander of the Faithful by the Christians of the city of ———. When ye came against us we asked of you security for our lives, children, goods, and co-religionists, and undertook that we should not in our cities nor in the surrounding country build any fresh monastery, church, cell, or retreat, neither should we repair any that were ruined, nor such as were within land pegged out by Moslems by night or by day ; that we should open wide our doors to the passengers and beggars, and give three days' hospitable entertainment to such Moslems as pass by us ; that we should harbour no spy in our churches or houses, that we should entertain no rancour against the Moslems, that we should not teach our children the Koran, that we should not promulgate our religion nor invite anyone to embrace it, that we should prevent none of our relatives from embracing Islam if he wishes ; that we should pay honour to the Moslems, and rise and offer them our seats if they wish to sit down : that we should not imitate any Moslem fashion in attire, such as hood or turban, shoes, or parting of the hair ; that we should not speak their language nor employ their patronymics ; that we should not ride with saddles, nor gird on swords, nor take any weapons, neither carry them upon use

that we should not use Arabic legends on our seals, nor sell wine; that we should shear the front of our heads, and wear our proper costume, wheresoever we are; that we should gird ourselves with the *zonarion* on our waists, and display no crosses nor any of our books in the streets or market-places of the Moslems; that we should not strike the *nákús* in our churches, save very gently; that we should not raise our voices in recitation in our churches when there are Moslems present, that we should not make processions on Palm Sunday or Easter Day, that we should not raise our voices at funerals, that we should not display fires in any of the Moslem streets or market-places, that we should not bury our dead in their neighbourhood, that we should not take as slaves such as have fallen into Moslem plunder-lots, and that we should not pry into their houses.

"Now, when I brought this contract to Omar, he added thereunto: 'Nor should we strike any Moslem.' All this we have taken upon ourselves and upon our co-religionists, and have received in exchange a guarantee of safety. And if we violate any of those conditions whereto we have agreed and contracted, then there is no longer any covenant for us, and there shall be lawful against whatever is lawful against rebels and adversaries."

"Omar wrote to him to execute what they asked, and told him to add two clauses to those enumerated: that they were to buy no Moslem captives, and that whoever struck a Moslem should have annulled his covenant."[1]

To this covenant we may add certain rules regarding churches which Omar also imposed. He commanded that any church that had not already existed before Islam should be demolished, that there should be no storeys projecting from a church, and that no cross should be displayed outside a church, save a fragment at the top of the crucifix.

The text of the above charter displays a desire to persecute and oppress the Christians that is unlike what appears in the other charters and treaties that belong to the beginning of Islam; it is also unlike what is otherwise known of Omar's justice and gentleness towards the 'people of the Covenant' and can be inferred from the narrative of his life. That life exhibits veracity in thought, word, and deed, and so when

[1] Siráj, 283.

a Moslem injured a Christian it was Omar's custom to obtain satisfaction for the injured party, even though the Moslem were one of the most eminent of the Companions. Thus he obtained satisfaction for a Copt from 'Amr Ibn al-'Ás and his son, asking since when they had made slaves of mankind, when their mothers had borne them free.[1]

At first sight, then, there would appear to be a contradiction between these virtues and the text of this charter, and it might be supposed that the charter was a forgery of latter times, as we supposed was the case with the "Prophet's Charter." The cases, however, are different, as there is greater evidence in favour of the genuineness of Omar's charter. We ought, then, to consider the evidence by which it is assigned to Omar, and then the causes of the apparent discrepancy between it and his character.

§ 34. ASCRIPTION OF THE CHARTER TO OMAR.

We regard it as probable that Omar gave a charter to the Christians of Syria, agreeing with the above in sense if not in expression, for the following reasons:—

1. The charter is to be found in Mohammedan works with its original text handed down by a series of authorities. The author of the work whence it has been taken, Al-Turṭúshí, himself a writer of the sixth century A.H., has given such a list of authorities going back to the original narrator, in the style of the most accurate chroniclers, which indicates that he got it from a good source.

2. "The Kings' Lamp," the name of the book of Ṭurṭúshí, is an important political and literary treatise, and is not a work of entertainment; its author was, moreover, one of the most learned men of Spain, having been the associate of Abu'l-Walíd al-Bájí, from whom he learned 'disputed questions,' and got a diploma; he further studied Inheritance, Mathematics, and Literature, going to Baghdad and Cairo and

[1] Siráj, 286.

reading with Abú Bakr al-Sháṣí and Abú Mohammed al-Jurjáṇí. He then went to Syria, where he settled, and taught, acquiring a reputation as an authority of law, and a model of learning, virtue, asceticism, and chastity. He was, however, a fanatical hater of Christians, whom he thought proper to humiliate. Once he visited Al-Afḍal. He admonished Al-Afḍal till the latter burst into tears, when Ṭurṭúshí recited the following verse:—

> "O thou, whom 'tis right to obey,
> Whose power we uphold and admire;
> The Prophet who raised thee so high,
> The man at thy side deems a liar."

He pointed to the Christian, whom Al-Afḍal ordered to leave the room.[1] Possibly this fanaticism of Ṭurṭúshí induced him to embody in his work a charter which most of his predecessors wished to leave in obscurity owing to its apparent contradiction to the character of a Pious Caliph. We are not inclined to charge Turṭushí with fabricating the charter himself, as such an act is unlikely in a man of such a reputation for sanctity.

3. Most of the articles in this charter are to be found in the law-books, where the rights of the people of the Covenant are dealt with, and indeed in almost literal agreement with Ṭurṭúshí's text.[2] Most of them are therefore to be found in books that are earlier than Ṭurṭushí's time, e.g. treatises on politics and administration, in some of which reference is made to the charter itself. Thus in the treatise on politics by Máwerdí (ob. 450 A.H.), seventy-five years earlier than Ṭurṭúshí, we find the following under the head "Poll-tax and Land-tax":—

> "If the convention with the Christians include entertainment of passing Moslems, such entertainment is to be for three days and no more, even as Omar covenanted with the Christians of Syria for the entertainment with food for three days of passing Moslems; they are not to be compelled to slaughter sheep or fowls, and the Moslem horses are not to have oats given them: this, moreover, he enjoined on the people of the country as opposed to those of the towns.

[1] Khillikán, i, 479.   [2] Hidáyah, 574.

Further, in the poll-tax contract, there are to be imposed on them two conditions, one incumbent, the other commendable. The former contains six clauses: (1) They shall not criticize or misquote the Koran. (2) They shall not charge with falsehood nor ridicule the Prophet of God. (3) They shall not criticize nor find fault with the Islamic religion. (4) They shall not have intercourse, licit or illicit, with a Moslem woman. (5) They shall not tempt a Moslem to leave his religion, nor make any attempt on his property or life. (6) They shall not assist the enemy nor harbour his spies. These six duties are obligatory without express specification. They are only stipulated in order to call attention to their gravity, and any violation of them after their stipulation shall be sufficient to annul the covenant.

"The latter or commendable condition also contains six clauses: (1) They are to wear some distinguishing mark, such as the yellow badge or the girdle. (2) Their houses are not to be raised to a greater height than the Moslem houses. (3) They are not to let the sound of their *nâḳûs* be heard. (4) They are not to drink wine openly before the Moslems, nor display their crosses. (5) They are to bury their dead quietly. (6) They are not to ride horses, whether of good or bad strain,[1] etc."

This passage of Máwerdí agrees almost literally with the text of Omar's charter, except that it is arranged in heads and clauses. It follows, then, that Omar's charter was known before the composition of the "Kings' Lamp"; and we may add that the historian Ibn al-Athír alludes to it in such a way as to show that he acknowledged its genuineness. Under the year 484 he says: "A rescript of the Caliph was produced enforcing the employment by the people of the Covenant of the yellow badge and the wearing of what was stipulated by Omar, Commander of the Faithful."[2]

4. When the first Caliphs in the early centuries wished to renew the charters of the people of the Covenant, especially the Christians, they made stipulations similar to those contained in Omar's charter, e.g. the adoption of a distinct attire. This shows that the charter goes back to the first century. The first Caliph who did this was Omar II, renowned for his piety, and for his

[1] Máwerdí, 138. [2] Athír, x, 76.

determination to follow the steps of his namesake and grandfather on the mother's side, Omar I. He was the first Umayyad Caliph who wished to reinforce on the people of the Covenant the conditions imposed by Omar, most of which had fallen into abeyance, especially the regulation regarding costume, the Christians having adopted the Moslem attire and taken to the turban. Omar II compelled them to abandon the turban, and wear characteristic garments, and to avoid all resemblance to Moslems. Similarly, the other Caliphs who persecuted the Christians all returned to the rulings of Omar, as will be seen.

§ 35. Omar's Charter and Omar's Character.

The apparent contradiction between Omar's character and the charter is worth considering, and the following may be said on the subject.

The most striking characteristics of Omar were his justice, his ruthlessness, his free-mindedness, and his severity. His piety was combined with extreme zeal in the cause of Islam, and the desire to propagate and extend it. His justice went to such lengths that he was prepared to give judgment against his own son or against his own self. He was, indeed, a personification of justice, and to this day the Moslems take his rulings for models, and endeavour to imitate him, without as yet succeeding. His zeal for Islam was also unrivalled, and in all his words and actions he ever had an *arrière pensée*, viz. the propagation of Islam, the elevation of its torch, and the combination of the Arabs in its support. Justice, indeed, compelled him to give equable treatment to the people of the Covenant, but his desire was the propagation of Islam, and this showed through his justice. Although, therefore, he granted religious liberty in his empire and permitted the people of the Covenant to retain their rites, priests, and churches, he forbade them to build fresh churches, in order that Christianity might be circumscribed, and that Islam might prevail over it and finally extinguish it. Justice compelled him to favour the Arabian Christians of 'Irák by way of compensation for the help they had given the Moslems in the conquest of that province; for this reason he in their case substituted alms for poll-tax; but his anxiety to combine the whole Arab race under the banner of Islam led him to stipulate that they should not train their children in the Christian religion.[1]

§ 36. CONTENTS OF OMAR'S CHARTER.

The contents of the charter fall under four principal heads:—(1) That the Christians shall build no fresh places of worship. (2) That they shall entertain passing Moslems three days. (3) That they shall harbour no spies in their churches, and shall not plot against the Moslems. (4) That they shall not imitate Moslem attire, or mode of riding, that they shall not teach their children the Koran, nor engrave their names in Arabic on their seals. Without these stipulations they are to have no security for their lives, families, or possessions.

The first of these heads corresponds with Omar's passion for the spread of Islam and its dominance, as we have seen. The second was required by the condition of the Moslems in the conquered countries, where they were strangers amongst the people of the Covenant: the Arabs were accustomed to the entertainment of strangers, but the people of those countries had no such custom, whence Omar had to stipulate it for the comfort of the Moslems who were on their way to the wars or travelling on other business. The third and fourth conditions can also be shown to correspond with Omar's character, though for this purpose some preliminary observations are necessary.

§ 37. THE SYRIAN CHRISTIANS AND THE BYZANTINE EMPEROR.

The first point to be noticed about this agreement is that its terms were enforced on the Christians of Syria, not on the other

[1] Ma'árif, 193; Baládhuri, 183; Athír, ii, 259.

people of the Covenant in Syria, nor on the Christians of other provinces, e.g. the Copts, the Nabatæans of 'Irák, the Sabians of Harran, the Magians of Persia, and the Jews in various countries. Clearly this fact must stand in some relation to the severe clauses in the charter. Why were not the same terms enforced on the Christians in all Islamic countries, and why were not the Jews, Sabians, and other people of the Covenant included? It should be added that there is ascribed to Omar another charter [1] to the people of the Covenant generally, of which the terms contain no persecution nor oppression, but rather mildness, respect for rights and protection, so that it resembles the "Prophet's Charter" in most of its provisions. Our view, indeed, about this charter is similar to our view of the Prophet's Charter, on the ground that its phraseology is unlike the phraseology of that age, i.e. the commencement of Islam, and that it is not mentioned by any early Mohammedan writers; only its contents correspond with the spirit of that age, and it resembles most of the contracts that were drawn up with countries that surrendered peacefully, of which some have been given above. Such a charter would naturally be given by Omar to the people of the Covenant, because it agrees with his justice and mild treatment of them, and it is given to all classes of people of the Covenant inclusively.

The charter with which we are dealing was given to the Christians of Syria exclusively, who therefore were apparently to be persecuted when others were not, and this policy could only have been dictated by a sufficient motive. Our idea is that Omar made the conditions that have been discussed with the intention of guarding the Syrian country against a return of the Byzantines brought about by the machinations of the Christians there, who might well act as the spies of the Byzantines against the Moslems, owing to the religious bond between them, a bond which in the East is stronger than any other, and has been so from the most ancient time to our own. Every Eastern community would rather be ruled by a tyrannous co-religionist

[1] Dictionary of Administration as above.

than a just ruler who was of another religion. History affords much evidence of this proposition, as does our own time, notwithstanding the religious lukewarmness that characterizes it; there is not an Eastern community but would prefer to be ruled by a man having the same religion as itself, without troubling whether he were just or unjust. A Christian prefers a Christian ruler, a Moslem a Moslem ruler still; how much more, then, in those times, when religion and politics were so closely connected?

The Syrian Christians, then, were subjected to the poll-tax, and were under the domination of the Moslems; but all the time they maintained their religion with its rites, with prayer in their churches performed as it had been performed before the Moslem conquest, and with priests and bishops coming to them from Constantinople or Antioch; their language was the language of the Byzantine Empire, and their creed its creed. We have further shown elsewhere that the Islamic conquest took, at the beginning of Islam, the form of a military occupation, the Moslems making no alterations in the religious ceremonies, personal affairs, or judicial decisions of the Christians, and acknowledging the sovereignty of the Byzantine emperor to some extent over the Syrian Christians. If any act were committed which interfered with that sovereignty the Byzantine emperor had a plaint against the Caliph, especially in what concerned the churches. And, indeed, the Caliphs observed their compacts scrupulously in this matter, till the Umayyads became powerful and violated the sanctity of those compacts, as they violated other arrangements sanctioned by the Pious Caliphs.

Al-Walíd Ibn 'Abd al-Malik, it is said, hearing the sound of the *nákús*, asked what it meant; and being told that it was in a church, ordered the church to be demolished, and began the work of demolition with his own hand, the Moslems enthusiastically aiding. The Christians then laid a complaint before the emperor at Constantinople, who wrote to Al-Walíd to the effect that the church had been allowed to remain by his predecessors: if they had been right, he must be wrong, whereas if he were right, they must have been wrong.[1] His protest, however, was ineffectual. The anecdote shows that at the commencement of Islam the Christians of Syria were under the protection of the Byzantines, or at any rate regarded the Byzantine emperor as the protector of their churches, just as they now regard certain of the European powers. Further, their minds were saturated with affection for the Byzantine Empire, owing to the teaching of their priests. They may, indeed, have had certain religious grievances against the empire, but when they found themselves under Arab domination they began to regard their former conditions as far preferable. This is not unusual in nations that are accustomed to subjection to others. They cannot remain constant, and are not ready to submit to a religious head. Moreover, their priests and bishops were endeavouring to renew their attachment to the Byzantine emperor: the conquest was recent, and the emperor still hoped to recover his sovereignty over the country, relying on the aid of his fellow-Christians who were in the neighbourhood of the Moslems, whom he might hope to use as spies.

Some of the Syrian Christians used, indeed, to go to great lengths in this matter, bringing Moslem intelligence to the Byzantines, harbouring Byzantine spies in their houses, and assisting them in carrying out their researches. A Christian might often come between two Moslems, dressed like them, and with an Arabic name like theirs on his seal, having committed some of the Koran to memory, in order to give them the impression that he was one of themselves. The conquest of Syria was still incomplete, and Omar was afraid it might still be undone, owing to its distance from the centre of government. Out of some such fear, then, he stipulated that the Christians of Syria should not imitate the attire or the mode of riding of the Moslems, that they should harbour no Byzantine spies, and that they should not plot against the Moslems.

[1] Mas'údí, ii, 113.

For a similar reason Omar forbade his viceroys to employ as agents the people of the Book, alleging that they took bribes, and that they were attached to each other; some, indeed, suppose that this prohibition was taken from one uttered by the Prophet in a discourse held by him on the day when he went to the field of Badr.[1] The prohibition could not be enforced, since the Moslems were compelled to take into their employ persons who could do accounts and write, especially at the beginning of Islam, when the books were still kept in the languages of the conquered countries.

Hence we hold it most probable that Omar wrote or got the Christians of Syria to write a charter, of which the above contains the real conditions, even if it be not the actual text, which may very well have been subsequently altered. And the reason of its severity is to be found in Omar's fear of the Christians of Syria, who among the Easterns came nearest to the Byzantine Church. The Copts hated the Byzantine Church, and aided the Moslems to conquer Egypt and oust the Byzantines. The charter, then, was not dictated by fanatical hatred of Christianity or the desire to persecute. Afterwards, however, its conditions were extended by the Moslems to the whole of the people of the Covenant, whereas Omar had intended it only for the Christians of Syria.

§ 38. The Umayyads and the People of the Covenant.

Such, then, was the condition of the tolerated sects when the Umayyads succeeded to the Caliphate. They had no fear of a Byzantine invasion of Syria, where was their capital; moreover, they had possession of the coast, were dominant over the whole country, and could raid the Byzantines by sea. None the less they oppressed the people of the Covenant by increasing the poll-tax among their other efforts to amass money with the view of obtaining partisans, as well as

[1] Siráj, 214.

enjoying luxuries. They increased both poll-tax and land-tax, and extorted both with violence, and went so far in their oppression as to take poll-tax from converts to Islam. And meanwhile they tortured and humiliated those who remained steadfast to their religion, on the ground that they were neither Arabs nor Moslems. Mankind with them consisted of three classes: Arabs, clients, and people of the Covenant. This, indeed, agreed with the view of Mu'áwiyah, who divided the inhabitants of Egypt into three sorts as follows: men, quasi-men, and non-men; the three meant the Arabs, the clients, and the allies, i.e. the Copts, respectively.[1]

When the Copts found that conversion to Islam would not exempt them from the poll-tax nor from its extortion by violence, some of them bethought them of taking the monk's robe, since monks were exempted from the poll-tax. The Umayyad viceroys, perceiving their object, proceeded to impose poll-tax on the monks, and became so vindictive that some wanted to enforce it on the dead as well as the living, by making the survivors pay poll-tax for their dead relatives.[2] Many such incidents are recorded for the Umayyad period, and have been related in the second part of this work (p. 21), with illustrations of the modes employed by the Umayyads for plundering the property of the people of the Covenant.

This process was carried on by the Umayyads, who overlooked the charter of Omar, until the Caliphate came to his grandson and admirer Omar II, who, amongst other instances of imitation of Omar I, wrote to his viceroys bidding them restore the provisions of the charter. His letter to them contains the charge to order non-Moslems to give up wearing turbans, and put on distinctive attire, imitate Moslems in no respect, and also to permit no unbeliever to have a Moslem servant,[3] and forbidding the viceroys to take people of the Covenant into their employ. He also forbade the Christians to beat their hammer while the Call to Prayer was going on.

The Umayyads were so keen about amassing money, for

[1] Makrízí, i, 50. [2] Id., i, 295. [3] 'Iḳd, ii, 262; Athír, v, 31.

the reasons which have been stated, that, finding the people of the Covenant better able to assist their design than others owing to their skill in accounts and in writing and the business of the land-tax, they employed them against their wish; and they cared little whether thereby the propagation of Islam and the circumscription of Christianity were furthered or not. Else they would not have made Khalid al-Kasri governor of the two 'Iraks, a man whose mother was a Greek Christian, and to please whom he favoured the Christians in his province, so that the latter became prosperous in his days. He wished his mother to embrace Islam, but when he could not persuade her to do so he built her a church behind the south side of the great Mosque at Kufah, and when the mu'eddhirr wished to call to prayer the hammer was beaten for her also.[1] Khalid employed Christians and Magians in offices over the Moslems, contrary to the injunctions of Omar II, and gave them a free hand in the government, so as to be able to rule the Moslems with despotic power. The mother of the famous poet Omar Ibn Abi Rabi'ah was a Christian, who died with a cross suspended from her neck.[2] In Umayyad times the Christians used to enter the mosques and walk about them without interference from anyone. The Christian poet Al Akhtal used to enter the presence of the Caliph 'Abd al-Malik without leave, when drunk, with a cross on his breast, without opposition. They used to permit him to do this because they required his aid in satirizing the Helpers.[3]

When an Umayyad Caliph wanted to promote a Jew or a Christian he would invite him to embrace Islam; but there was nothing to prevent his refusal unless, indeed, the Caliph had a spite against him, and could dispense with his service. In such a case the Caliph might avenge himself. Thus a certain Sham'alah, a Persian Christian, entered the presence of an Umayyad Caliph, who bade him embrace Islam. He declared that he would never do so: in any case, only when

1. Aghani, xix, 59. 2. Ibid., i, 32. 3. Ibid., vii, 74, 78.

he wished to of his own free will. The Caliph, furious at this reply, ordered some of the flesh to be cut off his thigh, to be roasted, and given him to eat. To Al-Akhtal, 'Abd al-Malik once made a proposal that he should embrace Islam, and be given a fixed sum out of the booty, and 10,000 dirhems on the spot. "How about wine?" he asked. "What is the use of it?" asked the Caliph; "its beginning is bitter, and its end intoxication." "It may be so," replied the poet, "but all between is such that compared with it your whole empire only counts as a drop of water from the Euphrates licked off the finger-tip." The Caliph laughed.

The Umayyad viceroys oppressed the Christians by extorting their money, and paying honour to anyone who facilitated such extortion. Makrízí's work contains some chapters dealing with the ruin of the Copts by these methods, which should be consulted.[1]

§ 39 SUMMARY.

To conclude, then, the Umayyad dynasty was an Arab dynasty, the basis of whose policy was the desire for conquest and arbitrary power. The monarchs compassed these ends by the aid of the clan-patriotism of the Kuraish and by winning partisans. This clan-patriotism led to the re-division of the Arabs into tribes such as had existed in pagan days, with the further divisions representing home-patriotism of various sorts. They carried to an excess their partisanship for the Arabs and their contempt for the non-Arabs, clients, and people of the Covenant or tolerated sects; their need of partisans forced them to amass wealth, which again had to be extended in conciliating adherents; and the need for it led them to commit injustice in acquiring it They laid hands on the alms-money, and appropriated the booty; they saw that their rivals the 'Alids made a just claim to the Caliphate, their arms being religion and piety, and when their respective claims were debated the 'Alids

[1] Makrízí, i, 79, 312, 493.

prevailed; so they poured contempt on religion and derision on those that concerned themselves therewith, and took refuge in craft and cunning, and discarding generosity, while going to excesses in violence and cruelty. They became notorious for this, nor is this character disputed by any of the historians, even of their own lineage. For Abu'l-Faraj, the author of the *Aghání*, was himself an Umayyad by descent,[1] and the chief crimes of the Umayyads are to be learned from his book.

The merit of maintaining their dynasty belongs to three Caliphs, all of them celebrated for political ability and astuteness, each of whom reigned for about twenty years: Mu'awiyah (41–60), 'Abd al-Malik (65–86), Hisham Ibn 'Abd al-Malik (105–125). When the 'Abbasid Manṣur became Caliph he took for his political model Hisham.[2] The most religious of the line was Omar II, but he was born out of season, and his reign was short. Had it not been for these rulers the dynasty must have terminated speedily, since the throne was bandied about among a series of weak Caliphs, who were debauchees and voluptuaries. The first of these was Yazíd Ibn Mu'awiyah (ob. 64), who was devoted to hunting, and spent his energy on acquiring falcons, dogs, apes, and lynxes; he was also fond of drinking bouts, and was imitated by his viceroys, who drank wine openly. In his time the singing art came to the front in Meccah and Medinah, and musical instruments were used, having been previously unknown to the Moslems.[3]

Another of these debauchees was Yazíd son of 'Abd al-Malik (ob. 105). He was known as the debauched Umayyad; coming after Omar II, he followed a very different line from that Caliph. He was devotedly attached to two slave-girls, Salamah and Ḥabbabah, and spent most of his time in their society. One day Ḥabbábah sang:

> "There's some heat 'twixt the jaw and the collar:
> One can't cool, no, nor soften, nor swallow";

and Yazíd was so enthralled by the song that he almost flew.

[1] Athír, viii, 229. [2] Mas'údí, ii, 132. [3] Id., ii, 68.

The girl told him that she had a request to submit; his answer was that he was going to fly. "To whom will you leave your people?" she asked. He answered, "To you," kissing her hand. Going out one day for a pleasure excursion in the neighbourhood of the Jordan, while he was drinking with Ḥabbabah, he threw a grape-stone at her, which got into her throat, would not go down, and caused her to fall ill and die. For three days he would not let her be buried, but continued to kiss and caress her, and gaze at her, weeping, till the body could no longer remain unburied, and he permitted the interment. He then returned to his palace, in grief and distress, when he heard a slave-girl sing the following song:

> "What pain for the lover who sees with a groan
> His beloved's abode a wilderness lone";

whereat Yazíd shed tears. After her death he survived seven days, during which he showed himself to no one, in accordance with the advice of his brother Maslamah, who was afraid he might do something which would ruin his reputation.[1] His reign altogether was only four years.

Another was Al-Walíd Ibn Yazíd Ibn 'Abd al-Malik, who was a drunkard and profligate, chiefly concerned with the chase and with wine, of which he had reservoirs made deep enough for him to plunge into[2] and drink from. His first act on becoming Caliph was to send for the minstrels from Medinah and Meccah, and also to summon to his court a number of debauchees and ne'er-do-wells to be his boon companions. He, too, went to excess in drunkenness and debauchery, but his reign did not outlast a year.

The Arabs were highly displeased with the debauchery of the Umayyads from the time of Yazíd Ibn Mu'awiyah, of whose appointment to the Caliphate they disapproved. Naturally their displeasure at the conduct of the succeeding debauchees was yet greater. Some verses are preserved in which a poet warns them against nursing wolves, and feeding

[1] Athír, v, 57. [2] Aghání, iii, 90.

them with their own flesh, or tearing their own stomachs open with their hands.

The conduct of these winebibbers was very different from that of the astute Umayyads whom we have mentioned, none of whom drank wine, or took part in any sort of revelry or debauchery. Even Hisham Ibn 'Abd al-Malik, who came towards the end of the dynasty, neither drank wine nor permitted it to be drunk in his presence,[1] but reproached and punished those who drank.

So when the Umayyad Caliphs plunged into excesses of the sort described, and this was coupled with their fanaticism against non-Arabs, with their contempt of clients, and their habitual ill-treatment of the people of the Covenant and the other villagers, whose property was habitually pillaged by Moslem troops when they passed through,[2] people began to talk to each other of the speedy termination of the dynasty. And, indeed, after a few years it had passed away and the 'Abbasid dynasty took its place.

[1] Aghani, v, 167. [2] Athír, v, 146.

CHAPTER III.

§ 1. First Persian Period.

From the Caliphate of Saffáḥ, 132 A.H., *to that of Mutawakkil,* 233.

We call this period Persian, although it comes within the 'Abbasid age because the dynasty of the time, though Arabian in respect of its sovereigns, language, and religion, was Persian in respect of its politics and administration. The Persians won the victory for it, maintained it, organized its government, and administered its offices. Persia provided its viziers, governors, scribes, and chamberlains. The Persians were induced to aid the 'Abbásid dynasty by the chauvinism of the Umayyads, which has already been described, and by the Umayyad contempt for the clients, who were mainly Persians. Hence the Persians gave their aid to anyone, 'Alid or Schismatic, who had a grievance against the Umayyads. They were, indeed, more inclined to favour the 'Alids, owing to the appearance of justice which their claim displayed, since they wished the sovereignty to be bestowed on the Prophet's son-in-law or the sons of the Prophet's daughters. The 'Alids kept sending their agents over 'Iraḳ, Fars, Khorasan, and other countries that were at a distance from the seat of the Caliphate, and allegiance was readily promised them by the Persians, hoping to escape Umayyad tyranny.

Then arose the 'Abbasid pretenders, who won the sovereignty with the help of Abu Muslim of Khorasan, and who counted on the internal dissensions of the Arabs and the dislike of the Yemenite tribes to the Umayyads. Only the Muḍarites were on the Umayyads' side. Abú Muslim therefore solicited the aid of the Yemenites, and thereby accomplished his design. This shall now be explained.

§ 2. THE TRANSFERENCE OF THE CALIPHATE TO THE 'ABBÁSIDS.

The 'Alid party.—When the Umayyads came forward, became supreme, and usurped absolute power, the 'Alids were claiming the Caliphate and endeavouring to obtain it : the first of the line who sought it after 'Alí himself was his son Hasan, who, however, resigned his claim in favour of Mu'áwiyah in the year 41. The partisans of the faction in Kúfah were indignant at his resignation, and made disturbances ; the governor of Kúfah at the time, the astute Ziyád, "his father's son," took severe steps to extinguish the disturbance, and slew many of the adherents of 'Alí, among them Ḥujr Ibn 'Adí and his followers. The rest of the faction continued vigilantly to await the death of Mu'áwiyah on the chance of the popular choice falling on one of 'Alí's sons, in which case the sovereignty would come back to the Prophet's house. It did not occur to these persons that Mu'áwiyah would appoint his son to succeed him. When they learned that he had taken this step they were indignant, and this feeling was accentuated by their knowledge that the heir-apparent was a dissolute man, who preferred the chase to administering the affairs of an empire. This feeling is expressed in an epigram by 'Abdallah Ibn Hishám al-Salúlí :

> "We 're filled full of wrath, and were we to drain
> The blood of Umayyah, our thirst would still pain :
> While wasting your people, ye still without care,
> Ye sons of Umayyah, go hunting the hare." [1]

The most eminent of the 'Alids at that time was Husain son of 'Alí : when in the year 60 Mu'áwiyah died, and his son

[1] Mas'údí, ii, 50.

Yazíd succeeded, Ḥusain refused to do homage; and, indeed, most of those pious persons who swore allegiance regarded that act as a violation of decency.[1] Ḥusain was in Medinah, and when he was asked to swear allegiance he fled to Meccah. Most of his partisans were, however, in Kúfah, and these wrote to him, urging him to come to them and promising him their assistance. He obeyed them, but when he had got near Kúfah they declined to give him any effective aid; the governor of Kúfah, 'Ubaidallah Ibn Ziyád, sent an army against him, and in the battle that ensued he was killed; that famous death took place on the 10th of Muharram of the year 61 A.H.

The 'Alid faction afterwards regretted their supineness, and came forward after the death of Yazíd and the proclamation of Marwán Ibn al-Ḥakam in the year 64, demanding vengeance for Ḥusain's blood, and taking the title "the Penitent." They drove out 'Ubaidallah Ibn Ziyád, who was still governor of Kúfah, and set up a governor of their own, who, however, was overcome by 'Ubaidallah. Then there arose Mukhtár Ibn Abí 'Ubaid the Thaḳafite, an ambitious man, anxious like many others to seize the opportunity which the disturbed state of affairs offered for the plunder of property: he was a man of great schemes, and coming to Kúfah he demanded vengeance for the death of Ḥusain, and called on the people to swear allegiance to Mohammed Ibn al-Ḥanafiyyah, brother to Ḥusain on the father's side. He was followed by a number of Kufans, whom he designated "God's bodyguard." He attacked 'Ubaidallah Ibn Ziyád, defeated him, and slew him with most of those who had been concerned in Ḥusain's death; only Mohammed Ibn al-Ḥanafiyyah was not a party to his undertaking, and he sent to Mukhtár to decline it. Mukhtár therefore substituted 'Abdallah Ibn al-Zubair in his proclamation, this man having put himself forward as a claimant to the Caliphate, somewhat as Husain had, for his father Zubair had been

[1] Athír, iii, 252.

a pretender to the Caliphate after the death of 'Uthmán, as we have seen. 'Abdallah stayed in Meccah, asking the Moslems to swear allegiance to himself; Mukhtár was not, indeed, sincere in his advocacy of the claims of either, since he doubtless wanted the Caliphate for himself; and when 'Abdallah became aware of his intention he appointed his brother Mus'ab governor of 'Irák, and sent him to fight Mukhtár; Mus'ab succeeded in killing Mukhtár in the year 67.

After the death of Ḥusain the 'Alid faction was split in two. One section asserted that the right to the Caliphate belonged to the children of 'Alí by Fáṭimah the Prophet's daughter; whereas the other held that after the death of Ḥasan and Ḥusain it went to their brother Mohammed Ibn al-Ḥanafiyyah, this sect being called the *Kaisánís.* The other sect was, however, the more energetic and the more prominent of the two. After the death of Ḥusain they swore allegiance to his son known as 'Alí Zain al-'Ábidín; and the right to the Caliphate was supposed to continue in his descendants till the number of twelve imáms—'Alí, Ḥusain, 'Alí Zain al-'Ábidín, Mohammed al-Bakír, Ja'far al-Ṣádiḳ, Músá al-Káẓim, 'Alí al-Ridá, Mohammed al-Taḳí, 'Alí al-Naḳí, Ḥasan al-'Askarí, Mohammed al-Mahdí. Many minor subdivisions of Shí'ís (partisans of 'Alí) were also formed, which swore allegiance to different descendants of 'Alí, such as the *Zaidites,* who swore it to Zaid son of 'Alí son of Ḥusain, the *Ismá'ílís,* who swore it to Ismá'íl son of Ja'far al-Ṣádiḳ, etc.

Whenever the Umayyads heard of the appearance of any of the 'Alid missionaries they did their utmost to put him to death. And they did indeed kill many, by poison, crucifixion, etc. Hence those who carried on the 'Alid propaganda concealed themselves for fear of an onslaught. The 'Alids themselves during the supremacy of the Umayyads were in distressed circumstances and were likely to die of starvation, and some had no higher ambition than the support of their families. When, however, Khálid al-Kasrí, the Umayyad viceroy, took office in 126, he had compassion on them and supplied them with money, so that they again began to pretend to the Caliphate.[1] This Khálid was a man of remarkable character: although a viceroy in the employ of the Umayyads, he assisted the 'Alids, and gave posts to the people of the Covenant, as we have already stated.

§ 3. The 'Abbásid Faction.

Among other pretenders to the Caliphate were the descendants of the Prophet's uncle 'Abbás, who, however, made no actual attempt at seizing it during the prosperous days of the Umayyads, though they carried on a secret propaganda. They and the 'Alid faction were on good terms in the times when they were persecuted and in distress, as being both of the Háshim clan and enemies of the Umayyads before Islam: and, indeed, persecuted factions become tender towards each other at all times.

The 'Abbasids continued to maintain strict secrecy as to their propaganda, while remaining in Humaimah, in the Balká district of Syria, until the Umayyads became weak, and then they thought the time had come to show themselves. In the meantime the Kaisání faction, which maintained the claims of Mohammed Ibn al-Hanafiyyah, was urging those of his son Abú Háshim, who, in the course of his visits from Medinah to the Umayyads in Syria, passed by Humaimah. In the course of one of those visits paid to Hishám Ibn 'Abd al-Malik, that Caliph found him to be possessed of eloquence, capacity, and statesmanship. Knowing also that he aimed at being Caliph, the Umayyad took fright, and had him poisoned with milk on his way back to Medinah. Abú Háshim felt the poison in him as he journeyed, and turned aside to Ḥumaimah, where at the time the head of the 'Abbásid faction was Mohammed Ibn 'Alí Ibn 'Abdallah Ibn 'Abbás, in whose house Abu Háshim was entertained. When the latter perceived that his end was near, being

[1] Athír, v, 129.

unwilling that his rights as Caliph should lapse, he, being far away from his home, bequeathed the Caliphate to the aforesaid Mohammed. There were present a number of his own party, whom he entrusted to Mohammed, and whom he recommended to Mohammed's care. When Abú Háshim was dead, Mohammed became keen to acquire the Caliphate, and felt confident of success, because he had the whole of the Kaisání faction on his side. So he began to despatch missionaries secretly. He died, however, before success had been achieved, and bequeathed his claims to his son Ibráhím known as *the Imám.*

Ibráhím now began to despatch emissaries, beginning with Khorasan, in whose inhabitants he placed greater reliance than in those of any other province, because the bulk of the Kaisání faction were to be found in Khorasan and 'Irák, and the inhabitants of both provinces had repeatedly assisted the 'Alids. Sending out the same emissaries as had been employed by Abú Háshim, he told them to obtain oaths of allegiance to the Family of the Prophet, without specifying whether 'Alids or the 'Abbásids were meant. The people of Khorasan, wearied out with the Umayyad despotism, were quite ready to promise allegiance to the Family of the Prophet, supposing that the sovereignty would be shared by the two branches. Meanwhile Ibráhím was able to get the co-operation of the great general Abú Muslim of Khorasan, who achieved success and installed an 'Abbásid in the Caliphate, as is well known.

§ 4. MANSÚR'S OATH OF ALLEGIANCE TO THE 'ALIDS AND HIS RECANTATION.

When the Háshimites—'Alids and 'Abbásids—perceived the breaking up of the Umayyad power, they met at Meccah, the chief men on both sides being present, and debated concerning the approaching downfall of the Umayyad dynasty, and the question which of the members of the Prophet's family should succeed; among those who took part in this assembly were Abu'l-'Abbás al-Saffáḥ and his brother 'Abdallah Ibn Mohammed Ibn 'Alí Ibn 'Abbás, better known as Abu Ja'far al-Manṣúr, with other members of the 'Abbásid family. They agreed to swear allegiance to the most eminent of the 'Alids of the time, viz. Mohammed Ibn 'Abdallah Ibn Ḥasan al-Muthanna Ibn Ḥasan Ibn 'Alí called 'the Pure Soul'; they swore allegiance to him owing to his personal eminence and his acknowledged superiority. Among those who swore on that occasion was Al-Mansúr himself.[1] Possibly this oath was what kept the 'Alids quiet and prevented their pretending to the Caliphate during the dispatch of the 'Abbásid emissaries, assuming that it had been agreed that the sovereignty should be shared between the two families. And, as we have seen, the 'Abbásid missionaries worked in the name of the Family of the Prophet, not in that of the Imám Ibráhím or any other member of the 'Abbásid branch.

The emissaries of the 'Alid faction, who had been advertising the claims of the 'Alids in 'Irák, Fars, and Khorasan, before the transference of the oath of allegiance to the 'Abbásids, had no choice but to acquiesce in that transference. Among these emissaries was Abú Salamah al-Khallál (vinegar merchant) al-Muthri (the rich), of Fars. His residence was in Ḥammám A'yan, a suburb of Kúfah. This man was a vigorous champion of the rights of the 'Alids, and had employed his wealth and personal influence on their behalf. When he learned how the oath of allegiance had been transferred to the 'Abbásids, he repressed his indignation, and waited to see how this would be taken; presently he heard that the Imam Ibráhím had sent Abú Muslim as his emissary into Khorasan with the famous charge, "Kill all suspects." As the heads of the 'Alid family obeyed this man, Abú Salamah did as they did, fully expecting that the sovereignty would be put in commission between the two factions.[2] When he heard that Marwán Ibn Mohammed, the last of the Umayyad

[1] Khaldún, iv, 3; Athír, v, 243; Fakhrí, 147. [2] Faraj, ii, 120.

Caliphs, had executed the Imám Ibráhím, he bethought him of returning to the defence of the 'Alid claims.[1] Presently, however, there came to him the brothers of the Imám Ibráhím, including Abu'l-'Abbás al-Saffáḥ, with the remaining members of the family, and finding it generally assumed that the sovereignty had been transferred, Abú Salamah, who was their entertainer, felt unable to transfer it back: whence it remained in the possession of the 'Abbásids. Meanwhile Abú Muslim and the other heads of houses and generals were fighting against the Umayyads in Khorasan, Fars, and 'Irák; and when they had won the victory and secured possession of Khorasan and the neighbouring countries, they came to 'Irák and there proclaimed Abu'l-'Abbás. The 'Alids had therefore to remain quiet, fearing the might of the wave of success which swept all before the 'Abbasids, while still retaining some hope that the sovereignty might after all be shared between the two families.

The 'Abbásids were aware of Abú Salamah's secret intention to transfer the Caliphate to the 'Alids; they therefore accused him secretly before Abú Muslim, who suborned a man to kill him in Kúfah by a sudden assault, while circulating the rumour that the man had been killed by a Schismatic; and they killed many more besides of those whose loyalty they doubted, until they were left in possession of the field.

The family of Ḥasan Ibn 'Alí had already, as has been seen, sworn allegiance to one of their number, Mohammed Ibn 'Abdallah, in Medinah, when the same oath had been taken by the other members of the Háshim clan, including Abú Ja'far al-Mansúr; when they learned that the Umayyad dynasty was over, and that allegiance had been sworn to Abu'l-'Abbás al-Saffáḥ in the year 132 A.H., they came to Kúfah to demand from Abu'l-'Abbás the fulfilment of the oath of allegiance already given. Abu'l-'Abbás endeavoured to appease them by gifts of money and estates; among these visitors was 'Abdallah Ibn al-Ḥasan, father of the 'Alid

[1] Mas'údí, ii, 150.

pretender. Suffah treated him with honour and offered him as much money as would satisfy him, leaving it to him to name the sum. He named a million dirhems, a sum which, he said, he had never beheld. Saffah had not in his possession that amount, so he borrowed it from a banker named Ibn Abi Mukrin, and handed it over to the old man. It so happened that while ʻAbdallah was with Saffah some jewels were brought which the ʻAbbasid soldiery had taken from the late Caliph Mohammed Ibn Marwan. Saffah began to handle the jewels in the presence of ʻAbdallah, who wept at the sight. Being asked why, he said : "To think that such jewels should be in the possession of Marwan's daughters, whereas my daughters have never even seen the like !" Saffah presented him with the jewels, and then ordered a banker to purchase them of him for 80,000 dinars, or about a million dirhems. Saffiah continued to entertain his guest ʻAbdallah honourably, while studying his disposition. Finding by the aid of spies that the old man was a victim of avarice, he loaded him with wealth, and sent him back to Medinah, to distribute his gains among his poor relations, who were well pleased therewith.

Nevertheless, ʻAbdallah continued to enterain ambitious hopes for his son,[1] to whom allegiance had already been sworn, and the ʻAbbasids continued to regard him with alarm, and Saffah to conciliate him with gifts of money. At the death of Saffah in 136 he was succeeded by his brother Mansur, an energetic man, who cared not what crimes he committed with the object of securing his own sovereignty. His first consideration was to find out what sentiments were harboured by the family of Hasan in Medinah, to whom he had formerly given an oath of allegiance. He therefore sent spies to Medinah, and wished to make trial of the people he feared. Forwarding the usual stipend to the people of Medinah, he wrote to his governor there to give it to the recipients personally, and not to sent it to anyone ; to watch

[1] ʻIkd. iii. 27.

carefully the Hashimites and see whether any of them failed to present themselves, and to take special note of the two sons of 'Abdallah, Mohammed and Ibrahim. The governor carried out the Caliph's orders, and wrote to the effect that only the two persons named had failed to present themselves to receive their stipend. Mansur then felt convinced that they were meditating an insurrection, and that they had only kept quiet during his brother's reign because he had paid them special honour, and provided them plentifully with money--a course which Mansur did not think fit to imitate. Finding their resources straitened, the 'Alids of Medinah made up their minds to revolt, and sent their emissaries into Khorasan and elsewhere to summon their partisans to swear allegiance to them. Mansur, hearing of this, despatched, agents to seize their letters on the road, and adopted further expedients in order to apprise himself of their secrets. He also desired the two sons of 'Abdallah to be brought before him, and wrote to their father to produce them ; he, however declared that he did not know where they were. It now become Mansur's main anxiety to get rid of them and of the other 'Alid pretenders to the Caliphate, especially those of the descendants of Hasan, who resided in Medinah. He accordingly sent orders to his governor at Medinah to arrest them all and send them to 'Irak, whither they accordingly were sent loaded with chains, and with irons on their necks and feet. They were also mounted without cushions. But the two sons of 'Abdallah had hidden themselves and could not be brought. The Hasanids who were brouhgt, being more than ten in number, with the exception of one or two were killed by Mansur's command.

Mohammed, however, to whom allegiance had been sworn, not having gallen into the trap, Mansur ordered his governor at Medinah to make a strict search for him ; Mohammed was therefore compelled to come forward openly as a claimant to the sovereignty, and received the oath of allegiance from the people of Medinah, who had first consulted their leading jurisconsult, Málik Ibn Anas, who advised that they should openly espouse Mohammed's cause. When they objected that they had already sworn allegiance to Manṣúr, he replied that that oath had been given under compulsion, and that which had been sworn to Mohammed was more binding since it had been given before the other.[1] Another great jurisconsult, Abú Ḥaníſah, took the same view, and declared that Mohammed was the better man and had the better right. Manṣúr bore these utterances in mind, and both the lawyers had to suffer for their freedom of speech. When in the year 145 Manṣúr got Mohammed into his power and executed him, he persecuted them both, and had a beating inflicted on Málik for his decision that an oath imposed by force was not binding, and imprisoned Abú Ḥaníſah for refusing the judgeship, as is well known.

Manṣúr's repudiation of the oath which he had taken to Mohammed Ibn 'Abdallah produced a powerful impression on the minds of the 'Alids, who had not imagined that a member of the Prophet's family could act in the spirit of the Umayyads. They began to regret Umayyad days, and wish they might return. It is stated that during Mohammed Ibn 'Abdallah's revolt against Manṣúr he heard a poet lamenting the Umayyads, and burst into tears. His uncle asked him how he, who was engaged in such an enterprise against the 'Abbásids, could bewail the Umayyads? He replied that although they had good cause to complain of the Umayyads, they had found the 'Abbásids still more godless, and the 'Abbásid conduct still less justifiable. The Umayyads had some virtue and some generosity which failed in Manṣúr.[2]

§ 5. Expedients of the 'Abbásids for the Maintenance of their Authority.

Execution on suspicion.—We have seen that when the 'Abbásids began to urge their pretension to the Caliphate,

[1] Athír, v, 251; Khaldún, iv, 3. [2] Aghání, x, 106.

they were in the midst of two great dangers : on the one hand, they were compelled to fight with the Umayyads and gain over their partisans ; on the other, they had to secure themselves against the ʻAlids, who had a prior claim to the sovereignty. Events had taught them that a dynasty cannot be supported by religion and piety only, as had been the case in the time of the Pious Caliphs and as the descendants of ʻAlids had designed. For the ʻAlids had failed to achieve success because they based their pretensions only on the nobility of their ancestry, the genuineness of their piety, and the facts the Muʻawiyah had succeeded only by cunning and scheming, and that ʻAbd al-Malik had only maintained himself in power by violence and ruthlessness. When, therefore, throught the bequest of Abu Hashim to Mohammed Ibn ʻAli the ʻAbbasid sovereignty had been transferred from the ʻAlids to the ʻAbbasids, as has been shown, and from Mohammed Ibn ʻAli it came to his son Ibrahim the Imam, and this man was fortunate enough to secure the services of Abu Muslim of Khorasan, Ibrahim made this man, in whom he found the requistie energy and astuteness, commander of his captains and emissarics, and gave him the injunction which served as the pivot of ʻAbbaside policy, of which the following is the text :--

> " You are one of us, the Family of the Prophet. Observe my injunction. Observe this tribe of Yemen, stick to them and dwell among them, because our purpose can only be accomplished through them. Be suspicious of Rabiʻah in regard to them. Mudar is the enemy in the neighbourhood ; kill any one of them about whom you are in doubt : and if you can manage to leave no one in Khorasan who speaks Arabic, do so. Kill any lad five spans long of whom you have suspicions."[1]

These were the injunctions which Abu Muslim received from the Imam Ibrahim before starting, and he acted accordingly, killing anyone whom be doubted or suspected. The number of victims dispatched by him in the course of his mission

[1] Arthir, v, 165.

amounted to 600,000, all of them killed in cold blood, without fighting, and in the course of a few years ;[1] and among them were eminent members of the 'Alid faction, including the Chief *nakibs* censors), and some of the most distinguished emissaries, e.g. Abu Salamah al-Khallal, who aided the 'Abbasid cause with his wealth, just as Abu Muslim aided it with his sword, and had won the title Minister of Mohammed's family, just as Abu Muslim had the title General of Mohammed's family. No sooner had Saffah asked Abu Muslim's advice in his case, and charged him with the intention of transferring the Caliphate to the 'Alids, than Abū Muslim advised that he should be slain, and he was slain, and with him those whom he had appointed as governors over different regions. The same was the treatment meted out to Sulaiman Ibn Kathir, also one of the foremost 'Abbasid agents, a venerable old man who had spared no pains to win victory to their cause. After the execution of Abu Salamah, Abu Muslim heard the same against him as had been bruited against the other, and summoned him (Sulaiman) to his presence, when he asked him whether he remembered the injunction of the Imam, "Slay whomsoever you respect." Sulaiman said he remembered it. "Then I suspect *you*," said Abu Muslim. Sulaiman implored him by God not to suspect him. Abu Muslim told him his adjurations were useless, since it was clear that he harboured treachery against the Sovereign, and ordered his head to be struck off.[2] Naturally many more were killed by them outside the faction of 'Ali, among them princes and generals ; and these murders were effected by various ruses and by actual treachery. Such a case was that of Al-kirmani and his children and chief adherents.[3] So many were slaughtered that the Moslem world grew weary of his ways, and it came to be the rule that if ever a man were summoned to an audience with the Caliph he would make his will, and prepare grave clothes and embalming materials. Some of the chief of the 'Abbasid faction, also grew indignant,

[1] Athir, v. 227. [2] Id., v. 208. [3] Id., v. 183.

and declared that they had not followed the family of the Prophet with the intention of spilling innocent blood and doing iniquity, and more than 50,000 persons joined this movement. Abu Muslim sent against them an army, which defeated and put them all to death.

§ 6. Mansur and the 'Abbasid Dynasty.

By such measures as this, Abu Muslim prepared for the 'Abbasids the road to the sovereignty, and assisted them first by dirving the Umayyad sovereign from his throne ; nor was he satisfied with securing it for Saffah and killing Marwan Ibn Mohammed, the last of the Umayyad Caliphs, but urged the new sovereign to kill all survivors of the Umayyad house, either by suggesting it himself or by employing the poets to alarm the Caliph. Abu Muslim is supposed to have charged the poet Sudaif to recite his ode in the presence of Saffah, when Sulaiman, grandson of the Caliph 'Abd al-Malik was also there, having received a promise of protection from Saffah, who treated him kindly, and had also given a similar promise to the other members of the Umayyad family. Sudaif then on this occasion recited the following verse :--

"Be thou not deceived by their smiles .
When behind there are treason and wiles :
Ply the sword and the scourge till the race
Of Umayyad's swept off the earth's face."

Saffah was induced by these lines to order Sulaiman to be killed. Another time, when there were about 70 members of the Umayyad family with Saffah, another poet entered and recited some similar composition ; the Caliph had them all killed, and spread mats over their corpes, and a feast was instituted while the groans of the victims were still heared.[1] There is, however, another story concerning their death, in which it is stated that were killed by Saffah's uncle,

[1] Fakhri. 134. 'Ikd. ii. 279.

'Abdallah Ibn 'Alí, who was a notorious hater of the Umayyads. All agree in asserting that they were slain in the year 132 A.H., after an amnesty had been granted them: somewhat as the Mamluk princes were killed at the beginning of the nineteenth century.

It is most probable that Abú Muslim advised the 'Abbásids to slay them lest they should stand in the way of the new dynasty, and that he told Sudaif to recommend that measure in his verse. Nor was Sudaif's poem dictated by affection to the 'Abbásids, but by detestation of the Umayyads, and the desire to avenge the wrongs of the 'Alids, to whose faction he himself belonged; he had supposed that the sovereignty would be shared between the two branches of the Prophet's house, and when he found Manṣúr seize it for himself he resented this action and proceeded to satirize the 'Abbásids. Manṣúr, hearing of his compositions, ordered his minister to seize Sudaif and bury him alive, which was done.[1]

When the 'Abbásids had slain all the members of the Umayyad family whom they had in their power, they aimed at exterminating them in other countries as well; and few of them escaped, the most important survivor being 'Abd al-Rahmán Ibn Mu'áwiyah Ibn Hishám, who fled westward and founded the Umayyad dynasty in Spain, as shall be explained. The work of exterminating the Umayyads was undertaken by the aforementioned 'Abdallah Ibn 'Alí, who went so far as to exhume their bodies and mutilate them, in order to avenge the wrongs done by the Umayyads to members of the family of 'Alí, and especially to Zaid son of Zain al-'Ábidín. He had the corpse of Hishám Ibn 'Abd al-Malik exhumed, and finding it still preserved he scourged it 80 times and then burnt it.[2]

When Manṣúr had got rid of the Umayyads, Abú Muslim did his utmost to free his master from the possibility of rivals among his 'Abbásid relatives; among these was 'Abdallah Ibn 'Alí, who had already been mentioned. This person

[1] 'Ikd, iii, 32. [2] Khillikán, ii, 205.

aspired to the Caliphate, and was therefore attacked at Manṣúr's order by Abú Muslim, who defeated him in battle, and obtained possession of all the spoils and arms in his camp. Mansúr next wished to turn his attention to the descendants of Ḥasan, who were his rivals in claiming the Caliphate, but found himself fully occupied with Abú Muslim himself, who, he feared, might oust him, Manṣúr, from his throne; such was the influence, the renown, and the presumption which he had reached. Manṣúr became, therefore, fully determined to kill Abú Muslim, that he might be free to deal with the 'Alids; he accordingly charged him with the intention of depriving the 'Abbásids of the sovereignty, and held that he deserved death in accordance with the injunction of the Imám.

Manṣúr's intentions with regard to Abú Muslim dated from the days of his brother Saffáḥ, who, however, was unwilling to attempt such a deed; on ascending the throne, Manṣúr made up his mind to carry it out, but first employed his victim to fight with his uncle 'Abdallah Ibn 'Alí, thus using one of his two enemies to overthrow the other, so that it might afterwards be easier for him to deal with the survivor. When, therefore, Abú Muslim had overthrown 'Abdallah, Manṣúr found a means of making Abú Muslim come to him from Khorasan—the story is too long to be repeated here. Abú Muslim was brought into Manṣúr's presence as a visitor who had no cause for alarm, but Manṣúr had placed some armed men behind a curtain. Abú Muslim's sword was taken from him, and Manṣúr began a conversation with him, wherein he proceeded from complaint to rebuke, till the moment agreed on had arrived. Manṣúr then clapped his hands, the armed men came out of their ambush, and killed Abú Muslim. This happened in the year 137. Manṣúr commanded the body to be wrapped in a rug, and then sent for some of his ministers, and asked whether they advised that he should be killed, not letting them know that this had already been done. One of them replied that if a hair of his head had been injured he had best be killed at once. Manṣúr then pointed to the rug, and when the man saw Abú Muslim's corpse therein he told Manṣur that he might regard that as the first day of his Caliphate.[1]

When Abú Muslim had been dispatched Manṣúr waited to see what his friends in Khorasan would do, being aware that by this assassination he had incurred a serious risk. And shortly afterwards there was a serious insurrection in Khorasan, the insurgents being called the Ráwandís. These insurgents would have made short work of Manṣúr had he not found a champion in Ma'n Ibn Zá'idah, who slew them to a man. Still, Manṣúr felt no security against the recurrence of similar troubles, and so built the city of Baghdad, and fortified it well that it might serve as a protection against disaster should such threaten. He then set about clearing his empire from the 'Alids, and fought with Mohammed Ibn 'Abdallah and killed him; then he turned his attention to 'Abbásid competitors, among whom was his uncle 'Abdallah Ibn 'Alí, who had been defeated by Abú Muslim, but not yet killed; Manṣúr succeeded, by sending him a promise of amnesty, in bringing him to his court, where he was imprisoned with his two sons. Private information reaching him that his cousin 'Ísá Ibn Músá intended to revolt, he being at the time governor of Kúfah, Manṣúr pretended ignorance of this, and sent for him, after having devised a scheme which he concealed from his most intimate associates. When the man arrived, Manṣúr went out to meet him, and welcomed him warmly, then presently dismissed those of his staff who were with him, so that they were left by themselves. He then addressed him thus: "Cousin, I am about to inform you of a matter which you only are fit to know, and the burden of which you only can assist me in bearing: are you such as I deem you to be, and ready to do what will ensure the continuance of your prosperity, which is bound up with the continuance of my empire?" 'Ísá replied that he was the Caliph's slave, and ready to obey him in all

[1] Mas'údí, ii, 167.

that he wanted done or not done. Manṣúr then told him that their common uncle 'Abdallah was disaffected, and harbouring intentions of a sort that justified his execution, which indeed was necessary for the security of the throne; 'Ísá was therefore to take him and slay him secretly. 'Ísá assented, and, his uncle being delivered over to him, proceeded with his charge to Kúfah. Manṣúr's idea was this: if 'Ísá killed his uncle 'Abdallah, the latter's relations would demand vengeance, and Manṣúr would hand 'Ísá over to them to take it, so that he (Manṣúr) would be rid of the two at once. 'Ísá, however, had some suspicion of this plot, for indeed suspicion was rife at that time owing to "the injunction of the Imám," and consulted some of his friends, who warned him of the probable consequences; he therefore kept his uncle alive in prison, and when Manṣúr demanded that he should be produced, produced him alive. Manṣúr killed him in a building founded upon salt.[1]

There are many other examples of the cunning and unscrupulousness to which Manṣúr resorted in order to consolidate his empire. He would grant an amnesty and then violate it; this we saw him do in the case of his uncle 'Abdallah, and he did the same in the case of Ibn Hubairah, the Umayyad governor of Wásiṭ. When Saffáḥ was proclaimed he sent his brother Manṣur to fight against Ibn Hubairah; envoys were interchanged, and it was agreed that Ibn Hubairah should be given a certificate of amnesty from the 'Abbásids. Such a document was made out by Manṣúr, and Ibn Hubairah spent forty nights studying it with the aid of experts to make sure that it was valid; when he had satisfied himself that it was, he returned it to Manṣúr, who transmitted it to Saffáḥ, requesting him to pass it. And Manṣúr's original idea had been to keep faith in this case; but Abú Muslim, who was still alive at the time, urged Saffáḥ to kill Ibn Hubairah, urging that a level road was spoiled if a stone was thrown on it, and that Ibn Hubairah was such a stone. Then when Ibn Hubairah came to Manṣúr to demand his protection, Manṣúr broke faith and slew him,[2] just

[1] Mustaṭraf, i, 63; Athír, v, 257. [2] Khaldún, ii, 279.

as he afterwards treated Abú Muslim himself, as we have seen. Mansúr accordingly became notorious for violation of his word, and became talked about on that account. When the 'Alid Mohammed Ibn 'Abdallah rose in Medinah, and Manṣúr was afraid of him, the latter wrote offering Mohammed a certificate of safety, and promising to treat him well. Mohammed replied asking what sort of certificate he meant to give, that of Ibn Hubairah, or of his uncle 'Abdallah, or of Abú Muslim?[1]

Manṣúr and Abú Muslim provided models of cunning and unscrupulousness to those that came after. It must be observed, however, that these qualities were employed by them only in dealing with such persons as competed with them for the sovereignty, in whose case a suspicion was sufficient to make them murder; but their rulings in other cases were exceedingly just and merciful, as shall be seen. Whoever aspired to the Caliphate or anything therewith connected was treated by them as a criminal and any candidate for the office or agent for such candidate was in danger of his life, and when summoned to appear before the Caliph would wash and perfume his body in preparation for his end.

Manṣúr also served as a model for 'Abd al-Raḥmán Ibn Mu'áwiyah, founder of the Umayyad dynasty in Spain, who had fled from 'Irák to Syria and thence to the West to escape death, and who, having been assisted by his followers and especially by a client named Badr, who played the part of Abú Muslim in establishing him in the throne, when securely seated paid no gratitude to Badr, but imprisoned him, and afterwards drove him out of the country so that he died. The same reward was meted out by him to the chief partisans by whose help he had profited. This shall be described later on.

The ingratitude of the 'Abbasids to their benefactors became so notorious that the Caliphs themselves used to indicate it to persons who were unable to discover it. When Al-Amín learned that Táhir Ibn Husain was devoting himself to the cause of Ma'mún, of whose troops in Khorasan he was general, and

[1] Athír, v, 254.

having defeated the army of Amín was near putting an end to the rule of the latter, Amín wrote to him thus: "In the Name, etc., cannot you see that since the foundation of our dynasty no one has ever upheld our cause but has been rewarded with the sword? Look out for yourself if you do not stop."[1] And in fact when Ma'mún was supreme, having won his place by the sword of Ṭáhir, he wished to kill Ṭáhir on some such plea as that advanced by Manṣúr in the case of Abú Muslim. He therefore presented him with a slave whom he had himself trained, with orders to the slave to poison Ṭáhir, which he did.[2]

§ 7. 'ABBÁSID POLICY IN THE TREATMENT OF THEIR SUBJECTS.

Persian Clients.—We have seen that the 'Abbásid dynasty was established by Persian aid, as well as that of other subject races, among them Clients and People of the Covenant, who, having causes of resentment against the Umayyads, helped the Prophet's family to overthrow them. The most important community by whom the 'Abbásid enterprise was supported was that of the Persians.

Persians and Arabs before Islam.—The Persians were an imperial power, who from ancient times had established dynasties, governed large masses of men, and laid down laws. In the fullness of their might they had waged war against Greece and Rome, and there had arisen among them great captains, scholars, and philosophers, who had translated works of learning and philosophy into their language. In ancient history they had played a great part, and besides the royal house, the *dihḳáns*, and the knights, there were in Persia many noble houses, among which seven counted as the noblest. On the mounds of Istakhr, the capital of ancient Persia, and other ancient cities there are legends engraved similar to those left by the Pharaohs, the Greeks, and the Romans.

[1] Mas'údí, ii, 213. [2] Khillikán, i, 237.

Within the Persian empire there were many Arab tribes residing on the borders of Persia in Mesopotamia and 'Irák. These were subject to native kings under Persian protection, the Mundhirs of Ḥírah. The Persians not unfrequently acquired the Arabic tongue, and even composed Arabic poems: even the kings were not averse to this pursuit. It is asserted that Bahrám Ibn Yezdejird was brought up among the Arabs at Ḥírah, and there learned Arabic and composed Arabic verses.[1] Arabs were employed in Persian bureaux to write or to interpret between them and Arabian visitors from Ḥijáz, Yemen, or Nejd, especially after the inclusion of Yemen in their empire at the time of Kisra Anushirwan.

The most famous among the Arabian scribes employed in the Persian bureaux were the family of 'Adí Ibn Zaid, who belonged to a Muḍarite clan. 'Adí, his father, and his grandfather, were all expert writers, at a time when few of the Arabs could write at all. They served in the Persian bureaux. The grandfather, Ḥammáz Ibn Zaid Ibn Ayyúb, wrote at the court of Nu'mán in Ḥírah; he entered into friendly relations with the Persians, and when his son Zaid was born he gave him in charge of a *dihḳán*, who was his friend and also a member of the court. This *dihḳán* brought him up, and taught him Persian, so that he grew up with a mastery of both languages, and the *dihḳán* requested Kisra to make him postmaster, a dignity which was only conferred on sons of *Marzubáns*. Zaid was promoted at court till he came to be consulted by Kisra on all matters of importance. His son 'Adí received a good education, pursuing the same studies as the sons of the knights, and acquiring skill in the Persian game of polo. Kisra promoted him, and made him clerk in his bureau in Madá'in He became a man of great power and influence, and received audiences of Kisra with the chief ministers, and was sent on important embassies to the Byzantine Court and elsewhere. If ever relations became strained between Arabs and Persians, and the former revolted, 'Adí acted as mediator. At the death of the

[1] Mas'údí, i, 113.

Arabian king in Ḥírah, Kisra would not appoint a successor without asking the advice of 'Adí. This gave offence to and excited the envy of the kings of Ḥírah, who were Yemenites, whereas he was of Muḍar; one of them therefore slandered him to Kisra, who had him executed. He was, however, succeeded by his son Zaid Ibn 'Adí as secretary for Kisra to the Arab kings in matters concerning them and also concerning the private affairs of the Persian kingdom; and it was Zaid's business to collect the yearly dues paid by the Arabs to Kisra.[1]

In short, before Islam Arabs rendered the same sort of service to their Persian overlords as were after the rise of Islam rendered by the Persians to the Arabs their masters. Moreover, the Persians in the might of their sovereignty and the width of their empire before Islam used to call themselves the Free Men or the Masters, and regard the rest of mankind as their slaves. They were the victims of the same delusion as befell the Arabs after them, and as befalls all nations that obtain imperial power: they become inflated with pride, and suppose themselves superior to all besides.

When Islam appeared and the place of the Kisras was taken by the Caliphs the Persians felt sore, especially when they had to undergo oppression and humiliation from the Umayyads. They were constantly revolting and as constantly being repressed by the Umayyads, who exceeded all bounds in their tyrannical and humiliating treatment. They trained artillery at their cities and slew the inhabitants, so that they exterminated the most of the noble houses and the chief knights who had gathered in old times at Istakhr.[2] They cannot be blamed for helping every insurgent who rose against the Umayyads. At last they succeeded in gaining the supremacy for the 'Abbásids, which they regarded as a victory for themselves, as they hoped to escape the Arab chauvinism which was directed against themselves and to regain some of their former sovereignty.

[1] Aghání, ii, 20. [2] Athír, iii, 49.

§ 8. Employment of Persian Clients.

When the 'Abbásids had seized the reins of government they established their capital in the midst of their faction in 'Irák, making their headquarters first at Kúfah, then at Háshimiyyah, till Manṣúr built Baghdad on the Tigris, and made it the metropolis of the Caliphate. They promoted the Persian clients, and especially the natives of Khorasan, whom they made their intimate associates and ministers, particularly such as had fought on the side of Abú Muslim when he was securing the Caliphate for them, the most famous of these ministers being Khálid Ibn Barmak, grandfather of the Barmecides, who was one of Abú Muslim's officers, and was present at many of his battles, where he gave an excellent account of himself, and did good service to the cause of the Prophet's family. His father Barmak was one of the Magians of Balkh, where he was minister to a Fire-temple called Nubhar, and in that capacity both he and his son acquired fame. This Barmak was highly esteemed among the Persians; his son Khálid embraced Islam, entered the army of Abú Muslim, and being both astute and resolute he gave the 'Abbásids no occasion to doubt his sincerity, as Abú Muslim had done. Saffáḥ promoted him to the Vezirate, in which he was retained by Manṣúr, whom he served after Abú Muslim's death in a campaign against the Kurds who had overrun Fars;[1] the same office was held by his descendants, Yaḥyá, his son, and Ja'far, his grandson, in whose time the Barmecides were overthrown, for causes that shall be mentioned.

The 'Abbásids similarly employed clients in a variety of important posts. Manṣúr was the first who did so, giving the management of his affairs to clients and slaves, and setting them over the Arabs. He was imitated by his successors down to the fall of the dynasty, as shall be seen. At his death he bequeathed a third part of his estate to his freedmen,[2] and left

[1] Khillikán, i, 106. [2] Fakhrí, 210.

injunctions that they should be honourably treated. The following passage occurs in his injunctions to his son Mahdí: "Look well unto thy freedmen and treat them well, promote them and increase their numbers, for they are thy support should any adversity befall thee. . . . . I also charge thee that thou treat well the people of Khorasan, who are thy supporters and thy faction, that gave their money and their lives to place thee on the throne, and love for thee will never depart from their hearts. I charge thee that thou do well unto them, and forgive any of them that offend, and recompense them for what they have done, and when any of them dies thou shalt be in his stead unto his widow and orphans."[1]

It was, indeed, natural that the 'Abbásids should pay honour to the people of Khorasan, when these had preferred the 'Abbásids to their own wives and children, and fought with their opponents; the Arabs, however, used to regard the favour accorded them as anomalous at the first, when they came to the Caliph's court and saw men of Khorasan going and coming and entering the presence of the Caliph as though they were his relatives, whereas the Arabs had to stand at the gate and could only with difficulty obtain admission. Thus there is a story that the Arabian poet Abú Nakhílah visited Manṣúr, and when he asked for an audience could not obtain it; and all the time he saw men of Khorasan going and coming and mocking him, as an uncouth Arab. A friend, seeing how he was treated, asked how he liked the régime; he replied:

> "Of most of the people you see in this place
> You don't know the country and can't tell the race;
> There are robes which they open and presently fold,
> And hoods that are purchased for riches untold
> For the freedman of freedmen or slave of a slave:
> One wonders how much can the Treasury save?"[2]

When Mahdí, Manṣúr's son, wished to discuss any question he would summon his court to a debate, and ask the clients to speak first.[3] Their treatment was similar in other cases. The

[1] Athír, vi, 7. [2] Aghani, xviii, 148. [3] 'Ikd, i, 53.

court, the ministers, and the staff were after a little largely composed of Persians. Persian officials set in order the government bureaux, they settled the administration, they furnished the viziers, generals, viceroys, secretaries, chamberlains; a Persian dynasty might be said to have been installed, since most posts were hereditary, like the Caliphate itself. Similarly, the vezirate and the viceroyalties had a tendency to be appropriated to certain families—those of Barmak, Wahb, Ḳaḥṭabah, Sahl, Ṭáhir, etc.

The chief governmental powers were concentrated in the vizier, who appointed and deposed other officials; and the man invested with the vezirate would naturally bestow those offices on his own adherents and partisans; in consequence the whole condition of the inhabitants of the countries altered, a feeling of security began to prevail, and men were able to devote themselves to trade, manufacture, or agriculture. They forgot the Umayyad oppression and tyranny; labour became free, and religion also became free; Arab chauvinism departed, and the community began to enjoy the blessing of safety.

When the Turks became supreme at Court, and the power of the Persians had declined, which occurred after the time of Ma'mún, as will be seen, the clients still continued to retain their influence at headquarters, and on them the Caliph relied in both private and public affairs, whether as secretaries or as generals. Only the Persian clients no longer enjoyed any special favour: the clients so privileged were a mixture of various races, all, however, called clients, and all ready to sacrifice themselves in the service of Caliph or prince.

§ 9. The People of the Covenant in 'Abbásid Times.

When the Persian clients began to administer the government and set in order the bureaux they found that they required the assistance of members of tolerated sects in 'Irák and Syria, these persons having a special knowledge of book-keeping and secretarial work, and also of the land-tax, besides other accomplishments. To secure their help they held out to them the prospects of various paid offices and rewards, enabled them to live with comfort, and promoted them to honourable places. Feeling confidence in the new government, they trooped to Baghdad and placed their brains and their pens at the disposal of the 'Abbásids, in return for the liberal treatment, and especially the religious toleration accorded them. The 'Abbásids gave them posts in their bureaux, and made them overseers of their treasuries and their estates.

Of the money-testers or bankers most were Jews; many of the clerks were Christians. Christians were often at the head of the War Office, and this post was of such importance that its occupant, though a Christian, often had the chief persons in the realm hurrying to kiss his hand. Among Christian heads of the War Office in 'Abbásid times we may notice Málik Ibn al Walíd, to whom the appointment was given by Al-Mu'taḍid, and Israel the Christian, who held it for Al-Náṣir li-dín Allah. These members of tolerated sects at times even rose to the vezirate. Abu'l-'Alá Ṣá'id Ibn Thábit was deputy-vizier in the time of Al-Muttaḳí.[1]

Justice and religious toleration of this style spread from Baghdad to the Fáṭimide dynasty in Egypt, and members of tolerated sects acquired great importance under it. The vezirate or secretariate, as it was there called, was held by many of them, and they acquired great political influence. The Fáṭimide Al-'Azíz billáh had a Christian vizier named 'Ísá Ibn Nestorius, and another Jewish vizier named Manasseh. Christians and Jews were powerful in their days.[2] Other influential members of these sects in the Fáṭimide empire were the Christian Fahd Ibn Ibráhím, secretary to Barjwán, the most powerful man in the days of Ḥákim bi-amrillah. He was permitted to sign for Barjwán, and he was given the title Prince. The Christians became so powerful in his time that they were almost controllers of the whole realm.[3] The ministry was largely composed of

[1] Viziers, 95; Faraj, ii, 149. [2] Athír, ix, 32; Suyúṭi, ii, 17.
[3] Maḳrízí, ii, 4 and 31.

them in the times of both Ḥákim and Ḥáfiẓ.[1] The War Office clerks were ordinarily Jews.

Besides this the Caliphs and governors used to employ Jewish and Christian physicians, interpreters, and scribes, especially Syrian Christians. These persons did good service to Islamic civilization by translating learned works from Greek, Persian, and Syriac, as well as other languages, into Arabic. This has been dealt with in the third part of this work, where we have illustrated the favour shown these tolerated communities, and the promotion and honour accorded them. They included Christians, Jews, Magians, Samaritans, Ṣabians, and others. All of them enjoyed complete security, and earned stipends from the treasuries of the Caliphs and princes

At the commencement of the 'Abbásid period the Caliphs paid high honour to bishops, and gave them audiences. The Caliph Hádí was in the habit of inviting the Bishop Timotheus on most days to discuss religious topics with him. Many a difficulty was examined by the two together, and these debates were collected by the bishop in a book which he composed. Hárún al-Rashíd used to deal with him in the same way,[2] and other Caliphs did the like. They also neglected the injunctions of Omar I recommending oppression of Christians, and forbidding them to build new churches,[3] to assemble at festivals, or to take office under the Government. The 'Abbásids rendered intercourse easy for them, and displayed respect for their religion. At times the Christians even presented the Caliphs with icons of saints, and these were accepted.

§ 10. Persecution of tolerated Sects in 'Abbásid Times.

This did not prevent the occasional persecution of the Christians by Caliphs, who thought fit to revive the injunctions of Omar and demolish churches. The policy of autocrats varies with their individual characters, and some of the 'Abbásids took to persecuting Christians with or without cause. Such

[1] Id., i, 406. [2] Ta'ríkh al-Masháriḳah (MS.), 143. [3] Maḳrízí, ii. 511.

persecutors were Hárún al-Rashíd and Mutawakkil. The latter, who died in the year 247, was a fierce persecutor, probably the fiercest in the whole series of 'Abbásids. He ordered that all churches built since the commencement of Islam should be demolished, he forbade the employment of Christians in Government offices, and the display of crosses on Palm Sunday; he also gave orders that wooden figures of demons should be fixed on their doors, that they should wear yellow cowls, and a zonarion round the waist, that they should ride saddles with wooden stirrups with two globes behind the saddle, that the men's clothes should have inserted a couple of patches of colour different from that of the clothes themselves, each patch to be four inches wide, and the two patches were also to be of different colours. Any Christian woman who went out of doors was to wear a yellow tunic without band. There were other regulations of the same sort made by him as well.[1]

Oppression of this sort is not surprising on the part of Mutawakkil, who was equally vindictive against the other Government officials, who took severe measures against the 'Alid faction, and massacred scholars and writers. His persecution of the Christians was not altogether unprovoked,[2] since they had given help to opponents of the Government. In the year 241 the Moslems of Hims had attacked their governor with the assistance of the Christians. When the governor reported this to Mutawakkii, the latter sent orders to expel the Christians and demolish their churches. This was one of the causes of his vindictiveness.[3]

The same is said of the orders given in Rashíd's time to demolish churches in the frontier provinces, and to compel the 'people of the Covenant' to adopt a different attire and a different mode of riding from those employed by Moslems.[4] Hárún issued these orders on his return from warring with the Byzantines at Heraclea; and it is most probable that the Christians resident in the frontier province had assisted their

[1] Khaldún, iii, 275; Athír, vii, 20; Makrízí, ii, 494.
[2] Ta'ríkh al-Masháriḳah, 146. [3] Athír, vii, 29. [4] Id., vi, 82.

co-religionists in spying out Moslem affairs, and had allowed their churches to be employed for this purpose. Rashíd's measure was probably intended as a punishment to them for this disloyalty, and confined to the Christians of the frontier province. The difference in attire was also probably enforced owing to their habit of disguising themselves as Moslems and so carrying on espionage. For, except in this matter, Hárún was one of the most just and gentle of the Caliphs towards the people of the Covenant; thus, when one of the viceroys of his brother Hádí had demolished certain churches in Egypt, Rashíd on becoming Caliph ordered them to be rebuilt.[1]

A similar account is to be given of the persecution of Christians in Egypt during Fáṭimide rule which occasionally took place, though ordinarily, as has been seen, there was religious toleration, and Christians were greatly favoured. The first case of interference on the part of the rulers with their churches and services was in the year 395, when Ḥákim was Caliph. It was occasioned by the great promotion given to members of their community in his day, whence they became, as it were, the ministry; their power and wealth led to elation, and they began to ill-treat the Moslems, especially in the time of 'Ísá Ibn Nestorius and Fahd Ibn Ibráhím. Al-Hákim was irritated thereby, and in his case irritation led to uncontrollable fury. He ordered those two ministers to be executed, and took stringent measures against the Christians. They were to wear the yellow badge and tie the zonarion round their waists, to hold no Palm Sunday processions; all church property was seized and confiscated. No Christian was to be allowed to buy a slave. Their churches were demolished, and they themselves were to be forced to embrace Islam. Other fierce edicts of the same style were issued, the like of which the Christians have never endured before. Probably this was the most violent persecution which overtook them during the whole period of Islamic civilization.[2] Nor can that civilization be blamed for it, since its author was a madman.

[1] Makrízí, iv, 511. [2] Id., ii, 495.

Persecution of the Christians was probably suggested to Ḥákim by a war between Byzantines and Moslems which had just taken place, in which the Byzantines had demolished a number of mosques, among them a mosque in Constantinople. Hákim thus retaliated on their co-religionists in his dominion. Among the churches destroyed by Ḥákim was that of the Resurrection at Jerusalem. When Ẓáhir became Caliph after Ḥákim a truce was agreed to between him and the Byzantine emperor in the year 418. It was agreed that the mosque in Constantinople and the Church of the Resurrection should be rebuilt, and that those who had ostensibly embraced Islam in the days of Hákim should be allowed to return to Christianity if they desired. Many did so.

Possibly the cause which led Ḥákim to take those measures may have been trivial, but being augmented by his fanaticism and folly it made him order slaughter and demolition It should be added that he often issued to his Moslem subjects ridiculous orders, such as resembled sheer madness. Such were the edicts prohibiting the eating of mallows, or watercress, or brewing of beer; forbidding women to show themselves or walk in the streets; enjoining the abuse of ancestors, and cursing them, these curses to be engraved in mosques, on the doors of booths, and in cemeteries: and various others, equally pointing to unsoundness of mind. All of them appear, however, to have had some ground, though often a weak one. The reason for the prohibition of the mallow was that it was a favourite food of Mu'áwiyah Ibn Abí Sufyán, the enemy of the 'Alid faction, to which the Fáṭimides belonged. Watercress was forbidden because it was called after Ayeshah, the Prophet's wife, and enemy of 'Alí; and the herb called *mutawakkiliyyah* because it was called after the Caliph Mutawakkil, an enemy of the 'Alid faction. The drinking of beer was forbidden because 'Alí disliked it.[1] His other follies and eccentricities similarly had some motive, though inadequate—among them persecution of Christians and destruction of churches. Moreover, he recalled

[1] Maḳrízí, ii, 341.

these decrees for some trivial cause or for no cause at all, and ordered the churches to be rebuilt,[1] and gave the Christians permission to revert to their religion, a permission of which many availed themselves, though, as has been seen, this took place in the time of his son Záhir. One of his eccentricities was to build schools and appoint professors and teachers of law, afterwards killing those teachers and demolishing the schools. Another was to compel his subjects to lock up the streets in the daytime and open them at night, an edict which prevailed for some time.[2] That a man of this sort should persecute is not surprising, nor does such persecution leave any stigma on either the dynasty or the nation to which he belonged.

The worst persecutions to which the Christians and Jews had to submit took place in the period of decline, in the middle generations of Islam, especially after the Crusades, which did much to stir up fanaticism on both sides. The Christians recollected how the Moslems had been preferred to themselves and how their rulers had persecuted the Christian religion; and the Moslems' irritation against their Christian subjects was increased by the secret help which the latter gave the Franks. Hence the Moslem governors adopted violent measures against them. The Christians of Kárá, between Ḥimṣ and Damascus, used to kidnap Moslems during the Crusades and sell them secretly to the Franks. When in 664 the Sultan Ẓáhir returned from one of his campaigns he ordered the inhabitants of the place to be pillaged, the aged to be killed, and the young to be made servants; these were then reared with the Turks in Egypt and made into a corps with officers of their own,[3] a sort of anticipation of the Janissaries of the Turkish Court.

After the Crusades mutual detestation rose to such a pitch between the Moslems and the 'people of the Covenant' that each of these parties did its utmost to annoy the other. When the Government was in the hands of Moslems the Christians were in the inferior position. If a Moslem street took fire, Christians and Jews were suspected of arson, and the Government

[1] Athír, ix, 86. [2] Suyúṭi, ii, 17. [3] Abu'l-Fidá, iv, 4.

would order them or their places of worship to be burned.[1] Such fanaticism was the inevitable result of those dark ages. Christian Governments used to treat Moslems in their power as badly or even worse. Moslem captives used to be threatened with death if they did not turn Christian.[2] If they took a Moslem city by storm they would strike their hammers in the mosques.[3] When in Spain the Christians conquered the Moslems they forced the Moslems to wear a badge such as the Jews and tributaries had been compelled to wear. At a still later period the Spanish Christians gave the Moslems their choice between death and embracing Christianity, and they became Christians to a man.[4]

§ 11. Anti-Christian Fanaticism of the Mob.

It has been observed that the Caliphs and governors promoted the Christians in the public service and lavished on them wealth and honours, the reason being the need for their services at the commencement of 'Abbásid civilization as translators, physicians, calculators, scribes, etc., officials with whom an administration cannot dispense, and whose place the Moslems, all of them occupied with the cares of sovereignty, could not undertake to fill. On the other hand, the governors used to promote Moslems to official posts in preference to 'people of the Covenant.' just as the Umayyads used to prefer Arabs above non-Arabs. Hence there sprang up mutual jealousy between the lower orders of Moslems and Christians. This was only natural in a state in which two nationalities or two communities strive for office, and the same state of things exists in our own day.

This jealousy first appeared in the professional or artisan classes, who naturally gather round caliphs and governors, hoping to earn their living by supplying the necessities of civilization or furnishing amusement and entertainment—such

[1] Maḳrízí, ii, 8; Abu'l-Fidá, iv, 117; Siráj, 189.
[2] Athír, vii, 29. [3] Id., viii, 62. [4] Nafḥ al-ṭíb, ii, 1269.

as poets, minstrels, scribes, accountants, etc. Persons of the upper classes, the nobility, men of wealth, and ministers, did not share this jealousy or fanaticism; they were in the habit of regarding men as they were, without considering to what religion they belonged. Thus the Sharíf al-Raḍi, who addressed to the Caliph al-Ḳádir the following verses :—

"Commander of the Faithful, we
Are branches of one noble tree.
Deep-rooted both alike in fame,
Our boast on boasting days the same,
Only that thou hast monarch's state
While I'm not so adorned by fate"—

composed a famous dirge on the Sabian Abú Isḥáḳ, beginning :

"Ah! see whom they carry outside to the tomb,
The light of the Council, now turnèd to gloom."

This dirge was not approved by the populace, and some told him that a *Sharíf* (member of the Prophet's family) ought not to have bewailed a Sabian. He replied, "I only bewailed his worth."[1]

The populace and those who courted their favour, in order to obtain privileges or posts, displayed a fanatical aversion to Christians, and tried to injure them by lodging complaints against them with the rulers. When the ruler was resolute he would not listen to these calumnies. There is an anecdote that a Christian was in the year 284 charged by some Moslems at Baghdad with having reviled the Prophet. A crowd assembled and called on Al-Kásim Ibn 'Ubaidallah, the vizier of Mu'taḍid, to inflict the legal punishment. The vizier, being convinced that the man was innocent,[2] refused to comply. The case was brought before the Caliph and made a great stir. The Spanish Caliph Al-Ḥakam at the beginning of the third century of A.H. crucified one of his governors for wrong done to the children of the people of the Covenant.[3]

[1] Khillikán, i, 13; ii, 2. [2] Athír, vii, 192. [3] Id., vi, 137.

When the dynasty approached decrepitude this fanaticism spread from the populace to the upper classes. People were anxious at that time to win the favour of ministers by flattery and similar arts, hoping to gain some emolument. Compelled to devise expedients to aid them in their designs, they would concoct plots and invent calumnies. The easiest mode of advancing oneself in an Islamic government was simulation of piety, since religion and politics were so closely associated; and one mode of displaying piety and zeal in the cause of Islam was to attack other religions. When the head of the Government was weak he would be taken in and be induced to persecute. For this reason the tendency to persecute the tolerated sects, especially the Christians, grew as the Islamic empire advanced towards decrepitude. It was especially strong in the middle ages of Islam, following on the Crusades. The rulers and occupants of academical posts openly declared their contempt for all non-Moslems, whom they would fiercely persecute and treat as enemies. Mutual enmity began to strike deep roots, each party trying to injure the other, till the Christians were anxious for deliverance from Moslem rule by any means whatever. Hence, when the Tartars advanced to attack Baghdad in 656, the wishes of the people of the Covenant were in their favour. This mutual detestation came to a head before the last reformation, i.e. about a century ago, and appeared in official transactions, especially in countries at a distance from civilization. I have been shown a form of burial certificate issued by the religious tribunal in Diyár Bakr for a Christian who died there. This curious document runs as follows:—

"*From the religious Tribunal in Diyár Bakr.*

"To the Metropolitan of the Syrian infidels, vile of appearance and belief: whereas the accursed infidel Jacob of thy persuasion has dropped off the hooks, that his foul carcase may be interred there has gone forth the merciful edict from the religious guide of his place, after the taking of the poll-tax;

and though the earth may decline to receive his filthy carcase, yet that it may not pollute the air we have given leave according to law that it be buried within your city above named, according to your false religion, to be added to the company of Hell. This permit had to be given that there might be no opposition on the part of anyone. Given Jumádá i, 26, of the year 1203."

No Moslem or Christian of our time could read this document without incredulity and astonishment, and were it not for our belief in the veracity of our authority we also should have doubted its genuineness, and our belief was confirmed by the assurance given us by another friend that one of the patriarchal houses in Cairo contains a number of permits similarly conceived. Since the beginning of the present renaissance this fanaticism has begun to decline, and we hope that as the renaissance ripens the fanaticism will receive its deathblow.

§ 12. MUTUAL JEALOUSIES BETWEEN CHRISTIANS.

Consideration of the vexations which the Christians underwent in the best period of Islamic civilization suggests that a frequent cause of it was calumniation of one Christian sect by another, e.g. the Nestorians and Jacobites in 'Irák. Influential Christians often dealt more severely with their co-religionists than did the Moslem rulers. So when 'Ísá Ibn Shahlá was appointed court physician, he took the opportunity of oppressing the Metropolitans and Bishops and appropriating their wealth. He even wrote to the Metropolitan of Nisibis, demanding a vast quantity of church vessels, with the following threat: "Do you not know that the king himself is in my hand? If I like I can make him ill, if I like I can make him well." The Metropolitan sent this letter to the Caliph's chamberlain Rabí', and 'Ísá was punished by the Caliph.

This state of things is also illustrated by the treatment of the famous translator Hunain Ibn Ishák by the physician

Bakhtishú' Ibn Gabriel, who envied the rank which the translator had acquired at the Caliph's court. He desired, therefore, to ruin the translator by means of their religion. He had an icon made of the Madonna and Child, and ordered one of his adherents to take it as a present to the Caliph (Mutawakkil) at a time specified by him. Going to the Caliph's court at the appointed time he took the icon from the servant's hands and placed it before Mutawakkil, who admired it greatly. Bakhtishú' then began kissing it over and over again in the Caliph's presence till the Caliph asked him why he did so. His reply was, "Whom should I kiss if not the image of the Queen of the worlds?" Mutawakkil asked whether this was the practice of all the Christians? "Yes," he replied, "and indeed they kiss it even more fervently than I do, as being in your presence; but though we Christians do pay her such high honour, yet I know of one man in your service, and in receipt of your gifts and favours, who despises her and spits upon her—a heretic and atheist who does not believe in the unity of God nor another world, who masquerades as a Christian, whereas in reality he is an infidel who does not believe the prophets." The Caliph asked who this person was, and Bakhtishú' replied, "Ḥunain the translator." The Caliph then said he would summon the man to appear, and if the charge against him proved true he should be exemplarily punished: condemned to lifelong imprisonment with constant renewal of pains and tortures. Bakhtishú' requested that the order to produce him might be delayed till he (Bakhtishú') had left the Caliph's presence for a brief period. This being granted, Bakhtishú' went directly to Hunain and informed him that an icon had been presented to the Caliph, who had admired it. "If," he said, "we leave it with him and praise it, he will despise us, saying, 'Here is your Lord with His Mother portrayed.' The Caliph asked *me* what I thought of it, and I told him it was the sort of image that might be put up in a bath or similar place of no consequence, and when he asked me to spit on it I did so." Ḥunain, supposing this to be true, when summoned by the Caliph did as Bakhtishú' had told him and spat on the icon, when the Caliph ordered him to be imprisoned, and sent for the Catholikos Theodosius, who when he saw the icon began to kiss it fervently, with great emotion. Taking it in his hand he then began to implore blessings on the Caliph. The Caliph invited him to sit down with the icon on his lap, which the Catholikos begged the Caliph to leave with him. The Caliph then asked the Catholikos what that man deserved who spat on an icon. His reply was that if he were a Christian, and did so knowingly, he should be prohibited from entering a church or receiving the communion, and the Christians should not be permitted to hold any converse or dealings with him. The Caliph then presented the icon to the Catholikos with a reward, and ordered Hunain to be beaten with ropes and scourges, his houses to be pulled down, and himself to be imprisoned; nor was he released from prison till the Caliph fell ill, when, requiring his advice, he let him out.[1]

§ 13. RELIGIOUS LIBERTY.

Mutawakkil, as we have seen, was a persecutor of Christians and other people of the Covenant. Other, more moderate Caliphs are likely to have exhibited even more regard for Christianity than that displayed in the above anecdote. In that anecdote it appears that the Caliphs required that a Christian should be a sincere Christian. They did not require him to embrace Islam unless he chose to do so. Besides this the Moslems used to take part with the Christians in their feasts, Christmas and Palm Sunday, and go out with them to places of amusement, as though they were all one community.[2] This practice was not confined to Syria and 'Irák. In Egypt also the Moslems no less than the Christians used to celebrate the Christian feasts; the Caliph used to distribute largesses at Christmas and Epiphany, and the Egyptians used to make merry together.[3]

[1] Uṣaibi'ah, i. 194. [2] Athír, viii, 113; Faraj, ii, 156. [3] Maḳrízi, i, 494.

If the Government ever instituted any public benefaction the Christians shared therein like the Moslems. Especially was this the case with hospitals and infirmaries. They were built for the reception of both Moslems and members of tolerated sects; only when there was no room for both were Moslems preferred.[1]

It must be understood that at the best time of Moslem civilization religious liberty was granted by the rulers to all the various sects and denominations of their subjects. Fanaticism was never carried to the extent of compelling any community to embrace Islam, even in the days of the Umayyads, who oppressed all non-Arabs so severely in their desire to extort money. We have seen what was done by Khálid al-Ḳasrí and others in their time. The 'Abbásids were much juster and more tolerant than the Umayyads, and in consequence religious innovations multiplied in their days among the Magians and others. The Islamic sects also multiplied greatly. The most tolerant of the Caliphs was Ma'mún, who was himself a Shí'ite, but had for viziers a Sunnite, Yaḥyá Ibn Aktham, and a Mu'tazil, Aḥmad Ibn Alí Duwád.[2] The extent of his religious toleration may be inferred from his supporting the Mu'tazils in their doctrine that the Koran was created. This doctrine is ascribed originally to the Jew Labíd al-A'sam, who is supposed to have tried sorcery on the Prophet. This Labíd declared the Law to be create, and afterwards the Koran to be create. He was followed by his sister's son Ṭálút, who was followed by Abán Ibn Sam'án, and the last by Al-Ja'd Ibn Dirham in the days of Hishám Ibn 'Abd al-Malik, the Umayyad. He proclaimed the doctrine that the Koran was create, and its matter objectionable; that its eloquence was not miraculous, but could be equalled or even surpassed by human effort.[3] This irritated Hishám, who sent the man to Khálid al-Ḳasrí, governor of the two 'Iráks, with orders to execute him. He, however, merely imprisoned him. The Caliph urged his execution, and at last Khálid brought him out on the Day of Sacrifice, and after

[1] Usaibi'ah, i, 221. [2] Khillikán, ii, 223. [3] Makrízi, ii, 346.

praving said : "It is my intention to-day to sacrifice Al-Ja‘d Ibn Dirham, who asserts that God did not converse with Moses, neither take Abraham for a friend. God's name be hallowed from what Ja‘d asserts. Thereupon he cut the man's throat.[1] When Marwan Ibn al-Hakam became Caliph he adopted the doctrine of the Creation of the Koran, in Ja‘d's sense ; and when Ma'mun became Caliph he encouraged the Mu‘tazils. Perhaps he got his Mu‘tazilism from his tutor Yahya Ibn al-Mubarak. His doctrine was followed by the Caliph Wathik, to the great scandal of the Moslems, who termed him an Unbeliever,[2] as indeed they had called Ma'mun "Commander of the Unbelievers."[3] Then followed the persecution in the days of Mutawakkil. The Moslems were divided into two parties, the Caliphs going against the Mu‘tazils and expressing the strongest disapproval of the doctrine that the Koran was create. Poems bearing on the subject were composed in which the Mu‘tazils were upbraided and charged with infidelity. A specimen is the ode of Abu Khalaf al-Ma‘afiri :

"No, by Him who lifts the sky
Without pillar we can spy ;
None but atheists do prate
That the Koran is create.
"Tis the word revealed by
Men's Creator from on high."[4]

In general we may say that compelete liberty of thought was allowed in these times on religious questions. No man was forced to abandon or adopt any creed. Often each member of a household followed a separate faith. So of Abu'l-Ja‘d's six sons two were Shi‘tes, two Murjites, and two Kharihis.[5]

The policy adopted by the ‘Abbasids with reference to their subjects, both Moslem and people of the Covenant, was one of benevolence, justice, and tenderness. Examples have been given in the second part of this work of the justice and gentleness of the early ‘Abbasid Caliphs. Special benevolence

[1] Athir, v, 123; vii, 28. [2] Id., vii, 8. [3] Id., vi, 131.
[4] Nafh al-tib, ii, 158. [5] Ma‘arif, 156.

was manifested by them towards Persians and other influential members of the client communities. When the 'Abbásids had obtained the government and control of the army and treasury they promoted these persons to honour and authority. But when they conceived the slightest doubt as to their sincerity they pounced down upon them, as was done in the case of the Barmecides and other viziers of the first 'Abbásid period.

§ 14. ARABIAN CHAUVINISM IN THE 'ABBÁSID AGE.

Policy of Dividing.—Mansúr's attention was directed to the Arabs as being chauvinists, who, if they could unite, could obtain control of the government and accomplish whatever they desired. He was aware that they were courageous in the pursuit of justice and in open condemnation of injustice, and impatient of injury; and it will be remembered of what treachery and violence he was guilty with the object of securing his throne, conduct which high souls could not brook. His anxiety concerning them was increased by the language which he heard them employ when he was on pilgrimage, language which indicated their intolerance of injustice, containing phrases vexing to himself. When performing the circuit of the Ka'bah he heard a man praying thus: "O God, I complain unto Thee of the manifestation of injustice and corruption on the earth, and the covetousness that intervenes between right and its claimants." Mansúr went to a corner of the mosque, and calling the speaker asked the reason of his prayer. The man asked for a promise of amnesty before telling the truth. When this had been granted he told the Caliph that he it was who intervened between right and its claimants. Mansúr asked how he could be a victim of covetousness, when all the gold and silver, all the sweet and sour in the empire were in his possession. The man replied: "God has given thee charge of the Moslems and their goods, and thou hast set between thyself and them a wall of brick and mortar, with doors of iron and armed guards, whom thou hast commanded to admit only this one and that, instead of telling them to admit those that are oppressed and in misery, the hungry, naked, weak, and poor. There is not one of them but has a claim on this wealth of thine."

This and similar utterances awoke Manṣúr to the courage of the Arabs, whom he bethought him of humiliating. He began therefore to devise means for this end. For the Arabs there was a special register of stipends according to their lineage and rank, and containing the names of both Muḍarites and Yemenites. When Mansúr had finished strengthening his position by defeating 'Alids and Khárijís, etc., and had built and fortified Baghdad, with barracks for his troops, he began to consider of whom these troops consisted. He found there were three great detachments—Yemenites, Muḍarites, and men of Khorasan. Now it happened in the year 151 that some of the army mutinied, and fought with him at the "Golden Gate," his palace in Baghdad. He began to fear the repetition of such mutinies, knowing that his government depended on the army, and should the troops unite against him they could deprive him of it. He was also aware that each detachment had a hankering after one or other of the 'Alid or other pretenders, and that it would be perfectly easy for the army to transfer the government to a new dynasty.

The doyen of the 'Abbásids at this time was Ḳutham Ibn 'Abbás Ibn 'Ubaidallah Ibn 'Abbás. He was highly respected by the whole clan and took precedence among them. Mansúr consulted this person, telling him of the mutiny of the troops, and his fears lest they might unite to eject the 'Abbásids from the government. He wished to have Ḳutham's advice. Ḳutham's reply was that he had a notion, which would be spoiled by being revealed, whereas if allowed to be kept a secret it might be executed, and would secure Manṣúr in the Caliphate and cause his army to fear him. The Caliph could not imagine how any plan connected with the Caliphate could be executed without his knowing it. Ḳutham replied that if he was not trusted he ought not to be consulted, but if he were trusted he should be left to execute his plan. Mansur gave him leave to execute it. Kutham went home and called a slave, to whom he gave the following instructions: "To-morrow go to the palace before me, and when you see me come in and, getting between the high officials, rise up, seize the rein of my mule, and conjure me by the Prophet, by 'Abbas, and by the Commander of the Faithful to stop and hear a question and reply to it. I shall rebuke you harshly, but don't be afraid; repeat the question. I shall then strike you, but repeat your adjuration, and ask me which of the two tribes is the nobler, Yemen or Mudar. When I answer, leave go of the mule and you are a free man."

This plan was carried out. Finally, in reply to the question, Kutham said, "Mudar is the nobler, because of it is the Prophet of God, the Book of God, the House of God, and the Caliph (or vicegerent) of God". This reply angered the Yemenites, because he said nothing in their favour, and one of their captains cried out, "This is not so, the Yemenites have some things in their favour too," and told his slave to rein up the Sheykh's mule. This he did till he nearly made the mule go backwards. The Mudarites were then indignant at the Sheykh of their tribe being treated in this way. One of them commanded his slave to strike off the hand of the Yemenite's slave; and the feelings of the two tribes were mutually embittered. Kutham then went into Mansur's presence. From that time the Arabian army was divided, the Mudarites, Yemenites, and Khorasanites forming separate factions. Kutham informed Mansur that he had divided the troops into parties, each of which would be afraid to innovate for fear of being repressed by the other two.[1]

When Mansur's son Mahdi came from Khorasan he was met by his relatives from Syria, Kufah, Basrah, etc., who congratulated him on his arrival. He presented them by way of recompense with gifts of money and apparel, and Mansur did the same. Kutham then suggested to Mansur the following stratagem. He should send his son Mahdi across the Tigris

[1] Athir, v, 285.

and establish him in that quarter of Baghdad, with a portion of the army. There would then be two Baghdads, and if either revolted, the revolt could be repressed with the aid of the other. The suggestion was adopted, and helped to secure the dynasty, Mahdi built a city on the other side of the Tigris, which he called Rusafah, employing the 'policy of division.'

During 'Abbasid times the power of the Arabs steadily declined, while that of the Persians increased. In Rashid's time the empire was divided between two powerful elements, one a Persian and the other an Arab, each of whom endeavoured to obtain exclusive power. The Caliph's court was also in two parties, Persian and Arabs, centreing round Rashid's two sons Ma'mun and Amin. The mother of the latter was an Arab and a Hashimite, Zubaidah ; whereas the former was the son of a Persian slave-girl, purchased by Rashid in order to give him an heir, since Zubaidah's pregnancy came late. 'Abdallah al-Ma'mun, the slave-girl's son, was born before Muhammad al-Amin, son of Zubaidah.[1] Jealousy sprang up between these two women, similar to the historical feud of Sarah and Hagar, wives of Abraham. It infected the Court and the employes of the Government. The Hashimites and other Arabs were in favour of Amin, the Persians of Ma'mun. The chief representative of the Arab faction was the family of Rabi' Ibn Yunus. This Rabi' traced his pedigree to Kaisan, freedman of Al-Harith, freedman of 'Uthman son of 'Affan, so that his grandfather was freedman of a freedman. Rabi' became one of Mansur's clients, and was made janitor, afterwards vizier. Mansur was very fond of him, and placed great confidence in him. One day Mansur asked him what he desired, and he replied, "Your affection for my son Al-Fadi." "Why *affection* rather than anything else?" the Caliph asked. "Because," he replied, "If you are fond of him, his least service will appear great to you, and his worst offence small." Rabi' died in 170 A.H. when Hadi was Caliph. When Rashid became Caliph he appointedthe Barmecides viziers. Al-Fadl son of Rabi'

[1] Mas'udi, ii 211.

was vexed at the vezirate falling from his grasp, and wished to imitate and rival the Barmecides, but had not the necessary qualifications. His failure left great bitterness and resentment in his mind, and he endeavoured to calumniate them before the Caliph. His efforts probably helped their overthrow.

§ 15. Decline of Arab Chauvinism with the Fall of Amín.

Ma'mún, besides his Persian parentage on the mother's side, had been brought up in the family of Ja'far Ibn Yaḥyá the Barmecide, who endeavoured to obtain the succession for him,[1] and educated him to favour the Persians. Al-Faḍl Ibn Rabí' was no less anxious to secure the succession for Amín, and when after the overthrow of the Barmecides Rashíd died, it was Al-Fadl who urged Amín to cancel the succession of Ma'mún. The brothers disputed the succession,[2] Ma'mún being with his mother's kinsmen in Khorasan, while Amín was among his own people in Baghdad, and war broke out between the two parties. It was really a war between Persians and Arabs, since the Arabs over the greater part of the 'Abbásid domain were on the side of Amín,[3] whereas the people of Khorasan assisted "the son of their sister," Ma'mún, through the management of Al-Faḍl Ibn Sahl. Al-Amín in Baghdad endeavoured to stir up his army, by the counsel of Al-Faḍl Ibn al-Rabí'. The Arabs in the 'Abbásid army were enervated by the capital and its luxuries, and, being further divided by the policy that has been described, they were unable to make any effective resistance. When Al-Amín's condition had become desperate and he had no longer any money for the raising of troops, he called to his assistance the mob of Baghdad, including sharpers and knaves, who formed great gangs He ordered some of his commanders to persecute such persons as were wealthy or had in their possession deposits and pledges, Moslems and others; but this measure did no good, and the

[1] Athír, vi, 94. [2] Id., vi. 89. [3] Makrízí, i, 178.

war ended in a victory for Ma'mun, as shall be explained further on. The people of Khorasan thus robbed the Arabs of the Caliphate and handed it over to Ma'mun, just as they had formerly taken it from the Umayyads and given it to the 'Abbasids.

In Ma'mun's days the Persians became powerful, whereas the Arabs declined, so that he used to be often confronted by Arabs in the streets who complained of his neglecting them. They used to cry out, "Commander of the Faithful, look after the Syrian Arabs as thou dost look after the Persians of Khorasan."[1]

When Mu'tasim became Caliph in the year 218 he formed a corps of Turks and Farghanians, thereby giving Arab influence a decisive blow for the rest of the 'Abbasid period. He wrote to his governors in the different provinces, bidding them strike off the registers the names of Arab stipendiaries, and they obeyed, notwithstanding the protests of the Arabs, whose cause was lost with that measure,[2] and thenceforth they were kept out of public appointments. The last Arab governor of Egypt was 'Anbasah Ibn Ishak, cashiered in 242.[3] The Persians became masters of the empire, and they became more and more anxious to strip the Arabs of any privileges that they retained. Mardawij, who arose in Ispahan in the year 322, wished to take Baghdad, transfer the supreme power to the Persians, and put an end to the Arabian dynasty.[4] He did not succeed, although the influence gradually shifted to freedmen and slaves, as shall be seen.

§ 16. Shu'ubis and Arabis.

In the days of Ma'mun and his successors the Shu'ubs came forward openly with their attacks on the Arabs, while enjoying the favour of Ma'mun, who made them members of his staff, and bestowed rewards upon them. One of these was Sahl Ibn Harun, director of the public library, a vehement Arab-hater, others Abu 'Ubaidah the archaeologist and 'Allan the Shu'ubi.

[1] Athir, vi, 176. [2] Makrizi, i, 94, 311, 313. [3] Id., ii, 294. [4] Fakhri, 253.

These persons composed works dealing with the defects of the Arabs, and refuting those who preferred them to all other races.

The Shu'úbís asserted the equality of all human beings, and therefore were also termed Equalitarians. One of their arguments in refutation of the claims of the Arabs was that the Prophet himself had asserted the equality of all Moslems, whatever their nationality, in the maxim "All Moslems are brethren: the blood of one is as the blood of another; their protection includes the lowest of them; and they are one hand against all other men." Another maxim that was delivered in the Farewell Pilgrimage: "No Arab has any advantage over a foreigner save by virtue of piety." Similarly in the Koran: "The most honourable among you in God's eyes is the most pious." The Shu'úbís undertook the defence of all the nations of the earth at that time except the Arabs; when the Arabs boasted of their kings, the Shu'úbís would talk of the Pharaohs, Nimrods, Amaleks, Kisras, Cæsars, Solomon the Wise, Alexander the Great, and the Kings of India. If the Arabs boasted of the Prophets and messengers of God, they would talk of the prophets from Adam to their time, all of whom had proceeded from non-Arab races, except four—Húd, Ṣáliḥ, Ishmael, Mohammed. If the Arabs boasted of science, art, or philosophy, the Shu'úbís would quote the game of chess, the steelyard, and the astrolabe, and would boast of the philosophy of the Greeks, their poets, and their sciences, as well as of the sciences of the Indians, Persians, and others. One of the Shu'úbís in a Refutation was bold enough to say, "What, then, have the Arabs to boast of over the foreigner? They are like savage beasts, or ravening wolves, eating and preying upon each other, their men bound in chains like captives, and their women stuck behind them on camels' saddles, like captives."[1] Evidence of all this was brought from Arabic verses, proving how little they cared for honour. The Arab, they said, cannot get on without a Prophet to assist him.[2] They taunted them with the adoption of supposititious children, and composed verses libelling them; poets who composed such

[1] 'Iḳd, ii, 169. [2] Athír, vii, 57.

odes were Al-Hasan Ibn Háni', and Basshár Ibn Burd who however shifted from side to side.

The defenders of the Arabs also betook themselves to composing books in refutation of the Shu'úbís; the most famous work of this sort was by Ibn Kutaibah, which brought a series of rejoinders from their opponents; whatever the respective merits of these compositions, both politics and the nature of civilization settled the doom of the Arab state.

Overthrow of the Persian Viziers. Persian Viziers before the Barmecides.—We have seen how the 'Abbásid Caliphs promoted the Persian clients, and entrusted them with the most important offices, making of them viziers and governors. The Persians, growing mighty, aspired at absolute dominion, and bringing back the days of the Kisras. They knew, however, that this would not be possible except under the pretence of religion beneath the flag of an Islamic Caliphate. Probably it was some such hope which led them to join the faction of the Prophet's house in Umayyad times, and to aid that house in the quest after the Caliphate.

When allegiance had passed from the 'Alids to the 'Abbásids, and the latter were proclaimed Caliphs, Manṣúr appropriated the Caliphate to his own family, to the exclusion of the 'Alids, and fought with and killed the descendants of Ḥasan, after having slain Abú Muslim and other members of his own faction; and thereafter the Persians found it necessary to submit to his authority; but though they feared his violence, they retained their Shí'ite creed, and lay in wait for an opportunity to seize the government and create a Shí'ite dynasty.

The Caliphs were not blind to this, and took care not to fall into the danger; they therefore employed Persians in the highest offices of state, but were still vigilant, and if they detected in any of their ministers an inclination towards Shí'ism they cashiered or slew him. Hence the viziers concealed their inclination in that direction, and the Caliphs set spies to watch them in their houses. Thus Mahdí set a spy to watch his vizier Ya'kúb Ibn Dáwúd, originally an Arabian client, and at first clerk to the 'Alid Ibráhím Ibn Abdallah, descendant of Al-Ḥasan, and brother to that Abdallah who raised a revolt in Medinah and was slain by Manṣúr. Ya'ḳúb had at first joined his brother's revolt, but had then become loyal again, concealed his inclinations, and got into the service of Mahdí, who was greatly attached to him, and trusted him, so that he even gave him the title Brother, and had that edict inscribed in the registers; which gave the poet Silm al-Khásir occasion to compose the following ode:—

> "Inform the Prince whose sovereignty
> Has come by right from dispute free;
> A wortny helper hast thou won
> To right in Jacob, David's son."

Ya'ḳúb acquired such vast influence over Mahdí that he rendered it possible for his master to forget in dissipation the affairs of his empire, while Ya'ḳúb did the whole business; this was not pleasing to the Arabs, who made allusions to it in epigrams, which Mahdí heard without attaching any importance to them; thus, once when on pilgrimage he is said to have passed by a place where the following verse was written up:—

> "Mahdí, you would be a capital one
> If you had not got Jacob, David's son!"

Mahdí told his attendant to write under it "A fig for the writer of this verse, and ill-fortune befall him!"

When his enemies found no other means of altering the disposition of Mahdí towards him, they tried calumny of a sort to which the Caliph would be sure to attend. He was charged with harbouring Shí'ism, having taken part with the Shí'ites in their revolt. Mahdí made no mention of this calumny to Ya'kúb, but tried to put his loyalty to a test in the following way. He summoned him one day to a room where the furniture was all rose-colour, the Caliph himself in rose-coloured garments, and at his head a slave-girl of great beauty. Professing to be pleased with Ya'ḳúb, the Caliph presented him with all that was in the room, the girl included.

Mahdi then told him a matter of importance on which he wished his help, which was that there was an 'Alid from whom the Caliph wished to be delivered, and whom Ya'kub thereupon promised with solemn oaths that he would slay. Ya'kub then went home, sent for the man, talked to him, and finding him intelligent, was persuaded to spare his life, and helped him with money to get away. Meanwhile the slave-girl was listening in some part of the house, and told Mahdi what had happened. Mahdi sent and arrested the man, whom he concealed in the palace, and then brought Ya'kub and confronted him with the prisoner, after which he imprisoned Ya'kub for a number of years. He was not let out till the sixth year, by Rashid, through the intercession of his compatriot and co-religionist, Yahya Ibn Khalid the Barmecide. Rashid permitted him to stay in Baghdad or go whither he chose, and he chose Meccah, being quite decrepit. There he died in the year 187, the year of the overthrow of the Barmecides.

§ 17. The Bramecides and Their Place in the Empire.

After the death of Mahdi and Hadi, when Rashid became Caliph, he made the Barmecides his viziers, because their grandfather Khalid had been one of Abu Muslim's captains, and had given valuable help to the 'Abbasids. He was made vizier by Saffah, and employed by Mansur in his wars, as has already been mentioned. Khalid was a man of mighty intellect and broad mind, neither was he equalled by any of his children in generosity, wisdom, courage, or knowledge. In the year 148 there was born to his son Yahya a child whom he named Fadl, seven days before Khaizuran gave birth to Rashid: the two children were brought up together, and Al-Fadl was suckled by Khaizuran as well as her own son: the two were therefore foster-brothers, a fact expressed by Silm al-Khasir in the verse[1]

> "Al-Fadl and Harun the Caliph became
> Both nurslings of Khaizuran, most noble dame."

[1] Athir, v, 277.

When Hárún became a lad, Mahdí made Yaḥyá his tutor, and he grew up in Yaḥyá's family, and used to call him father. When Mahdí died in Jorjan in 169, the chief of the privy councillors were Yahyá Ibn Khálid and Al-Rabí' Ibn Yúnus. Rashíd was afraid of an outbreak if the death of his father should be known while they were at a distance from the capital, and asked for Yaḥyá's advice, who suggested what was wise until they returned to Baghdad, where the people were already in an uproar. In Baghdad there was Khaizurán, mother of Hádí and Rashíd, who sent to Yaḥyá and Al-Rabí' to ask for their advice; to which call the latter assented, but not the former, knowing that Hádí was jealous of her. Hádí was pleased with Yaḥyá's conduct, thanked him, and ordered him to look after Rashíd as he had done in Mahdí's time, and administered a rebuke to Rabí'.

The first thing that occurred to Hádí after seizing the reins of government was to cancel Rashíd's succession, and transfer it to his own son in order that the Caliphate might remain in the possession of his own descendants—as most of the Caliphs did in similar circumstances. Hádí revealed this intention to some of his courtiers, who assented, withdrew their oath of allegiance to Hárún, and proclaimed Ja'far son of Hádí heir-apparent, and even spoke slightingly of Rashíd in public gatherings. Hádí issued orders that a spear should no longer be carried in front of Rashíd, as was usual with the heir-apparent, and Hárún was avoided by the people, who declined to salute him. In this treatment Hárún was prepared to acquiesce, but Yahyá refused to do so, and urged him to adhere to his rights. Hádí was told that Yaḥyá was spoiling Rashíd, and sending for him asked what their relations were. Yaḥyá replied that the only relation between a slave and his master could be submission on the part of the former. "Why, then," asked the Caliph, "do you come between me and my brother, and spoil him?" "Who am I," asked Yaḥyá in reply, "to come between you? Mahdí brought him and me together, and ordered me to look after him; you repeated the order, and I have obeyed it" Hádí appeared satisfied with this answer. Yaḥyá took advantage of his good-humour, and said: "Commander of the Faithful, if you encourage people to violate their oaths, perjury will be thought lightly of by them; whereas if you let them abide by their allegiance to your brother, and proclaim Ja'far as his successor, the sanctity of the oath of allegiance will be maintained." The Caliph told him he was right, and dismissed him.

When Hádí met the captains who had advised him to cancel Rashíd's succession, they persuaded him to repeat the cancelling proclamation, and Hádí sent for Yaḥyá and imprisoned him. Yaḥyá wrote to him from prison, advising him that he had some good counsel for him. He was brought before the Caliph, who asked him what he had to say. He said: "Commander of the Faithful, supposing that event were to arrive which we shall never see, and indeed we pray God to take us away before it comes [meaning Hádí's death], do you think the people would allow Ja'far to be Caliph before he is of age? Would they be satisfied with a minor to lead prayer, pilgrimage, and war?" Hádí said he thought not. He went on: "Commander of the Faithful, have you no fear lest some one or other of the chief men of your party, e.g. So-and-so, may aspire to the Caliphate, and that others besides, who are not of your family, may also aspire thereunto, whence it might go away from your father's children? Most assuredly, if your father had not made your brother second heir, it would have been the best policy for you to do so. What, then, can be said of your depriving him when he is already installed? You had far better confirm your brother for the present: when your son is of age, compel Rashíd to withdraw, and proclaim Ja'far."[1]

Hádí died after only one year's reign, and Rashíd became Caliph. Yaḥyá was the first person who brought him the news of his accession, and took the ring to him while he was sleeping. Rashíd acknowledged his kindness, saying, "Father, you have set me in this seat by your luck and good administration, and therefore I make you ruler." Giving him his ring, he bestowed

[1] Athír, vi, 39.

on him the right to issue and cancel orders. He continued to hold him in great respect and to speak of him as 'father.' The following epigram was composed by a poet about his vezirate :—

> "The beams of the sun had been ailing, but when
> Hárún became sovereign they blazed out again :
> The bounteous Hárún, God's Prophet's right hand,
> While John, the vizier, carries out his command."

Yaḥya had several sons, of whom Al-Faḍl inherited the father's liberality and disinterestedness, Mohammed his high-mindedness, and Músá his courage and energy, while Ja'far inherited his eloquence and command of the pen. All of them were invested with the highest posts, and indeed ruled the empire, especially the two who have been named. Besides this they were renowned for their munificence, in which the example had been set them by their father Yaḥyá. A verb 'to Barmak' was derived from their name, signifying to be munificent.

Rashíd, wishing to do honour to Yaḥyá, assigned the highest posts in his empire to Al-Faḍl and Ja'far, and indeed divided the government between them. Ja'far was made ruler of the West from Anbár to Africa, Al-Faḍl ruler of the East from Shirwán to the extremity of Turkestan. Departing for Khorasan in 176, Al-Faḍl made it the centre of his government, abolished injustice, built mosques, reservoirs for water, and monasteries, and burned the rolls of arrears. He increased the army, and gave presents to visitors, as well as to his commanders and scribes. He did not remain there long, but left a deputy, and returned to 'Iráḳ in 179, where Rashíd received him honourably and made him vizier. After a little he decided to transfer the vezirate to Ja'far, and said to their father, "I should like to transfer the bureau of the seal from Al-Faḍl to Ja'far, but am ashamed to write to him to say so, so do you write instead of me." Yaḥyá wrote as follows : "The Commander of the Faithful, whom God exalt, bids you transfer the seal from your right hand to your left." Al-Faḍl replied, "I understand the wishes of the Commander of the Faithful with regard to my brother, and no favour that goes to him is removed from me, nor is any honour conferred on him taken away from me."[1]

Ja'far obtained great influence with Rashíd, and acquired a degree of favour to which no one afterwards attained. Rashíd even had a garment made with two collars, which he and Ja'far could both wear at once. Ja'far became absolute autocrat, who could obtain the sanction of the Caliph for anything he chose to order, such as the presenting away of half the kingdom or the hand of one of the Caliph's daughters. A good illustration of his autocratic power is to be found in the story about him and 'Abd al-Malik Ibn Ṣáliḥ the Háshimite. Rashíd was irritated against this 'Abd al-Malik, because, being a cousin of his, he aspired to the Caliphate. It happened that this person was present one day at a wine-party at Ja'far's residence. As he was about to depart, Ja'far asked him to name anything he wanted. The man complained of the unfriendliness of Rashíd. Ja'far replied, "The Commander of the Faithful is reconciled, and no longer bears any resentment against you. I owe you four million dirhems. They are paid, and here is the money; still, it is more honourable for you that they should be paid by the Caliph, and this will give better evidence of the kindliness of his feelings towards you." "Further, I should like to exalt the rank of my son Ibráhím by marriage with a daughter of the Caliph." "The Caliph gives him his daughter 'Aliyah." "I should like attention to be called to his rank by the raising of a banner over his head." "The Caliph makes him governor of Egypt." 'Abd al-Malik departed, leaving the company to marvel at the hardihood of Ja'far in promising all this on his own authority, and fearing that the Caliph would be incensed at Ja'far in consequence. Before the day was over, however, they learned that Rashíd had ratified the whole, saying, as each detail was brought before him, "Excellent!"[2]

Besides this he had a free hand in the disposal of the public treasury and the liberties of the people. Yet none the less, so soon as Rashíd suspected him of disloyalty he overthrew him

[1] Fakhrí, 186. [2] Khillikán, i, 106.

and the whole of his relatives with him. The historians give different accounts of the cause of the overthrow, which will form the subject of the following section.

§ 18. Overthrow of the Barmecides.

The Barmecides were Shí'ís, and their grandfather Khálid had sworn allegiance to the 'Alids before the 'Abbásids, like the rest of the population of Khorasan and Fars. When the 'Abbásids were victorious, and he saw how they dealt with Abú Salamah, then Abú Muslim, and others who wished to restore the Caliphate to the 'Alids, he thought it wise to abandon the cause of the 'Alids, and served faithfully first Saffáḥ, then Manṣúr. His son Yaḥyá and his grandsons were of the same principles as himself—at heart they were on the side of the 'Alids, and inclined to favour 'Alí's family, but they kept their inclinations secret, especially during the reign of Rashíd, who was a vehement persecutor of the 'Alids and their followers, whom he tracked out and executed.[1] From his youth he had hated the 'Alid faction, which was afraid of him before he succeeded to the throne; and when he became Caliph he ordered all the descendants of Abú Tálib to be transported from Baghdad to Medinah.[2]

This became so well known that poets who wished to gain Rashíd's favour lampooned the 'Alids, and Hárún was himself the subject of the satires of 'Alid bards. These latter did not venture to come forward openly in Rashíd's lifetime, but when he was dead and buried at Ṭús, Di'bil Ibn 'Alí produced a poem containing allusions to the massacres of 'Alids organized by the 'Abbásids, praise of the Prophet's family, and satire on Rashíd; it also called attention to the existence at Ṭús of the graves of Al-Riḍá and Rashíd side by side.[3]

The Barmecides disapproved of Rashíd's hatred of the 'Alids, and regarded his dealings with them as criminal,[4] though they had to suppress their wrath; still, they gave secret assistance to

[1] 'Iḳd, i, 42. [2] Athír, ii, 47. [3] Aghání, xviii, 57. [4] Ibid., xx, 76.

the 'Alid faction to the utmost of their ability; its chiefs used to assemble in the house of Ja'far (at that time head of the Barmecide family, the chief favourite with Rashíd) and complain of Rashíd's doings; and though Ja'far did his best to prevent Rashíd hearing of this, it was divulged by some of his numerous enemies in the Caliph's palace, most of whom were either Arabs or connected with Arab families. The most ill-disposed towards him among them and also the best able to injure him was Zubaidah, Amín's mother,[1] whom he had irritated by preferring her rival's son Ma'mún to hers; and she nursed resentment against him from the time when they had all gone to the Ka'bah for the purpose of suspending the documents appointing Amín and Ma'mún to the succession. When Amín had taken the oath in the accustomed style, and was going to walk out of the Ka'bah, Ja'far brought him back, and desired him to swear three times with a formula invoking God's wrath against him if he broke faith—a request which vexed his mother Zubaidah, who cherished resentment on account of it, and became one of those who urged the Caliph to destroy him; in addition to this there was the racial enmity between them. Besides this Ja'far had many ill-wishers among the Arab princes, and especially the family of Rabí' and the family of Mazyad al-Shaibání, whose influence at Court had been weakened by Ja'far, who had incited the Caliph against them.[2] There were also various Persian ill-wishers, even their uncle Mohammed Ibn Khálid, who helped the plot to effect their ruin.[3]

All these endeavoured to embitter the mind of Rashíd against the Barmecides, at times urging that they belonged to the 'Alid faction, at others asserting that they were playing the autocrat, at times declaring that they and their retainers appropriated the public revenues. Rashíd bore all this in mind, but had not forgotten the benefits which Yaḥyá had conferred upon him, and the services of his sons in putting his empire in order and restoring its prosperity. If therefore he was vexed

[1] Mas'údí, ii, 195.
[2] Athír, vi, 57; Khillikán, ii, 179.
[3] Athír, ii, 71.

at times by the aid which Ja'far appeared to give to 'Alids or to receive from them—for, indeed, when appointed governor of the West, Ja'far had installed a Shí'í as governor of Egypt[1]—still Rashíd kept quiet, biding his time.

§ 19. THE 'ALID FACTION IN KHORASAN.

The people of Khorasan and their neighbours of Tabaristan and the Dailemites had belonged to the 'Alid faction before the rise of the 'Abbasids, and had only sworn allegiance to the 'Abbásids in order to comply with Abú Muslim or out of fear of him. When they heard of his treacherous murder, they were angry and covenanted with one another to avenge his death. Before they could do anything, Mansúr had fallen upon the Káwandís, their brethren, who were followers of Abú Muslim, and then he built and entrenched himself in Baghdad, so that they were again compelled to bide their time; and thereupon he began to attack the 'Alids, and slaughter them, so that such as escaped fled to the extreme ends of the Islamic empire, Khorasan and the West, and began to send out their emissaries and proclaim their doctrine secretly. The people of Khorasan continued to be their firmest supporters, owing to their desire to punish Manṣur for the slaughter of Abú Muslim, and to abide by the league they had made against him.

The chief fears of the 'Abbásids were from the direction of Khorasan, because the faction of the 'Alids was there, and the people were brave and generally formidable, from the time when they had transferred the Caliphate from Umayyad to 'Abbásid hands. In the reign of Rashíd the chief exponent of 'Alid ideas was in Khorasan in the person of Yaḥyá, brother of Mohammed Ibn Abdallah, whom Mansúr had fought and slain; this person grew so powerful that Rashíd sent Al-Fadl Ibn Yahyá to deal with him. Al-Fadl induced him to come down from the Dailem country by offering him favourable conditions. Rashíd wrote a certificate of amnesty with his own hand, which was signed by

[1] Suyúṭi, ii, 10.

all the leading Háshimites. And when Al-Faḍl brought Yaḥyá to Baghdad, Rashíd kept his word, and assigned him a princely revenue.

Presently, however, Rashíd wanted to imprison Yaḥyá, perhaps being urged to take this step by some of the enemies of the 'Alids, but found himself unable to do so owing to the certificate of amnesty which he held ; so he consulted the lawyers, and one declared the certificate valid, whom Rashíd tried to refute ; then another, the Ḳáḍí Abu'l-Bakhtarí declared it invalid on some ground or other, whereupon Rashíd tore it up, determined to imprison Yaḥyá, and handed his person over to Ja'far, who regarded him as unjustly treated, since he had only come to Baghdad on the faith of the certificate. He thought fit, therefore, to employ his influence and dexterity in letting the man free, thinking Rashíd would not enquire for him. So he sent a communication to Yaḥyá in prison, who proceeded to implore him to fear God in his case, and not expose himself to the vengeance of the Prophet Mohammed in the next world, since he had assuredly committed no wrong, nor had he harboured any disloyal person. Ja'far, affected by what he said, bade him go whithersoever he wished, and when Yaḥyá objected that he could not go about safely sent with him an escort to conduct him into a safe refuge.[1]

§ 20. RASHÍD AND JA'FAR.

Ja'far's enemies watched his movements, and chief among them Al-Faḍl Ibn al-Rabí', who had aspired to succeed his father in the vezirate, when these Persians had come in his way, and appropriated it. He set spies to watch Ja'far, who informed him of Ja'far's action in the matter of Yaḥyá, of which he proceeded to inform Rashíd, who, however, rebuked Al-Faḍl, stating that Ja'far's action had been by his order. He then sent for Ja'far, and asked him to sup with him, and after handing him morsels with his own hand and talking to him as an equal,

[1] Khaldún, iv, 8 ; Athír, vi, 50, 70.

he asked about Yaḥyá, and Ja'far replied that he was in prison still. But when the Caliph asked Ja'far to swear by the Caliph's life that this was so, Ja'far, guessing what had happened, swore that it was *not* so. He then told Rashíd the whole story, asseverating that Yaḥyá was an innocent man; and Rashíd expressed approval of Ja'far's action, declaring that it agreed with his own intentions. However, he secretly nursed his wrath against Ja'far, and determined on his death from that moment. "God kill me if I do not kill you!" was his private observation when Ja'far left him. However, he waited for a favourable opportunity of carrying out his plan, being aware of the influence which the Barmecides had acquired with different classes of the population (including the Hashimites themselves) through their liberality.

Rashíd therefore wished to put Ja'far off his guard, and that he might not guess at the Caliph's intentions offered to make him governor of Khorasan, and taking the seal from him gave it to his father Yaḥyá and drew up a document appointing Ja'far governor of Khorasan and Sijistan—an appointment cancelled after twenty days.[1] Either, then, this appointment had been merely a blind, or the Caliph having made it became afraid of the consequences.

Among the enemies of the Barmecides was 'Alí Ibn 'Ísá Ibn Máhán, who accused Músá, brother of Yaḥyá, of treasonable correspondence with the people of Khorasan, urging them to forswear allegiance to Rashíd, and offering to come out to them. Rashíd believed this charge, and imprisoned Músá, though he presently discharged him; but that he was definitely alienated from the Barmecides appeared in various actions of his towards them. Thus Yaḥyá Ibn Khálid had been in the habit of entering the Caliph's presence without formal leave, and Rashíd hinted that he disapproved of this proceeding, from which accordingly Yaḥyá ceased. Also, it had been the custom of the slaves to rise up when Yaḥyá entered the Caliph's presence, and his henchman Masrúr was now told to forbid this. Yaḥyá

[1] Athir, vi, 61.

perceived the Caliph's alienation, and it formed the subject of general conversation, till people began to expect that the family would be overthrown, though no one ventured directly to tell them so. Hints, however, were occasionally thrown out by poets in their odes, as e.g. by Ibn Bakkar, who sang the following before Yaha:--

"What do people want of us,
Won't they calm abide?
They would try to bring to light
What we fain would hide."

Rashid was sensible of the momentous character of the step he wanted to take, and was afraid of the adherents of the Barmecides if he should make his onslaught on them; wishing, therefore, to ascertain the feelings of the Court on the subject, he supposed that the minstrels would best enable him to do so, because they had access to the people when they were merry and drunk, and drunkenness makes men reveal their secret thoughts and feelings. Asking his minstrel Ishak of Mausil what people were talking about, he learned from Ishak that the subject of popular conversation was that Rashid was about to arrest the Barmecides and put in office Al-Fadl Ibn al-Rabi'. Rashid, pretending to be angry, asked what business this was of his? So Ishak said no more.[1]

Rashid, moreover, employed spies to enter the houses and offices of the Barmecides and count their breaths', and whenever any incriminating glance or utterance attracted their notice they exaggerated it to the Caliph.

Among the spies of the Caliph were two Khazarite slaves, whom the Caliph had brought up and presented to Ja' far; these slaves used to inform him daily what went on in the salon of Ja' far. For Ja' far had a salon in which entertainment was provided once a week, where the grandees of the empire assembled with the most eminent Persians, who all wore garments of one colour, which were furnished by Ja' far, who

[1] Aghani, v, 113.

also wore the like. At one of these salons conversation turned on Abú Muslim and his ability, and how he had been able by himself to transfer the Islamic empire from one family to another; when Ja'far observed that this was no great exploit, nor did he deserve much praise, since he had accomplished it by the slaughter in cold blood of 600,000 persons: real ability would be shown by transferring the empire from one family to another without bloodshed.[1] The two Khazarites noted this remark and conveyed it to Rashíd, suggesting that Ja'far implied some intention on his own part to transfer the Caliphate from the 'Abbásids to the Persians or the 'Alids: which increased Rashíd's anger.

In the year of their overthrow (187), Rashíd was returning from pilgrimage with his mind fully made up to strike a blow. He made show of being pleased with Ja'far, and appointed him governor of the province of Khorasan, with the view of putting him off his guard, and also with the view of getting the seals from him under the pretence of the new appointment. He bestowed on him a robe of honour, and assigned him an army with a standard at Nahrawán; the people therefore set up their tents there, and stayed, making themselves ready for the further journey; the pick of Ja'far's adherents were then at Nahrawán, while Ja'far remained in Baghdad making his preparations for the journey to join them.

Ja'far had a Háshimite friend who was anxious for his safety, who, learning of Rashíd's attentions with regard to Ja'far and his family, wished to mediate: visiting Ja'far while the latter was engaged in his preparations for the journey to Khorasan, he began to discuss various topics, till he worked his way on towards the subject about which he had come to talk. The man's name was Ismá'íl Ibn Yaḥyá. He ended by saying, "You are about to start for a wealthy country, of vast extent and of wide dominion; if you would bestow some of your estates on the children of the Commander of the Faithful, this act would assure your place in his affections." Ja'far was displeased at

[1] Zínat al-Majális (Persian).

this, since apparently he had no inkling of what the Caliph had in his mind; and his reply was, "'Ismá'íl, your cousin's bread is due to my charity, and for the maintenance of his empire he is indebted to us; is it not sufficient that I have left him without a care for himself, his family, his court, or his subjects, that I have filled his treasuries, that I have managed all his important affairs, but he must needs covet what I have laid aside for my children and descendants? What, is he tainted with Háshimite envy and ingratitude, and is he too a victim of covetousness? Most assuredly, if he asks me for any of my property he shall rue it!" Apparently he meant that he would raise the standard of revolt in Khorasan; and when 'Ismá'íl heard his threats, and perceived how angry he was, he went away and hid himself, both from Ja'far and from Rashíd, as being suspected by both.

One of Rashíd's spies heard this conversation, and reported it to his master, who now determined to strike: possibly his first idea may have been merely to arrest Ja'far and imprison him; but when this menace came to his ears he made up his mind to kill him. He regarded it, however, as a serious step, and asked the advice of his wife Zubaidah, stating plainly what was revolving in his mind: "I am afraid that if these people become possessed of Khorasan the Caliphate may slip from my grasp." Zubaidah urged him to strike quickly, telling him besides, it is asserted, of improprieties committed by Ja'far in Rashíd's house,[1] connected with his sister 'Abbásah Rashíd therefore took advantage of the isolation of Ja'far from his friends and adherents who were in Nahrawán with his army, while he was himself in Baghdad, and sent his henchman Masrúr to bring him Ja'far's head. The story of the execution is well known. Rashíd then sent persons to surround the dwellings of his father Yaḥyá and all his children and his brother Al-Faḍl, by night, and imprisoned them all; and he further seized all their possessions, all their agents, their slaves, and their furniture, sparing only Mohammed Ibn Khálid, who was one of their accusers. The vezirate was then conferred by him on Al-Faḍl

[1] Itlídí, 113.

Ibn al-Rabí', their enemy. At a later period Rashíd repented of having slain the Barmecides, and wept when he thought of them.[1] Ja'far then met with the same fate at the hands of Rashíd as had befallen Buzurgmihr at the hands of Kisra Abarwíz; the Persian king killed his vizier on suspicion of heresy, and then repented [2]

Rashíd slew the Barmecides doubtless because he was afraid of their ousting him from the throne, acting on the 'Abbásid doctrine of killing all suspects: a principle by no means practised by them in dealing with their subjects, whom they used ordinarily to treat in accordance with the requirements of the law of Islam, of justice, and indeed mercy, tenderness, and generosity Rashíd especially was well known to weep when admonished and to relent when implored, as also to give liberally when asked, till his conduct in these matters became proverbial; but when he had to do with the 'Alids, their emissaries and their supporters, he had no fear of God.[3]

Amín and Ma'mún, or the Arabs and the Persians.—When the Barmecides had been slaughtered in this style the people of Khorasan were irritated, and their resentment against the 'Abbásid dynasty was redoubled: a new league was formed by them to avenge the death of Abú Muslim and the deaths of the Barmecides, and they kept watching for a favourable opportunity to arrive. Their hopes turned towards Ma'mún, because his mother was a Persian, and he had been brought up in the family of Ja'far the Barmecide, with an inclination towards the Shí'í faction. Shí'ism was not at that time a religious doctrine as it is now, but was applied to a political party, consisting of the adherents of the 'Alids, whether Persians or others. Love for the Persians and their political doctrine was implanted in the heart of Ma'mún from his tender years, and moreover Yaḥyá Ibn Khálid had selected for his attendant Al-Fadl Ibn Sahl al-Sarkhasí, who was a magian of Khorasan, not converted to Islam till 190, when he yielded to the

[1] Aghání, xvii, 76. [2] Mas'údí, i, 119. [3] Fakhrí, 17.

persuasion of Ma'mun.[1] He sided with the 'Alid faction, being anxious to assist the Persians in Khorasan, and being a man of ability was promoted by Yahya till he became a member of his staff, and finally his steward. Al-Fadl, perceiving the ability and intelligence of Ma'mun, and expecting that he would one day be Caliph, paid court to him, and endeavoured to win his favour. Ma'mun responded to these attentions and promoted him, till Al-Fadl aspired at nothing lower than the vezirate.

It is recorded that before Ma'mun became Caliph, his tutor, observing his good opinion of Al-Fadl and the respect he paid him, spoke of this to Al-Fadl, and said, "I shuld not be surprised if you were to get a million dirhems out of him." Al-Fadl replied that he associated with Ma'mun, not in the hope of getting any sum out of him either small or great, but in the hope that his seal might one day be authoritative in both East and West.[2]

When Rashid assigned the succession to his two sons he gave Amin 'Irak and Syria to the extreme West, and the right to the title Caliph after himself, while to ma'mun he assigned Khorasan and the rest of the East,[3] with the succession to the Caliphate after his brother Amin. All this was done through the machinations of Ja' far and other members of the 'Alid faction, among them Al-Fadl Ibn Sahl. In the year 192 Rashid wished to visit Khorasan, and bade his son Ma'mun remain in Baghdad till his return. Rashid being ailing at the time, Al-Fadl was afraid he might die on the road, in which case his (Al-Fadl's) efforts would be abortive; so he went to Ma'mun, and told him that he did not know what might happen to Rashid. "Khorasan is your province, and Amin has been preferred to you for the Caliphate; the mildest measure that he is likely to employ in your case is cashiering. He is Zubaidah's son, his 'uncles' are the Hashimites, and you know all about Zubaidah and her wealth. So you had better request the Caliph for leave to travel with him." Ma'mun acted according to this suggestion, and though the Caliph at first refused he afterwards granted

[1] Khillikan, i, 413; Athir, vi, 79. [2] Fakhri, 203. [3] Athir, vi 69.

the request. Doubtless his refusal must have been dictated by some motive; and, indeed, he was expecting his end, and saw that his children were employing spies to watch him and count his breaths,[1] and impatient at his survival.

Ma'mún then travelled with his father, and with them went Al-Faḍl, who on the march did his best to further the interests of Ma'mún, and made all the captains of Rashíd's army swear allegiance to Ma'mun, as well as others, and got Rashíd to promise Ma'mún all the money that was with them. Then Ma'mún took up his residence at Merv, the capital of Khorasan; and meanwhile Rashíd fell ill at Ṭús, while Amín was in Baghdad, not however without having spies in Rashíd's army, of whom the most zealous in his interest was Al-Faḍl Ibn al-Rabí', Rashíd's vizier after the Barmecides. When Amín received news of his father's serious illness he sent to Ibn Rabí' and others of his adherents, desiring them to proclaim him successor; and when in 193 Rashíd died, Ibn Rabí' contrived in the absence of Ma'mun at Merv that all who were in the army should join Amín's party; they obeyed him owing to their anxiety to return to their homes and families in Baghdad, and forgot the oath which they had already sworn to Ma'mún. The treasure in the camp was all taken to Amín, his proclamation was accomplished, and presently Al-Faḍl Ibn Rabí' advised Amín to cancel his brother's succession to the Caliphate, and Amín did as he advised.

§ 21. Al-Faḍl Ibn Sahl and 'Alí al-Riḍá.

When Ma'mún heard of his father's death and return of his followers to Amín, taking with them the wealth of the camp, and having broken their oath to him, he feared for his life, and gathering his adherents in Merv, asked their advice, telling them that he was no match for his brother. They, however, encouraged him and promised him their assistance; and

[1] Athír, vi, 83.

Al-Faḍl took care to point out to him that he was established among his mother's relations, that the people had sworn him allegiance, and that if he would only be patient he (Al-Fadl) would guarantee him the Caliphate. This straightforward promise satisfied Ma'mún, who promised to be patient, and said that he rendered Al-Faḍl responsible for the rest. To Al-Faḍl he further gave the title "Of the two headships," viz. of the pen and the sword.

Al-Fadl worked his hardest in Ma'mún's cause, which was indeed his own and that of his country and nation; he conciliated the people and fortified the frontiers. The enmity between the two brothers waxed stronger and stronger, and communications were cut off between Khorasan and Baghdad. Each of the two removed the name of the other from the *khuṭbah*; armies were sent into the field, and terrible battles were fought in which victory was on the side of Ma'mún, whose followers were Persians led by Ṭáhir Ibn al-Husain; finally, Baghdad was taken, and Amín killed in the year 198, his head being brought to Ma'mún in Khorasan. And when Ma'mún saw Al-Fadl's promises realized he became an instrument in Al-Faḍl's hands, and ventured to oppose him in nothing. Al-Faḍl became autocrat, and made his brother Al-Ḥasan governor of the mountain provinces, 'Irák Fars, Ahwáz, Ḥijáz, and Yemen, on condition, however, of his remaining in Baghdad. He further took advantage of the opportunity to restore the Caliphate to the 'Alids, whose representative in Khorasan at the time was 'Alí Ibn Músá al-Riḍá Ibn Ja'far Ibn Mohammed Ibn 'Alí Ibn al-Husain, known as 'Alí al-Riḍá, whom Al-Faḍl did his best to get appointed by Ma'mún as his successor to the Caliphate. It is uncertain whether Al-Faḍl stipulated this as a condition of his assisting Ma'mún in obtaining the Caliphate for himself, or merely recommended it without actual stipulation. Ma'mún accepted the suggestion, whether in order to keep a promise, or by way of compliance with a view to subsequent treachery, or because he really had a high opinion of the 'Alids, imbibed during his infancy, when he professed to belong to the

'Alid faction.[1] In the year 201 he proclaimed 'Alí his successor giving him the title Al-Riḍá (i.e. God's good pleasure) of the family of Mohammed ; he also ordered his army to abandon the 'Abbásid colour, black, and take to the 'Alid colour, green ; and a rescript to that effect was sent all over the empire.

When the news of this reached Baghdad the Háshimites made a great outcry, in which their adherents joined ; they refused to swear allegiance to 'Alí, declaring that the Caliphate must not leave the 'Abbásid family. They supposed the edict to be a plot contrived by Al-Fadl Ibn Sahl, and objected to his brother Ḥasan remaining prefect of Baghdad. Finally, they determined to depose Ma'mún and proclaim his uncle Ibráhím Ibn al-Mahdí Caliph. They accordingly proclaimed him Caliph with the title Al-Mubárak (the blessed). They also wrote a threatening letter to Ma'mún, telling him he would be killed if he adhered to his resolution.

Al Fadl Ibn Sahl kept this information a secret from Ma'mún, fearing lest he should take fright, repent, and cancel his proclamation ; thus deposing 'Alí, in which case all Al-Faḍl's labours would become abortive. 'Alí al-Riḍá was, however, informed of what was going on in Baghdad and was unwilling that all this stir should go on on his account, and that Ma'mún should not be told about it. Going in person to the Caliph, he informed him of the state of Baghdad, and of the proclamation of Ibráhím Ibn al-Mahdí ; Ma'mún regarded the story as strange and even incredible, having been informed that Ibráhím had merely been made in his (Ma'mún's) absence prefect of Baghdad. 'Alí assured him that Al-Faḍl had lied. Ma'mún then saw through the plot contrived by Al-Fadl, and recognized that the assistance given to himself by Al-Fadl had been for this object ; he regarded himself as justified in killing him, and suborned certain persons to assassinate him in his bath at Sarkhas, afterwards trying these persons and executing them for the murder.[2]

[1] Mas'údí, ii, 224.

[2] Athír, vi, 143 ; Fakhri, 199 ; Aghání, ix, 31 ; Khillikán, i. 414.

He considered, however, the question of proclaiming 'Alí Riḍá, being afraid to retract, and fearing in case he should do so a revolt on the part of the people of Khorasan, in which he might lose his life. He resorted therefore to treachery, and suborned some one to give 'Alí poisoned grapes, which caused his death.[1] This put an end to the occasion of the irritation of the people of Baghdad, who withdrew their allegiance from Ibráhím and returned to Ma'mún; Ibráhím, Al-Faḍl, Ibn al-Rabí', and all the adherents of Amín in the struggle took to flight, and Ma'mún entered Baghdad in the year 204 and fixed his residence there. In order to banish all suspicions that he harboured any affection for the 'Alids, he began to persecute them, prevented them from approaching him, and ordered them to wear black.[2]

Although, therefore, the influence of the Persians became again paramount in Baghdad, the 'Alid faction were depressed and compelled to keep their opinions secret till the end of the reign of Wáthiḳ. And when in 232 Mutawakkil came to the throne he started a violent persecution of the 'Alid faction, having been brought up from his youth among Arabian chauvinists, who detested the Persians and the 'Alid faction.

Among them were 'Alí Ibn Jahm, the Syrian poet, of the Banú Shámah, 'Amr Ibn Farrukh al-Rukhkhají, Abú Samt, a descendant of Marwán Ibn Abí Ḥafṣah, who used to curry favour with Rashíd by satirizing the 'Alids, he being an Umayyad client. These persons used in general to frighten Mutawakkil about the Shí'ite faction, and advise him to keep them at a distance, to humiliate and injure them. Next they recommended the abuse of those ancestors of the 'Alids whose high religious station was an article of general belief. Their words carried weight with him, and as he grew up he more and more detested the 'Alid faction and the Caliphs who had given that faction help, viz., Ma'mun, Mu'taṣim, and Wáthiḳ,[3] just as the instructions of the Barmecides had left their mark on Ma'mún, and inspired him with affection for the 'Alid faction.

[1] Athír, vi, 144; Fakhrí, 199. [2] Athír, vi, 156. [3] Id., vii, 22.

So when Mutawakkil became Caliph he commanded the destruction of the grave of Husain Ibn 'Alí, with all the surrounding buildings, and forbade people to approach it. He carried his hatred of 'Alí and his household to such a pitch that he even made of 'Alí a laughing-stock. Among his court attendants was a hermaphrodite called 'Ubádah, who used to tie a pillow to his waist underneath his garments, and uncover his head, which was bald, in order to mimic the Caliph 'Alí, and dance, repeating—

> "Here's the pot-bellied bald head
> Of Musulmans called head"

(meaning 'Alí); and hereat Mutawakkil would laugh over his cups.[1] From that time the Sunnite faction got the upper hand in the empire, being maintained by the Turks, as shall be seen. With the decline of the 'Alid cause in Baghdad the influence of the Persians declined; and with the Caliphate of Mutawakkil ends the first Persian period.

§ 22. SECRECY IN THE 'ABBÁSID EMPIRE.

The 'Abbásids were specially renowned for the keeping of secrets, and enjoined this practice on their clients and familiar associates, especially in matters appertaining to the maintenance of their dynasty. Illustrations of this have appeared in the dealings of the Caliphs with their generals and viziers from the commencement of the dynasty, especially in those of Manṣúr with his uncles and with Abú Muslim, etc., and of Rashíd with the Barmecides, and of Ma'mún with Al-Fadl Ibn Sahl, 'Alí al-Riḍá, and Ṭáhir Ibn al-Ḥusain. They regarded secrecy in their undertakings as an essential of success, as we saw in the case of Kutham Ibn al-'Abbás when he spread division among the detachments of the army by a device of which he did not wish to inform Manṣúr. Besides this they employed the aid of

[1] Abu'l-Fidá, ii, 40.

spies and watchers, and everyone spied everyone else. The Caliph set spies to watch the generals and viziers, and the viziers set spies to watch him. A man's slave or slave-girl was often a spy on his movements. The Caliph would set people to watch his own sons or brothers, the heir to the throne would set them to watch his father, as we saw was done by Amín and Ma'mún in the case of Rashíd. Ma'mún's spy was the henchman Masrúr, Amín's the physician Gabriel son of Bakhtíshú'. These persons counted the Caliph's breaths.[1]

When Ma'mún became Caliph, and had come to Baghdad, he set spies to watch Ibráhím Ibn al-Mahdí, and hired a man to attend him and report every word he uttered, whether in jest or earnest.[2] The other Caliphs did the like, especially towards the end of the dynasty; and, indeed, the growth of espionage is a sign that a dynasty is approaching its decline. The viziers then had spies to watch the Caliphs, and the Caliphs spies to watch their viceroys, this function being discharged by postmasters or officers of the intelligence department, in addition to the slaves, male and female, and singing women employed for this purpose. This was done for fear their authority might be undermined, and secrecy was maintained to an extraordinary degree. Ma'mún had his intelligence agent for every person, and would pardon every utterance except an attack on the monarch, revelation of a State secret, or improper allusions to the royal ladies.[3]

Owing to their secrecy the motives for many acts that took place in their time were obscure and imperfectly understood. Thus the historians have to conjecture the reason for the overthrow of the Barmecides, and differ seriously in their surmises. Of many a murder the author was unknown, and the victim was supposed to have died of eating grapes, or dates, etc., whereas his death was due to poison given him by his physician or housekeeper[4] at the instigation of some Caliph, general, or heir-apparent.

[1] Athír, vi, 83.
[2] Aghání, xx, 82.
[3] Mas'údí, ii, 225; Uṣaibi'ah, i, 171.
[4] Uṣaibi'ah, i, 182.

§ 23. Confusion of Genealogies after Islam

We have seen what care the Arabs bestowed on the preservation of their genealogies : they went so far as to despise one who was not born of two Arab parents. If his father were non-Arab he was called *mudharra,'* if his mother were a foreigner he was called *hajin.* If his mother were slave he was regarded as a slave, and only acknowledged as a son if he turned out well. The *hajin* did not inherit, and this was an illustration of the contempt felt for the non-Arab, as has been seen.

§ 24. Children of Slave-girls.

When Islam spread, and the Arabs conquered the Eastern nations, Persians, Turks, etc., numbers of slave-women were acquired in the course of the conquests. These women were employed as nurses, wet and dry, the younger ones being also made concubines. At first the Moslems used to disapprove of marriage with them, and despise their children, especially in the Hijaz, the centre of Arabian chauvinism ; but this ceased when there arose in Medinah three noble persons, all of them sons of slave-girls : 'Ali Ibn al-Husain, al-Kasim Ibn Muhammad, and Salim Ibn 'Abdallah. These surpassed the people of Medinah in jurisprudence, chastity, and learning. After their appearance the poeple took kindly to concubines.[1]

Nevertheless, the Umayyads continued to treat the sons of slave-girls with contempt, owing to their partisanship for Arabs as against foreigners. When 'Abd al-Malik learned one day that 'Ali Ibn al-Husain had married a slave-girl and manumitted her, he wrote to reproach him. 'Ali's reply was that God by Islam had raised the lowly and made good the defective, and substituted generosity for meanness. Hence no stigma was left on a Moslem. So the Prophet had married his handmaid and his slave's wife. When 'Abd al-Malik read his reply

[1] Ikd. iii. 229.

he observed that 'Alí Ibn al-Ḥusain found honour where most men find disgrace. It must, however, be borne in mind that after Islam had commenced the Arabs began to pay more honour to the *hajíns* (see above), supposing that in the pedigree only the male line counted. This view is expressed in the following lines :—

> "No man should be taunted because of his mother
> Being negro or Greek or Persian or other :
> The mother 's no matter ; the child 's of the father."

The Umayyads continued to treat the sons of slave-girls with contempt till the close of their dynasty. Thus, when Zaid Ibn 'Alí Ibn al-Ḥusain came forward as pretender to the Caliphate in the days of Hishám Ibn 'Abd al-Malik, he was taunted by the Caliph with his origin as a slave-girl's son. He replied that such an origin did not prevent a man from attaining the most exalted posts, seeing that Ishmael's mother was the slave of Isaac's mother, but in spite thereof God made him a prophet, made him father of the Arabs, and raised up out of his seed Mohammed, the best of mankind.[1] The fact that the Umayyads were such strong partisans of the Arabs of itself made the 'Alids more inclined to mix with them. Hence most of the 'clients' were of the 'Alid faction.

Both views then—that to be the son of a slave-girl was a disgrace, and that the mother counted for nothing in the pedigree—found representatives at the beginning of Islam.[2]

The nature of Islamic civilization was, however, too strong for the Umayyads and their desire to preserve the Arab pedigrees pure from admixture. Such admixture, therefore, took place even in the line of the Umayyad Caliphs, towards the end of whose dynasty sons of slave-girls were proclaimed sovereign. The first Caliph of this sort was Yazíd Ibn al-Walíd Ibn 'Abd al-Malik, proclaimed in the year 126 ; his mother was a descendant of Yezdejird son of Kisra, taken captive in Sugnd by Ḳutaibah, who sent her to Ḥajjáj, who presented her to Al-Walíd Ibn 'Abd al-Malik, to whom she bore

[1] Mas'údí, ii, 130. [2] Verses in illustration are given in 'Iḳd, iii, 230.

Yazid.[1] There is a story that the Umayyads objected to the proclamation of *hajins* as sovereigns, not out of contempt for such persons, but because of a notion that with a sovereign of this sort their dynasty would come to and end. In Yazid they found the fulfilment of this prophecy. He only reigned seven months: he was followed by Marwan Ibn Mohammed, whose mother was a Kurdish slave. And with him the dynasty inded.

§ 25. Caliphs whose Mothers were Slaves.

The 'Abbasid dynasty, unlike the former, was based on the clients, and in its time Arab chauvinism declined owing to the large admixture with foreign elements that had taken place; the status of the mother ceased therefore to court. Most of the Caliphs has slave-mothers, beginning with Ibrahim the Imam. Various races were represented by these mothers. Persians, Turks, Greeks, Kurds, Berbers, Abyssinians, Zanj, etc. Here is a list of some of the 'Abbasid Caliphs whose mothers were slaves:-

Caliph.	*Mother's Nationality.*
Ibrahim the Imam	Berber.
Mansur.	Berber.
Rashid.	Harash [?]
Ibrahim Ibn al-Mahdi.	Zanj.
Ma'mun	Persian.
Muntasir.	Abyssinian-Greek.
Musta' in.	Slav.
Mu' tazz.	[?]
Muhtadi.	Greek.
Muktadir.	Turk.
Muktafi	Turk.
Mustadi'.	Armenian.
Nasir.	Turk.

1. Athir. vi, 270; v, 147.

The other dynasties exhibit a similar state of things. The mother of the Fáṭimide Mustansir was a Sudanese slave, that of the Umayyad 'Abd al-Rahmán al-Dákhil a Berber. To this list we could add many sons of Caliphs who never ascended the throne, e.g. Mohammed Ibn al-Hanafiyyah, son of a black woman of Scinde.

If pedigrees were thus mixed in the case of the Caliphs, they were naturally much more so in the case of other ranks of society. Arabian pedigrees were kept pure only in pagan days, and at the beginning of Islam, to the middle of the Umayyad period; after that purity was confined to the father's side; on the mother's side they became exceedingly mixed. We at this time are aware that the child inherits characteristics from the mother no less than from the father, and often resembles the mother in character more closely than the other. After the second century of the Hijrah, except in the desert or where there was little communication with foreigners, the blood of the Arabs contained only a small Arab strain. Besides the influence of foreign blood they were greatly influenced by the climate and customs of the lands where they settled. The town Arabs of the third century A.H. were then different from the Arabs at the beginning of Islam; and the difference must be enormously greater between the latter and the town Arabs of the present day, whose ancestors have ceaselessly mixed and intermixed with foreigners, while on the other hand numbers of persons have falsely claimed Arab descent after the old Arab pedigrees had been lost. The word Arab has come to have a wider denotation, being extended to various countries. Syrians, Egyptians, inhabitants of 'Iráḳ, and of Morocco are called Arabs, whereas they are in truth a mixture of Arabs, Turks, Dailemites, Circassians, Greeks, Persians, Armenians, Georgians, etc. One who comes to these countries to settle is regarded at first as a stranger. When he has settled and founded a family his children are regarded as immigrants, but after a few generations they are called Arabs like the rest.

§ 26. FIRST TURKISH PERIOD.

From the Caliphate of Mutawakkil in 232 to the supremacy of the Dailemites in 334.

By this period we mean that in which the Turks (i.e. the army) became absolute masters of the 'Abbásid empire, as distinguished from the Persian 'Abbásid period, in which the Persian viziers obtained despotic power. Between the two periods there is no separating line; indeed, the two were for a time coincident.

§ 27. THE ORIGINAL TURKS.

The Turks are an ancient nation made up of tribes, clans, etc., whose homes were originally on the Altai Mountains, called also the Golden Mountains, in the centre of Asia, between India, China, and Siberia. They have a story about their supposed founder similar to the Roman myth of Romulus. Bartazina, the first Turkish leader, also suckled a wolf. When he came to man's estate he led them in their wars and raids with their tents and flocks, they being in the nomad state. They fought with the neighbouring nations, especially the people of China. Bartazina left several sons, who, having seen Chinese cities and Chinese civilization, wished to build cities after the same model. One of the commanders, however, dissuaded them, observing that the Turks were only a tenth in number of the Chinese, and that the strength of the Turks lay in their liberty. "When we feel ourselves strong enough to make war we raid; at other times we return to the nomad state. The people of cities are caught within their walls like birds in a cage." This argument seemed decisive, and the plan of city-building was abandoned. The state of the Arabs before Islam was similar; their nomad condition was one of the causes of their conquering.

The Turks therefore remained raiding and tent-dwelling nomads, increasing in numbers and power till about 400,000 of them got together; they fought for fifty years with Chinese, Persians, and Romans, and were ordinarily victorious. In the time of Justinian they made a treaty with the Romans, and relations remained friendly between them and Justinian's successors, and several embassies were interchanged. In the days of Khakan Dizabul ambassadors were sent by the Romans to him in the Altai Mountains, and the parties made a league to fight against the Persians, then under Kisra Anushirwan, whom they proved unable to overcome. By this tme they were spread over Turkestan, where some cities had been founded.

§ 28. THE TURKS AFTER ISLAM.

When Islam made its appearance and the Arabs spread over the world, the hoofs of their horses trod the country of the Turks, called by the Arabs "What is beyond the River." The Arabs conquered Bokhara, Samarcand, Farghanah, and Ashrusnah, as well as other portions of Turkestan, in Umayyad times. When the 'Abbásids became supreme those cities were subject to the Moslems, paying poll-tax and land-tax. As part of the poll-tax they were in the habit of sending children of the nomads of Turkestan, ordinarily taken captive and so made slaves of, according to the fashion of those days. Besides these other members of the race often fell into the hands of the Moslems during the wars, were given the name *mamlúks* (thralls), and were distributed among the palaces of the Caliph and his ministers. So they began to adopt the religion of Islam, like the other nations that had been subdued by the Arabs in that age, and to furnish slaves and clients, as has been shown above.

The Turks were distinguished from the other nations that had become subject to the Moslems by bodily strength, courage, skill in archery, ability to travel long distances on horseback, and steadiness in the field; together with neglect of learning, especially philosophy and natural science, with which few Turks occupied themselves while Islamic civilization lasted. When a Turk devoted himself to any study of this sort the fact was mentioned with astonishment. Thus, Ibn Athír, speaking of the astronomical attainments of Kutulmush, observes: "It is extraordinary that this Kutulmush, being a Turk, should have mastered astronomy with other studies." The Turks appear in Islamic history under a variety of names, according to their lesser or greater divisions, which were no less numerous than those of the Arabs.

§ 29. THE TURKISH ARMY IN 'ABBÁSID TIMES.

The first Caliph who employed Turks as soldiers was Manṣúr, but in his time they were a small corps of no political importance: chief importance belonged to the troops from Khorasan (Persians) and Arabs. When in the days of Rashíd the rivalry between Arabs and Persians came to a head, and with the fall of Amín Arab predominance was extinguished, the victory remaining with the Persians, who had helped Ma'mún, whose mother was one of themselves, town life had already exercised a deleterious influence on the Moslems, and taken from them the vigour requisite for the pursuit of empire. Ma'mún's brother Mu'taṣim reflected on this before he became Caliph, and his mother was a Turk, from whom he had inherited not only a fondness for the Turks, similar to Ma'mún's fondness for the Persians, but also many of the Turkish characteristics which have been enumerated. The courage and arrogance exhibited by the Persians after Amín's death made Mu'taṣim fear them on his own account. He had no confidence in the Arabs, whose chauvinism had departed, and who, spoiled by the luxury of town life, had lost their vigour. He therefore bethought him of obtaining support from the Turks, who were still vigorous nomads, courageous in war and patient of privations. He in consequence began to select vigorous Turks, whom he either bought of their masters in 'Irak or sent to look for in Turkestan or elsewhere. Many thousands were thus got together, men of good constitutions and personal beauty, whom he clothed in satin, with gilt cinctures and gilt ornaments, distinguished by their costume from the rest of the army.[1] Most of the Turks whom he got together were of Farghanah or Ashrusnah.

When he became Caliph the Turks were his helpers, and their numbers increased so fast that Baghdad became too small for them. They began to annoy the people in the streets, and great injuries were inflicted by them on the young and weak. Corpses of persons slain by them were often found lying on the kerb. One feast day when Mu'tasim was an parade an old man arose and addressed him as Abu Ishak ; the soldiers would have struck him, but Mu'tasim intervened, and asked the old man what he wanted. He said : "God give you no good reward for your conduct as our neighbour : you have brought these barbarians, your Turkish soldiers, to reside among us, and they have made our boys orphans and our wives widows, and killed our men." When Mu'tasim heard this he went into his palace, and was not seen riding in public till the next feast day, when after performing public prayer he did not re-enter Baghdad, but went looking for a camp for his guards and finally selected Samarra for the purpose. Pleased with this place he renamed it *Surra man ra'a*, 'delight of him that sees it.' Marking out sites for buildings there, he assigned sections to his Turks according to their tribes and their location at home. Separate streets were assigned to all the crafts and trades. Houses and other vast buildings were erected and water procured. The rumour went about that the royal residence had been transferred from Baghdad thither, and this led to a general concourse to the place, goods and other necessaries or comforts of life being conveyed in great abundance. Samarra remained the capital of the 'Abbasid empire from 221 to 279, when Mu'tamid went back to Baghdad.[2]

[1] Mas'udi, ii, 246. [2] Athir, vii, 281.

Mu'taṣim divided his *mamlúks* into detachments with commanders over them, according to military ideas of the time. Not only did he collect recruits by purchase or presentation, but he further encouraged the Turkish princes and chieftains to come to him and live under his protection. Such a recruit was Juff Ibn Yaltikin, a prince of Farghanah. Hearing this person described as a brave and dashing soldier, Mu'taṣim summoned him with other princes, all of whom were highly honoured by the Caliph. When Sámarra was built they were assigned plots there, and those assigned to Juff were called after him during many centuries.[1]

Most of the Turks when brought together by Mu'taṣim were idolators or Magians by religion; some, however, had already embraced Islam. The non-Moslems, however, soon changed over to Islam when once they had entered the army of the Caliph or received a Moslem training. Some only made an outward show of Islam in order to curry favour with the Caliph. Such a case was that of Ifshín, who remained a Magian, though he professed Islam in order to obtain a share of the spoils of war.

Mu'taṣim was exceedingly anxious to make his Turks maintain their original character, and was afraid of their adopting the habits of the towns, thinking that if they mixed with other nationalities their own national spirit and courage would decline. He therefore made purchases of Turkish slave-girls, whom he compelled his guards to marry, while prohibiting them from intermarriage with the other Moslems till they had children who might intermarry. The slave-girls mentioned were given fixed stipends, their names being entered in registers, so that no Turk could either divorce or abandon his wife.[2]

§ 30. The Turkish Army and Public Affairs.

This measure strengthened the power and influence of the Turks, who got control over the empire, especially after they had rescued it from Babak al-Khurramí, taken Amorium, and

[1] Khillikán, ii, 41.

[2] Ya'ḳúbí (Geogr.), 33.

so aided Islam. The chief voice in public affairs became theirs. These having been for a time in the hands of Persian viziers, were now under the control of Turkish captains—or perhaps were left to the mercy of the two. Many viziers during this period attained great distinction, e.g., Ibn Wahb, Ibn al-Furát, 'Alí Ibn 'Ísá, Ibn Muḳlah, etc. These persons vied with the Turks in obtaining influence at court, and plundering others by fines, trials for malversation, etc.

By this time the dynasty had passed its youth and begun to decline. The Caliphs, devoted to pleasure and amusement, were unable to direct public affairs; the office of Caliph could only be obtained by the aid of the Turkish guards, who would do nothing save for money. He who could obtain the help of the army was sovereign; national, tribal, religious, and local considerations counted for nothing. The Turks were the pivot of the movement, they being, as has been seen, people of courage and dash. Unscrupulousness and readiness to strike became the chief agents for the acquisition of sovereignty.

At the commencement of the 'Abbásid dynasty its soldiers were Muḍarite and Yemenite Arabs and Persians: by the latter we mean the population of the country between 'Iráḳ and the limit of Khorasan eastward as far as the river Jaiḥán (Jaxartes). These include the people of Khuzistan, Fars, Kirmán, Makran, Sijistan, Kuhistan, Khorasan, etc. All these had helped the 'Abbásid party by way of avenging themselves on the Umayyads, who had oppressed them, or else out of the desire for supremacy. Most of the soldiers were freemen, having been neither sold nor manumitted, and only called clients (or freedmen) in accordance with the nomenclature of the time, in reference to the fact that they were not Arabs. Out of their number the Caliphs selected certain persons whom they promoted to high posts in the public service, and these developed into viziers, viceroys, and savants. Invested by the Caliphs with governorships, they acquired independence, and founded independent dynasties under the protection of the 'Abbásid Caliphate, as will be seen.

When Muʻtasim became Caliph, and acquired his Turkish guard by purchase or persuasion, the army came to consist mainly of *mamliks*, whom the succeeding Caliphs were inclined to favour, assigning them post in their palaces, or giving them places among their private staff and escort. Some were promoted so high in the public service that they became commanders of the forces, and virtually desposts. Thus the administration shifted from the hands of the Persian clients, most of whom were of the Shiʻite faction, to the Turkish army, mostly Sunnite. Sunnism had taken hold of them from the time when Mutawakkil had publicly proclaimed persecution of the Shiʻites, and the Turks adhere to it still.

Their control of the palace began in the days of Mutawakkil, who became Caliph in 232. Exhibiting his dislike of the Shiʻah faction by his arbitrary measures with regard to them, he thought it necessary to favour the Turks even more than before, which increased their political ambition. Mutawakkil's son Muntasir urged them (or was urged by them) to murder his father, which they did, this being the first occasion when they made an attack on a Caliph. They made Muntasir his successor, whose reign, however, lasted only a few months, his guilty conscience accelerating his end.

He was succeeded by Mustaʻin in 240, who was succeeded by Muʻtazz in 251, and during this period the incluence of the Turks had increased enormously. A story illustrating their despotic power over the Caliphs is the following :-- When Muʻtazz was appointed his courtiers held a sitting, and, summoning the astrologers, asked them to see how long the Caliph would live and how long he would retain his Caliphate. A wit who was present said : "I know better than the astrologers how long he will live and reign." Being asked to specify the time he replied, "So long as the Turks please," and everyone present laughed.[1]

Muʻtazz was slain by them in a horrible way, being dragged by the feet to the door of the private apartments, and then stuck with pins. His shirt was then torn off, and he was placed

[1] Fakhri, 220.

in the sun, where, while he lifted his feet alternately in the torture of the heat, the Turks smote him with their hands.[1] Mustakfí was blinded by them and imprisoned till he died.[2] Káhir was reduced by them to such indigence that when they cast him into prison he was wrapped in a cotton *jubbah*, with wooden clogs on his feet.[3] It is not surprising that the Caliphs became a mere instrument in the hands of the Turks, the Caliph being on the winning side[4] whenever there was a struggle between them for power. Whereas at first the Turkish captains swore allegiance to the Caliph, presently the Caliph swore allegiance to them.[5]

When the Turks had obtained this promotion in the 'Abbásid empire, and their kinsmen who were at home learned thereof, they trooped to the capital in their hundreds and their thousands in order to obtain employment in the army. They were attracted towards Islam, and began to join it in thousands and myriads. In the year 350 A.H. 200,000 families, of no fewer than five members each, making in all a million souls, adopted Islam at once. In the year 435 there was a conversion of 10,000 families of Balasaghun and Kashgar, who sacrificed 20,000 head of sheep.[6]

The Turkish army of this period closely resembled the Prætorian cohorts of the Roman Empire, or the Bashi-Bazouks of the Ottoman Empire. Their services were at the disposal of anyone who would pay for them. Whoever aspired to sovereignty had to purchase them or hire them. In the course of years various detachments of them were formed, being called after their captains: so the Sájiyyah after Abu'l-Sáj, the Ṣaláhiyyah after Saláh al din; similarly the Asadiyyah, Nizámiyyah, etc. Wars often broke out between these detachments, when they strove with one another for influence or money. When in Búyid times the Dailemites obtained possession of Baghdad, a series of wars took place between the Turks and Dailemites and the Caliphs' slaves or freedmen; but every

[1] Athír, vii, 77. [2] Id., viii, 177. [3] Id., viii, 173.
[4] Id., ix, 264. [5] Id., viii, 176. [6] Id., viii, 210; ix, 216.

single dynasty that arose during this period employed the services of the Turks as soldiers, whether the dynasty was Shí'í or Sunní. They were brought successively from their Turkish homes to Baghdad and the other capitals of Islam, but rarely founded families. Hence they talked to each other in Turkish, though sometimes they learned Arabic, which, however, they were too proud to talk.

The governors and captains took great trouble in training their Turkish soldiery in military manœuvres, besides teaching them their religious duties: which last were taught them while they were still young. When a merchant brought a *mamlúk* to market, he would offer him to the commander or governor, who, if satisfied, would purchase the lad, and place him with his compeers, in charge of a Ṭawáshi (eunuch), to be educated. The first thing taught him would be such portions of the Koran as he had need to know. Under the Egyptian *mamlúk* dynasty each class of recruits had a jurisconsult, whose business it was to see them every day and teach them the Koran, Arabic writing, and the practice of the moral code of Islam, and to make them say their prayers. When the lad was old enough he was taught a little Mohammedan law; when he became a man he was taught various military accomplishments such as shooting or hurling the javelin. During the time when they were practising, no one, private or officer, would dare to address them or approach them. When the recruit was perfect in his exercises, he would be promoted from degree to degree till finally he might reach that of *amír* or commander; but he would only attain to this position if he proved to be of excellent character and talents. From the same class lawyers, savants, poets, and mathematicians [1] arose

The ordinary population, however, were in fear of the Turks and their violence, and were in terror if ever visited by them. For the Turks would quarter themselves in people's houses,[2] and do violence to their women and children. Among the populace of Baghdad they were in very bad odour.

[1] Maḳrízí, ii, 213. [2] Athír, ix, 264.

§ 31. SLAVES AND THEIR INFLUENCE ON THE 'ABBÁSID EMPIRE.

The first case of which we hear in which a slave came to the front in the 'Abbásid empire is that of Masrúr, slave of Rashíd, but even he only held a subordinate post. The first Caliph who promoted slaves and took pains to acquire a multitude of them was Amín, Rashíd's son, who, when he succeeded his father, looked out for eunuchs and paid high prices for them. He made them his private attendants both at night and in the day; he had them to wait at his table, and in general to carry out his orders. One particular class he called Farádís, and another (of Abyssinians) he called Ghurábís. His purpose in promoting those persons was neither self-defence nor the interest of his empire, but purely debauchery and wantonness. There is a poem extant in which the names of some of these slaves are recorded.[1]

§ 32. CAUSE OF THEIR INFLUENCE.

The eunuchs were of no consequence in the days of Ma'mún, Mu'taṣim, and Wáthiḳ. Only when the Turks had become supreme in the days of Mutawakkil and those that followed, and had begun to appoint, dethrone, and kill the Caliphs, one of the expedients employed by them for securing complete power over the nominal sovereigns was to keep them in custody before their accession, and imprison them in castles in order to weaken them. On the other hand, the Caliphs were disposed to imprison their relatives and children[2] for fear lest they should conspire with the Turks to depose and slay them. During the term of their confinement they had no associates except slaves and eunuchs. Getting to be on friendly terms with these, they learned by experience that their lives depended on the fidelity of these retainers, whom besides they found to be zealous in their cause. Especially was this true of the eunuchs, who were prevented by no other attachment, such as patriotism, from

[1] Athír, vi, 120. [2] Fakhrí, 297.

devoting themselves heart and soul to their masters' cause, and who could have no political ambition for themselves or their families. Whenever, therefore, an heir-apparent succeeded to the throne he did his utmost to conciliate his slaves by gifts and honours in order to make sure of their protection, should an attempt be made upon him by the Turks. It became the principle of the Caliphs to acquire great numbers of slaves, to promote and honour them, and ask their advice on all important occasions. And since "greatness is conferred by kings" these slaves acquired great power and influence till they were feared even by the Turks. During the Turkish period many of them rose from domestic service to taking the command of troops or governing provinces.

§ 33. Classes and Orders of Slaves.

When the numbers of the slaves increased in the Caliphs' palaces they were divided into classes and orders, known by special names, e.g., Greeks, Turks, Abyssinians, Armenians, Scindians, Berbers, Sclavs; they resembled the regiments of an army, and had salaries or wages assigned them.

The 'slaves' originally denoted the various persons of that rank who were employed in the Caliphs' and governors' palaces in various forms of domestic work. These persons were purchased of dealers, many of them having learned some trade, such as that of weaver, groom, cupper, baker, etc.; presently large numbers were acquired to help in defending the palaces in times of stress, their competence for this purpose varying with the amount of their purchase-money. These prices might vary from 100 to 1,000 dinars, or even more. In the palaces of some governors there were 500, 1,000, or even larger numbers of them. Those belonging to Bughá al-Sharábi, a Turkish captain, numbered 500; the Fáṭimide vizier Ja'ḳúb Ibn Killis had more than 4,000.

The detachments of slaves in the Caliph's palaces were called by special names, e.g., "the Lesser Lads," "the Lads of the State Apartments," "the Men of the Ranks," "the Men of the Stirrups," etc. The difference between the detachments of the Turkish army and those of the 'lads' was that the former, being in the employ of the State, were paid out of the public treasury, and were some bought, but others hired; whereas the lads, being employed in the private service or defence of the Caliph or governor, were his personal property, and supported out of his private estate. Detachments of lads might, however, be transferred to detachments of the army, or compelled to perform public service in their company, if circumstances required. The Caliph might of course purchase a number of slaves to defend him against his enemies, and this process could not be restrained. At times a detachment of slaves would obtain possession of the Caliph's or governor's person, and force him to do what they pleased. At times, too, the Caliphs found themselves forced to make a murderous onslaught on one detachment of slaves with the help of another.[1]

The eunuchs formed a peculiar class of slaves, specially employed in the hareems; of these, too, large numbers were procured, most of them being negroes by race. The people of Baghdad used to make the eunuchs butts for their wit and satire, calling after them in the streets with various jeers and insulting rhymes—

> "Mister no-power,
> Sprinkle the water and spread the flour!"

Or "Daddy Long-legs."

The eunuchs complained to the Caliphs of this treatment. In the days of Mu'taḍid the Baghdadese were severely punished for conduct of this sort. Some of the black eunuchs having been insulted in the year 286, appealed to Mu'taḍid, who ordered a number of their persecutors to be scourged.[2] Still, it often occurred that a eunuch rose to the rank of governor.

[1] Athír, viii, 126.

[2] Mas'údí, ii, 340.

§ 34. Generals and Viziers who were originally Slaves.

Muḳtadir, who became Caliph in 295, was the first of the series who acquired great numbers of slaves, favoured them, and promoted them to high posts. He possessed 11,000 slaves and eunuchs, Greeks and negroes,[1] and was also the owner of vast quantities of money and jewels. He reigned 25 years, and restored the Caliphate to its former lustre. He promoted his slaves, and relied on their assistance: the command of the forces and other important offices were conferred on them by him. In his time "Mu'nis the Slave" became prominent. Muḳtadir promoted him and made him his adviser, so that Mu'nis waṣ able to control public affairs, became commander of the forces, *Emír al-umara*, and Treasurer General and general autocrat. His services to the Caliph were ordinarily valuable; however, a misunderstanding arose between them, which after iteration led to an armed conflict, which ended with the death of Muḳtadir. His head was brought to Mu'nis, who, on seeing it, shed tears and beat his face.

The Caliphs only resorted to the practice of making slaves and eunuchs their masters when they wished to preserve their lives, or maintain their authority in the face of the imperious Turkish troops. Nor was this the exclusive practice of the 'Abbásids, for it was employed by most of the contemporary Islamic dynasties. Nor was it an Islamic invention, but had already been in vogue in most of the ancient empires. Thus Stephen the Freedman controlled the Roman Empire, and slew, appointed, and deposed as he liked; and so too did Solomon the Eunuch, etc.

In Islamic times many slaves became celebrated in high posts as generals, governors, treasurers, etc. Badr, slave of Mu'taḍid became general, and his name was engraved on shields and ensigns; he served his master well, and was finally

[1] Fakhrí, 234.

slain in his defence in the year 289 A.H.[1] Bajkan was originally a slave, and was promoted till he became Emír al-umará, the highest post in the 'Abbásid empire.[2] Jauhar, general of the Fáṭimides, who conquered Egypt for them and built Cairo, in the middle of the fourth century A.H., was a Greek slave. The honour paid him was so great that when he started from the West to conquer Egypt the children and retinue of the Caliph Mu'izz dismounted and walked before his horse.[3] Prior to him Káfúr al-Ikhshídí, a negro and eunuch, had become autocrat of Egypt in the year 355. Ya'nis the Sicilian eunuch was originally a slave of Mu'nis the slave, but nevertheless had risen in the public service and been appointed to governorships and got a share in the administration. Barjwán al-ustádh, a white eunuch, was promoted in the Fátimide realm to the post of vizier, which he held under the Caliphs 'Azíz and Ḥákim. He received the title Amín al-daulah, and indeed was the first person on whom it was conferred by a Fáṭimide Caliph.[4] The eunuch Ḳaráḳúsh, vizier of Saladdin, obtained the highest public offices in the Ayyúbid realm. 'Amíd al-Mulk, one of the chief Turkish generals, was a eunuch, as was also Shuḳair the Slave, postmaster for Egypt and Syria in the days of the Tulunids. Another slave and eunuch who attained high office under the Fáṭimides was Mu'taman al-Ḳhiláfah. The Slavs were similarly promoted under the Spanish Umayyads; and cases could also be cited of high office held by slaves and eunuchs under the Búyids and Seljuḳs, and other Islamic dynasties of those times.

§ 35. INFLUENCE OF WOMEN ON THE ADMINISTRATION.

Women have invariably great influence on men's actions in all ages and among all peoples, though the extent of that influence varies with the customs and morals of the particular nations. Where there is an absolute monarchy women are sure to have

[1] Athír, vii, 205. [2] Id., viii, 133. [3] Maḳrízí, i, 377 [4] Athír, ix, 49.

a powerful voice in the administration, even in Islam, where women's opinions are decried, and consulting with them is thought to lead to failure and misfortune: for, indeed, every eminent Moslem has delivered some maxim forbidding consultation with them and giving them a voice in the management of affairs. Thus, Manṣúr in his injunctions to his son Mahdí said, "Beware of giving women any control." Nakha'í made obedience to women a sign of the approach of doomsday. Abú Bakr held that reliance on women led to humiliation. 'Alí also uttered many apophthegms of the same import. Notwithstanding all this their influence was very great.

§ 36. The Queen-Mothers.

Part of the influence of women was due to the maternal right acknowledged by Islam, as has been explained in the paragraphs on Maternity. It was chiefly exhibited in the influence exercised by the Caliphs' mothers over their sons, especially in the middle period, when the Caliphs confined themselves to their palaces and put themselves under the control of their slaves.

Yet even at the commencement of the dynasty the 'Abbásids used to obey the princesses, who exercised a vast influence. The first queen-mother who played the part of autocrat was Khaizurán, mother of Hádí and Rashíd, a Ḥarashite by birth. She was greatly feared by her children, and killed any of them who thwarted or opposed her. She ruled absolutely in the days of her husband Mahdí, who implicitly obeyed her. When her son Hádí became Caliph she wished to govern in his stead, and to treat him as she had treated his father. Before four months had passed visitors were crowding to her, and cavalcades arriving at her gate morning and evening: which annoyed her son the Caliph. One day she preferred a request which he found himself unable to gratify. She said, "You *must* assent, for I have promised this to Abdallah Ibn Málik." Hádí cried out angrily, "A plague upon the —— son! I knew he would want it ; I shall certainly not grant it for you." "Then in that case I shall never ask you for anything again." "I do not mind that." When she rose up in anger to depart he cried out, "Stop ; may I be disowned by the family of the Prophet if I do not deprive of his head and of his property any general or councillor of mine of whom I hear that he has stood at you gate. What is the meaning of the cavalcades that come to you morning and evening ? Have you not anything to spin, or a Koran to read, or a chamber for privacy ? I warn you again and again not to open your door to Moslem, Jew, or Christian." The queen-mother went away in a passion, and never opened her mouth in his presence again. Presently he said to his courtiers : "Which is better, I or you, my mother or your mothers ?" They naturally replied that he and his mother were superior. He proceeded to ask : "Which of you would like to hear his mother talked about-- 'So and-so's mother has been doing this and that?' " They replied that none of them would like it. "Why, then," he went on to ask, "do you come to my mother, and talk about her doings ?" When the courtiers heard this they ceased their visits to the queen-mother. She resented this ; and hearing that he proposed annulling the succession of his brother Rashid and appointing his son Ja‘far successor, she ordered some of her slave-girls to kill him by covering his face with a blanket and sitting on it. This was done.[1]

When Rashid became Caliph she again became autocrat and amassed vast wealth, her revenues reaching 160,000,000 dirhems in the year, or nearly half the land-tax of the whole empire. After her death Rashid "played ducks and drakes" with her money. The wealth of other queen-mothers was similar. The Turkish mother of Muktadir, called Al-Sayyidah "the Princess," had an extraordinary influence on the statesmen of the time during her son's reign. She controlled affairs in his place, by an arrangement with the janitors and slaves. The viziers dreaded her and trembled at her name.[2]

[1]Athir, vi. 41. [2] Wuzara, 67.

by way of compensation for the help they had given the Moslems in the conquest of that province; for this reason he in their case substituted alms for poll-tax; but his anxiety to combine the whole Arab race under the banner of Islam led him to stipulate that they should not train their children in the Christian religion.[1]

§ 36. CONTENTS OF OMAR'S CHARTER.

The contents of the charter fall under four principal heads:—(1) That the Christians shall build no fresh places of worship. (2) That they shall entertain passing Moslems three days. (3) That they shall harbour no spies in their churches, and shall not plot against the Moslems. (4) That they shall not imitate Moslem attire, or mode of riding, that they shall not teach their children the Koran, nor engrave their names in Arabic on their seals. Without these stipulations they are to have no security for their lives, families, or possessions.

The first of these heads corresponds with Omar's passion for the spread of Islam and its dominance, as we have seen. The second was required by the condition of the Moslems in the conquered countries, where they were strangers amongst the people of the Covenant: the Arabs were accustomed to the entertainment of strangers, but the people of those countries had no such custom, whence Omar had to stipulate it for the comfort of the Moslems who were on their way to the wars or travelling on other business. The third and fourth conditions can also be shown to correspond with Omar's character, though for this purpose some preliminary observations are necessary.

§ 37. THE SYRIAN CHRISTIANS AND THE BYZANTINE EMPEROR.

The first point to be noticed about this agreement is that its terms were enforced on the Christians of Syria, not on the other

[1] Ma'árif, 193; Baládhuri, 183; Athír, ii, 259.

after the time of Mutawakkil, whom the Turks ventured to kill, an act which was the overture to a series of arbitrary appointments, deposings, murders, and blindings, executed by them on the Caliphs. The Caliphs, though responsible for the administration, were no longer able to carry it on; nevertheless, orders were issued in their names, while their hands were continually forced by the persons of influence in the palace—viziers, captains, slaves, freedmen, women, etc.—in most cases by viziers and captains. The man who could win most favour with the Caliph, or the most cunning and astute, would acquire paramount influence, and he, when once placed in control of the empire, would do his utmost to amass wealth, having no guarantee that his Caliph might not be displaced by another unfriendly to himself, or that he might not himself be ousted by the intrigues of his enemies. In such a case, unless he had money he had but a gloomy prospect. The captains constantly endeavoured to secure paramount influence in the palace by threats and calumnies, varying according to circumstances and persons.

In general it may be asserted that the influence acquired by generals and viziers was used for no good purpose. None of them looked for any personal advantage as the result of their labours and efforts other than the wealth they might acquire while their power lasted. The first object of the executive then came to be the amassing of wealth. A vizier who when appointed to office knows not what will become of him after a year or two, whether he may not be deposed, killed, or imprisoned, is unlikely to concern himself with anything else than acquisition by any possible means without care for the consequences. This was the principle posed by Ibn al-Furát, the greatest vizier of the period, in the phrase "It is better to move the affairs of the King in a wrong direction than to let them stand still aright."[1] The Caliphs, perceiving their greed, made a practice of fining each vizier whom they deposed and confiscating his property. Afterwards the process

[1] Wuzara, 119.

of fining was extended to all employés of the government, and even to ordinary citizens; in course of time it became the chief source for the procuring of money. A governor would fine the subjects, the vizier would fine the governors, and the Caliph the viziers. The amounts would vary with the rank of the victim. Finally, a special bureau was created to deal with fines, which ranked with the other government offices.[1] The fining process caused money to circulate just as trading did.

§ 38. VARIETIES AND AMOUNTS OF FINES.

The vizier Ibn al-Furát stated that having computed the money exacted of him by the Caliph, he had found it to be ten million dinars, and that the same sum had been exacted by himself of Al-Ḥusain Ibn Abdallah al-Jauhar (Ibn al-Jaṣṣás). It would seem, however, that he lost nothing, for by fining others they obtained what they lost by being fined. If anyone was fined a sum which he had not the means to pay immediately, he was allowed to pay in instalments, and help was given him towards procuring the money required. Thus in some cases the rank of the man fined was restored to him, his guise was altered, and he was established in a grand residence with handsome furniture and plate, to enable him to devise means of collecting money from various people.[2]

The different modes and occasions for fines became so numerous that every man of means or position was liable to incur one. The following is a table of the fines gathered by Ibn al-Furát in the time of Ráḍí. It illustrates the different sorts and amounts of the fines :—[3]

	DINARS.
From Ahmed Ibn Mohammed al-Bistámí, arrears (half) of fine imposed, A.H. 300	7,300
'Alí Ibn al-Ḥusain al-Bádhabíni, clerk, fine imposed for his administration in Mauṣil	11,000

[1] Wuzará, 306. [2] Faraj, i, 51. [3] Wuzará, 224.

	DINARS.
Mohammed Ibn Abdallah al-Sháfi'í, for his agency for 'Alí Ibn 'Isa	30,000
Mohammed Ibn 'Alí Ibn Muḳlah, for his administration	80,000
Mohammed Ibn al-Ḥusain called Abú Ṭáhir	100,000
Al-Ḥasan Ibn 'Alí 'Ísá, the coin-tester, for a deposit of 'Alí Ibn 'Ísá held by him	13,000
From the same, on his own account	4,000
From Ibráhím Ibn Mohammed al-Mádará'í	20,000
From 'Abd al-Wáḥid Ibn 'Ubaidallah, arrears of a fine imposed on his father	36,360
From Aḥmad Ibn Yaḥyá, for services rendered	10,000
From Ibráhím Ibn Aḥmad, for reconciliation	6,000
From Mohammed Ibn 'Abd al-Salám, for deposits lodged with him belonging to Mohammed Ibn 'Alí and Ibráhím al-Mádará'í	4,000
From 'Abd al-Wahháb Ibn Aḥmad Ibn . . . , for reconciliation	40,000
From Mohammed Ibn Abdallah Ibn al-Ḥárith, for the same	10,000
From Mohammed Ibn Aḥmad, for his administration at Mauṣil and elsewhere	250,000
From Ibráhím al-Mádará'í, arrears	15,000
From Abú 'Umar Ibn al-Ṣabáḥ, for arrears due from Ibn al-'Abbás Aḥmad	3,000
From 'Alí Ibn Mohammed Ibn al-Ḥawárí, who was killed also	7,000
From Hárún Ibn Aḥmad of Hamadhán	7,000
From Abdallah Ibn Zaid Ibn Ibráhím	2,000
From . . . . for his life	15,000
From 'Alí Ibn Ma'mún al-Iskáfí, who was killed also	60,000
From Yaḥyá Ibn Abdallah, for his dealings conjointly with Ḥámid	70,000
From Ḥámid Ibn 'Abbás, who was killed also	1,300,000
From Mohammed Ibn Ḥamdún al-Wásiṭí	150,000
From 'Alí Ibn 'Ísá	42,000
From Ibráhím, *jahbud* of Ḥámid Ibn 'Abbás	10,000

	DINARS.
From Al-Hasan al-Mádará'í	1,200,000
From the same	1,000,000
From Mohammed al-Mádará'í	1,001,000
From the same by another writ	10,000

	DIRHEMS.
From Abu'l-Faḍl Mohammed Ibn Aḥmad Ibn Bisṭám	20,000
From 'Alí Ibn al-Ḥasan al-Bádhabíní, by way of compensation for his conduct at Mauṣil, although he was killed...	500,000
From Abú 'Umar Ibn al-Sabáḥ, for arrears of fine due from Abú Yásir, guaranteed by him	100,000
From 'Ubaidallah Ibn Aḥmad al-Ya'kúbí	100,000
From Al-Hasan Ibn Ibráhím al-Khará'iṭí, compensation for the property of the Prince appropriated by him	100,000
From Al-Ḥusain Ibn 'Alí Ibn Nuṣair	100,000
From 'Alí Ibn Mohammed Ibn Aḥmad al-Sammán, on behalf of the heirs of Ḳurḳur	2,000
From Abú Bakr al-Jurjání, out of the estates of Ibn 'Ísá	10,000
From Al-Ḥusain Ibn Sa'd of Ḳutrubull	230,000
From Mohammed Ibn Aḥmad	1,500,000
From Abu'l-Ḥasan Ibn Bisṭám	3,000,000
From Aḥmad Ibn Mohammed Ibn Aḥmad Ibn 'Abbás	50,000
From Sulaiman Ibn al-Ḥasan Ibn Mukhallad... ...	230,000

§ 39. Spoliation of Goods.

A vizier would hold office for a year or two, after which he would be dismissed or resign, having in his possession some millions of dinars, in addition to estates and buildings, the whole of this wealth having been acquired by bribery and other forms of extortion. No vizier would ever appoint to a governorship without receiving from his nominee a sum of money called 'the vizier's perquisite.' The most curious example of corrupt appointments is that told of Kháḳání, vizier of

Muktadir, who on a single day appointed nineteen inspectors for Kúfah, obtaining a gratuity from each of them. If the governor or inspector nominated had not money enough to pay the sum stipulated by the vizier, he would pay part in cash and defer the rest till a time specified or not specified The Caliphs were aware of this procedure, but found no fault with it and made no attempt to stop it.

A governor appointed in this way, and owing part of the bribe promised to the vizier, would naturally feel no scruple about plundering the property of his subjects. Indeed, he had no other object in seeking his governorship. The governors therefore amassed wealth by tampering with the proceeds of the taxes, out of which they would spend one dinar and enter it as ten, or by extortion through bribery and the imposition of frightful customs on buyers and dealers in the towns,[1] or by despoiling the cultivators in the villages of part of their crops, of which in some cases they demanded a share. At times the governor would send his agents to the granary and divide its contents as he pleased. If the farmer objected he would be insulted, his beard shaved,[2] and he might receive blows besides. Some of the governors went so far as to appropriate whole estates.

A remarkable form of robbery was the following:—A vizier, governor, or other magnate, might seize someone's estate, without payment, and appropriate the fruits; when, however, land-tax became due, the original owner would pay it, for fear lest the person who had appropriated it should acquire a title to it, by the land-tax being entered in his name in the public books, in which case the title of the real owner would be extinguished.[3] The real owner would, in such a case, be compelled to go on paying the land-tax for years, till he was able to obtain justice from some equitable person who happened to come into power, or until he could find some expedient or plan for getting rid of the oppression.

Another form of robbery was to exact the land-tax two or

[1] Athír, xii, 129, 203. [2] Wuzara, 92. [3] Aghání, xx, 47.

more times; though at other times it suited the governor's interest to allow the land-tax to remain unpaid in consideration of some service rendered him by the owner of an estate. The sum so excused often amounted to a great deal. Thus, in the time of the vizier Ibn al-Furát a man named Abú Zunbur had estates covering an area of a hundred *farsakhs* square, which paid nothing whatever to the treasury.[1] Estates were often allowed to remain thus land-tax free when they belonged to persons of intrigue or address, or of influence with the Caliph.

§ 40. Espionage and the Rule about Brigands.

One method employed for the spoliation of goods was for the vizier or similar official to distribute a sum of money as a loan to the heads of the bureaux, judges, etc., with the understanding that the lender should be reimbursed at the expense of the provincials,[2] whereby the loss fell on the latter. Thus much annoyance was inflicted on the traders in the towns and the cultivators in the villages and country districts, and the earning of a livelihood was rendered difficult. Rights fell into abeyance; anyone who could devise an expedient for snatching property secretly or openly employed it. Thieves and pickpockets thronged the towns, while bandits similarly molested the country. The ranks of these were swollen by soldiers whose pay had been embezzled by covetous viziers or captains, and who in consequence attacked passengers and robbed them of their money and property, and, if complaint or action were brought against them, would excuse themselves on the ground stated. Highwaymen would attack trading caravans, and seize the goods on the pretence that the alms due from them to the Treasury had not been paid by the owners. The robbers would assert that this impost had been forcibly withheld, and that the goods were in consequence forfeit; and that they (the robbers) required them, owing to their poverty. When goods were seized under this pretext against the will of the owners, the act

[1] Wuzará, 94. [2] Ibid., 262.

remained unpunished, since the theory that the property was forfeit owing to non-payment of alms could be maintained, as also that the poor had a right to appropriate the alms whether the owners liked it or not.[1] The alms were in origin money taken from the rich Moslems and distributed among the poor. At the commencement of Islam they formed an important institution; about the middle of the 'Abbásid period the institution was neglected, and the bandits used this as an excuse for robbing the traders.

The general disorder led also to financial stress and a rise of prices in the towns; and besides this a series of civil wars broke out between the various parties, especially Sunnís and Shí'ís. Plots and accusations against leading statesmen were the order of the day; espionage became common in the palace and the bureaux of viziers and public clerks. Each official kept spies to watch the others and report what they were doing. The humbler citizens began to calumniate the better class and address to the Caliph or person in authority libels, containing charges against innocent persons by whose ruin the informers hoped to profit. And these were chiefly directed against retired statesmen or persons whose accession to authority the informers had reason to fear. Whole boxes filled with such libels accumulated in the offices of Caliphs and viziers; when they became a nuisance, or were of no further use, they would be burned.[2]

When disorder became rife at the capital and the viziers and captains became autocratic, the provincial governors thought fit to profit by this condition of affairs and establish independent dynasties. Thus the Islamic empire split into a group of states governed by Persian, Turkish, Kurdish, Arab, and other rulers.

§ 41. PARTITION OF THE 'ABBÁSID EMPIRE.

When the 'Abbásid empire had reached the state of disorder that has been described, being distracted between Persians and

[1] Faraj, ii, 106. [2] Wuzará, 72.

Turks, viziers and guards, slaves and women, and the majesty of the Caliphs had departed owing to the restraint placed on them and the contempt in which they were held, it was not difficult for the governors of remote provinces to detach themselves from the Caliphate, setting up an independent administration, and to appropriate the revenues of their provinces, thereby making themselves independent. This plan was first tried by those who were at the greatest distance from the capital. The first 'Abbásid governor who made himself independent was Ibráhím Ibn al-Aghlab, who set up a principality in North Africa in 184 A.H. His case, however, cannot be regarded as a result of the decline of the empire, since it occurred at the time of Rashíd, when the 'Abbásid dynasty was in full vigour; it was the distance which separated the province from Baghdad which enabled Ibráhím to do this. Of those rulers whose acquisition of independence was due to the decline of the Caliphate and the disintegration of the dynasty, the first were Persians, the next Turks, and the next Kurds, the order being the same as that in which they obtained power over the Caliphs. In each case the nation proceeded from the rule of a governor to that of a prince, and thence to that of a sovereign. The Persians who first secured independence were governors, who created small principalities, and afterwards great dynasties. The Turks and Kurds did the same. The sovereign families belonging to these races will be enumerated in order, to be followed by a list of the Arabian families, when we speak of the second Arabian period.

§ 42. PERSIAN DYNASTIES UNDER 'ABBÁSID SUZERAINTY.

The Smaller Dynasties.—When the Persians restored to Ma'mún the insignia of empire their influence with him was very great, and they became contemptuous of the 'Abbásid power. Presently the Turks obtained control over the Caliphs, after Mu'taṣim's time, tied their hands, and enfeebled their power, in which operations the Persians had a considerable share. When, however, they found their influence at the Court departed, they endeavoured to substitute for it independence in their principalities.

The captains and governors who acquired independence continued to acknowledge the spiritual sovereignty of the 'Abbásids, and desired independence under their suzerainty. The 'Abbásid empire thus split into a number of independent principalities, increasing by some law of progression. The following is a list of the Persian dynasties according to the order in which they became independent, with the names of the founders:—

DYNASTY.	PROVINCE.	DURATION.	FOUNDER.
Ṭáhirides	... Khorasan	... 205–259	... Ṭáhir Ibn al-Ḥusain.
Ṣaffárides	... Fars ...	... 254–290	... Ya'ḳúb Ibn al-Laith.
Sámánides	... Transoxania ..	261–389	... Naṣr Ibn Aḥmad.
Sájides	... Ádherbaiján ...	266–318	... Abu'l-Sáj.
Ziyárides	... Jurján	... 316–434	... Mardáwíj Ibn Ziyár.

We thus see how Persia became divided into a number of Persian principalities. The 'Alid faction revived, and realized to some extent the original object of their efforts in behalf of the family of 'Alí, viz. the restoration of the mighty power of Persia as it had existed before Islam. These principalities were, as appears from the table, of no long duration, and presently there arose the Búyid dynasty, the greatest Persian and Shí'ite dynasty, which arose in the East under 'Abbásid suzerainty.

§ 43. THE BUYID DYNASTY.

The supporters and promoters of this dynasty were Dailemites of Jílán beyond Khorasan, but the sovereigns themselves, the family of Búyah, were Persians. Their pedigree was traced to the ancient kings of Persia, and they were called Dailemites only because they inhabited the Dailem country. From the time of Rashíd the 'Alids had been endeavouring to propagate their doctrine in this region; and the last successful missionary of theirs was Al-Hasan Ibn ' Ali the Deaf (a descendant of Al-Husain), who preached the ' Alid tenets in the last years of the third century, and received a favourable hearing.

The immediate founder of the Buyid family was a man named Buyah (or Buwaihi), also called Abu Shuja', who had three sons--' Ali (afterwards ' Imad al-daulah), Hasan (Rukn al-daulah), and Ahmad (Mu' izz al-daulah). Buyan was himself in humble circumstances, and his sons enlisted in the army, which at that time was one of the most obvious means of obtaining a livelihood. ' Imad al-daulah was in the service of Mardawij, founder of the Ziyari dynasty, and was promoted under him till he was invested by him with the government of Georgia; presently his prosperity increased till he was able to write to the ' Abbasid Caliph, at that time Al-Radi (ob. 329), asking to receive in fief the provinces of Fars, on condition of his forwarding regularly a sum of money to the capital, which as we have seen, was an arrangement not unfrequently made in ' Abbasid times; the Caliph assented, and sent the robe of honour. His brother Hasan, called Rukn al-Daulah, obtained possession of Khwarizm, and presently the two brothers meeting the third brother, Mu' izz al-daulah, assembled in Shiraz, whence they journeyed westwards of Baghdad, in the days of Mustakfi (A.H. 334), who welcomed them, bestowed on them robes of honour, and gave them the titles that have been mentioned. Mu' izz al-daulah further was appointed Emir al-umara. The three brothers became absolute masters of the empire, obtained control over the Caliphate and deposed Caliphs and appointed others. They restored the prestige of the Shi' ah, and weakened the influence of the Turks, the ' Abbasid Caliphate still continuing in Baghdad. When the office of Emir al-umara was conferred on ' Abud al-daulah he assumed the title king (malik), being the first Islamic prince who was thus called. The reign of the Buyid family was from 320 to 447.

§ 44. TURKISH DYNASTIES UNDER THE SUZERAINTY OF THE 'ABBÁSIDS.

When the Turks grew as powerful in the 'Abbásid empire as has been described, and became an object of terror to the Caliphs, some of them became anxious to obtain governorships, as the Persians had desired. Making them independent principalities, they caused the rise of various Turkish branches of the 'Abbásid empire outside Fars, just as Persian principalities had arisen within that country. The following is a list of the Turkish principalities in 'Abbásid times, with the dates of their foundation, and the name of founder and locality :—

DYNASTY.	LOCATION.	DURATION.	FOUNDER.
Ṭúlúnid ..	Egypt ...	254–292 ...	Aḥmad Ibn Ṭúlún.
Ílekid ...	Turkestan ..	320–560 ...	'Abd al-Karím Sabaḳ.
Ikhshídí ...	Egypt ...	323–358	Mohammed al-Ikhshíd.
Ghaznevid ..	Afghanistan and India	351–582 ...	Alptakin.

The Turks rose step by step in the Islamic principalities as the Persians had risen before them, i.e. from the office of Emir to that of Sultan. That title was first assumed by Turks in Islam, and among the Turks first by the Ghaznevids, of whom was the Sultan Mahmúd Ghaznevi, conqueror of India and promulgator of Islam therein.

§ 45. THE SELJUḲ DYNASTY AND ITS BRANCHES.

These principalities were all branches of the Islamic empire, i.e. the Emirs or Sultans were viceroys of the 'Abbásid ruler, or generals, serving him, or serving one of his viceroys, who then became independent. The Persian principalities had sprung up in the same way, the two nations (Persians and Turks) struggling for influence, owing to their different national ambitions, and also to the difference between the Sunnite and Shí'ite systems.

With the rise of the Turkish principalities the Sunní system gained ground; for at the rise of the Búyid dynasty in 'Irák and Fars in the middle of the fourth century, and at the same time of the Fátimide dynasty in Egypt, Shí'ism grew powerful in the Islamic world, and Sunnism was depressed, while the 'Abbásid empire began to disintegrate. Then in the middle of the fifth century there arose the great Turkish dynasty known as that of the Seljucids, called after Seljúk, the founder of the line. It did not arise before it was wanted; it drew together the scattered fragments of the 'Abbásid empire, and strengthened its religious system, Sunnism, after it had grown feeble in the presence of Shí'ism in Egypt, Syria, 'Irák, Fars, and Khorasan; moreover, the Fáṭimide dynasty had extended its power over the West, and was near gaining control over the whole East as well. Then came the Seljúks from the extreme East, and, obtaining control over the 'Abbásid empire, pulled it together; and after it had been broken up into a number of independent principalities, ruled by Emirs who were Persians, Turks, Kurds, or Arabs, the Seljúks made it once more a single empire, ruled over by themselves, under the suzerainty of the 'Abbásid Caliph.

The founder of the Seljucid dynasty, Seljúk son of Yakák, was a Turkish Emir in the service of some of the Khans of Turkestan. He, learning of the break up of the 'Abbásid empire, aspired to become its master; knowing that he could never attain to this unless he became a Moslem, he embraced that religion, being followed therein by his tribe, all his army, and all his partisans. With all these he marched out of Turkestan in a westward direction, crossed the Jaxartes, and then proceeded step by step with conquests and the spread of their dominion till they had got possession of the whole 'Abbásid empire, and their authority stretched from Afghanistan to the Mediterranean. The Islamic world was then disputed between three rival powers, of which the greatest was the Seljucid in the east, the next the Fáṭimide in Egypt and the West of Africa, and the third the Umayyad dynasty in Spain. The Seljucid dynasty is not comparable with the smaller Turkish dynasties which had preceded it, since these latter were principalities which had sprung up within the 'Abbásid empire and separated themselves from the main trunk, whereas the Seljucid dynasty was independent from the start, and coming from the outside by force of arms won the empire; certainly the Íleki dynasty was similar in origin, but its effect on the Islamic empire was small.

The Seljúḳs fill a great space in the history of Islam, and during their time the Turks migrated in large numbers into Persia, 'Iráḳ, Syria, and other portions of the Islamic empire, to take up their abode and to earn their living under the protection of their compatriots. The Seljúḳs further were the first dynasty that built schools of the highest grade to which Islamic civilization attained, through Nizám al-Mulk, vizier of the Sultan Maliksháh, in the middle of the fifth century. Nizám al-Mulk was himself a Persian by origin, being descended from one of the *dihkáns.* His schools, hostels, monasteries, mosques, and hospitals were founded by him in the name of his Seljucid master.

The Seljúḳs formed a number of dynasties, which all branched off a single stem, and were called by a single name, but distinguished by the names of the localities where their rule severally extended. The chief of these is that of the Great Seljúḳs, from whom the other branches were derived; the following is a list of the whole number, with the length of their duration :—

1. Great Seljúḳs, 429–552.
2. Seljúḳs of Kirmán, 433–583.
3. Seljúḳs of Syria, 487–511.
4. Seljúḳs of 'Iráḳ and Kurdistan, 511–590.
5. Seljúḳs of Asia Minor, 470–700.

The reign of the Seljúḳs lasted altogether about three centuries, and extended from the frontiers of China to the frontier of Syria.

§ 46. TRANSFERENCE OF THE SELJUCID EMPIRE TO THE ATÁBEKS.

During the time of their power the Seljúḳs were in the habit of bestowing the governorship of provinces on members of their retinue called Atábeks (a Turkish word signifying Father Prince). This word, first used in the sense of minister, came to be employed in that of king. The Atábeks began gradually to make themselves independent in their provinces, until they had partitioned between them the whole of the Seljucid empire, except that in Asia Minor, which remained Seljucid till the Ottoman empire arose at the end of the seventh century. The following table gives the branches of the old Seljucid empire which fell to the Atábeks and others, and the length of time which these dynasties lasted :—

1. Burid of Damascus, 497–549.
2. Zengi of Al-Jezirah and Syria, 521–648.
3. Bektíjíni of Arbela, etc., 539–630.
4. Ortoḳi of Diyár Bekr and Márdin, 595–712.
5. Shahs of Armenia, 493–604.
6. Atábeks of Ádherbaiján, 531–622.
7. Salghari dynasty of Fars, 543–686.
8. Hazársabi dynasty of Lúristán, 543–740.
9. Khwárizmshahs, 470–628.
10. Ḳuṭlughi dynasty of Kirmán, 619–703.

These dynasties were all swept away by the Mongols.

§ 47. SELJÚḲS OF ASIA MINOR.

The Seljúḳ dynasty of Asia Minor remained standing when other branches had fallen, only it was parted into a number of divisions, over each of which a Seljúk family ruled, as follows :—

1. Mysia, family of Karási.
2. Pisidia, family of Ḥumaid.
3. Phrygia, family of Kirmiyán.
4. Lycia, family of Tákah.
5. Lydia, Sarukhán and Aidin.
6. Caria, Mentesha.
7. Paphlagonia, Ḳizil Ahmadli.
8. Lycaonia, Ḳarman.

These dynasties were extinguished by the Osmanlis in the eighth century.

§ 48. Kurdish Dynasties under 'Abbásid Suzerainty.

The Kurds are a hardy nation, most of them wild Bedouins, living in tents, and divided into clans and tribes, far less receptive of civilization than the Persians, Turks, and other Eastern nations that adopted Islam at the commencement of Islamic civilization; the various dynasties used to invoke their aid in their raid-like campaigns, just as they employed the Bedouins of Arabia. Their habitual location was in Kurdistan, Armenia, and parts of Mesopotamia, such as Mauṣil and Diyár Bekr, and the great body of the nation are still in those regions.

Owing to their retention of the Bedouin savagery the 'Abbásids employed few members of the race in government offices, nor did they produce any independent ruler of eminence nor any statesman or administrator, till a long period had elapsed since the commencement of Islamic civilization. The first person who established an independent Kurdish state in Islam was Husnúyah Ibn Ḥusain al-Barzugáni, leader of certain Kurdish tribes in Kurdistan in the middle of the fourth century A.H.; his power extended over the greater part of that region, including Dínawar, Hamadhán, Naháwand, Sermáj, etc. His authority was recognized by the Caliph at Baghdad, who gave his son the title Náṣir al-daulah. This dynasty lasted only from 348 to 406. Another Kurd who established an independent government was Abú 'Alí Ibn Marwán, who did this in Diyár Bekr in the year 380. His authority spread over Ámid, Arzan, and Mayyáfáriḳín; his successors, however, did homage to the Fáṭimides, and the dynasty terminated in 489.

§ 49. AYYÚBIDS.

The Kurds, however, made no considerable mark till the time of the Ayyubids. 564–648. The founder of this dynasty was Ṣaláh al-dín. He was one of the most notable Moslems in history, for wisdom, administrative ability, and personal courage, as well as power of organization. He built his throne on the fragments of the Fátimide empire in Egypt, where he paid allegiance to the 'Abbasids. He fought with the Crusaders and drove them out of Syria, and rescued Jerusalem from their hands. His exploits are indeed too celebrated to be recounted. The Kurds became mighty in his days, and were invested with governorships, and viceroyalties in Egypt, Syria, Kurdistan, Yemen, and Khorasan; at his death his empire was divided between his brothers, sons, and nephews, owing to which the dynasty had no long duration. They were ousted out of most of their provinces by their Turkish mamlúks, just as the Atábeks had ousted the Seljúḳs before. The mamlúks gave Egypt two dynasties, known as the Mamlúk Sultans, as will be stated.

Note.—It is worth observing that Islam exercised a special effect on the peoples of the East and drew them gradually towards civilization; they accordingly proceeded to the construction of states and empires in the order in which they had adopted Islam and in an order which corresponded to their distance from the centre of the Islamic world. First the Arabs adopted Islam and founded the Islamic empire of Arabia; they were succeeded by the Persians, the nearest of the Eastern nations to the Arabs; then by the Turks, who were beyond the Persians, and, when Islam spread among them, founded dynasties and organized governments; then the Kurds put in an appearance; they were indeed nearer to the centre of the

Islamic world than the Turks, but they civilized later, owing to the greater power of administration which the Turks possessed. Then Islam extended to Turkestan and the Tartar or Mongol regions beyond, and these advanced and raided the Islamic territory, first with no object save slaughter and plunder, but presently they were affected by the Islamic world to such an extent that they took to organizing dynasties and states. Much the same might be said of the influence of Islam in the West, especially among the Berber tribes in North Africa, as we have already seen.

§ 50 THE CALIPHATE AND THE SOVEREIGNTY, OR RELIGION AND POLITICS.

At the commencement of Islam the Prophet was chief of the Moslems in temporal and spiritual concerns, being their ruler, judge, lawgiver, priest, and general; when he made any one of his followers commander of a province he committed to him both forms of sovereignty, spiritual and temporal, and charged him to rule justly and to instruct his subjects in the Koran. Presently, however, he separated the two functions and assigned them to different persons. Thus in the year 8 A.H. he sent Abú Zaid al-Ansári and 'Amr Ibn al-Áṣ together, with a rescript inviting people to embrace Islam. And his instruction to them was as follows: "If the people are ready to pronounce the creed, and ready to obey God and His Apostle, then 'Amr is to be governor and Abú Zaid to lead prayer, as also to receive admissions into Islam and to teach the Koran."

This was not yet a principle, since in several cases the same person was to act as governor, collecting the land-tax and managing military operations, and also leading prayer. Yazíd Ibn al-Muhallab, when appointed governor of 'Irák by Sulaimán Ibn 'Abd al-Malik,[1] had to perform both offices. Still, it may on the whole be asserted that whereas the political and religious concerns of Islam were in the Prophet's time all concentrated in

[1] Athír, v, 10.

his person, they afterwards were separated and divided between a variety of officials; the Caliphate, however, remained as it remains until this day, a combination of a spiritual with a temporal office.

In origin, doubtless, the Caliphate is a religious office, undertaken by the Pious Caliphs with the object of accomplishing the task commenced by the Prophet, viz., the expansion of Islam and fighting the world in its cause. They were, however, compelled to undertake the management of the political concerns of the Moslems, since the sacred war necessitated arrangements of various sorts, such as the organization of an army for the protection of the provinces; and this involved the appointment of governors and the collection of land-tax. There was, indeed, a certain admixture of religion in all they did, the final object being in each case religious. It was for the sake of religion that they organized armies and conquered countries. And when Islam had spread far and wide, and become firmly established, so that there was no further need for the sacred war, the religious headship might well have become independent of the political headship, or the sovereignty might have split into two as has been the case with Christian nations.

The connexion, however, between government and religion in Islam is different from the connexion between the two in Christianity, since Christianity spread among the people before it reached the governing class; whereas Islam spread first among the governing class, and from them to the people. For the original Moslems were the Prophet's companions, who formed the class whence the Moslem generals and soldiers were derived; these spread Islam over the world and fought to win it the victory. When it had acquired strength and the Moslem dynasty was established, and the chieftains were anxious for worldly power, the existence of the Caliphate was one of the chief causes of their success, owing to the influence wielded by religion over men's minds at that time. It was only a religious banner that could make them unite, especially in the East, where the same state of things still prevails.

Pious Moslems, indeed, separated the Caliphate from the temporal sovereignty, and when Mu'áwiyah tried to acquire the first place, after the fashion of ambitious politicians, by astuteness and force, they opposed him and refused him the oath of allegiance. Only when 'Alí had been killed, and his son Ḥasan had resigned his claims to Mu'áwiyah, the Moslems were compelled to do the latter homage, such as they might pay to a king; but they disliked giving him the title Caliph, or acknowledging that he had any spiritual sovereignty. They were prepared to give him the title king. He, however, was determined to combine the two forms of headship, being aware that temporal sovereignty by itself would be of little use to him. There is a story that Sa'd Ibn Abí Waḳḳáṣ presented himself before Mu'áwiyah, after the sovereignty of the latter had been confirmed, and saluted him as king. Mu'áwiyah, laughing, asked him what harm it would have done Sa'd to have used the title Commander of the Faithful? Sa'd's answer was, "What, can you talk of this with a smile? I assure you that I had rather not have the post if it was to be acquired as you acquired it."

This shows that the Moslems did not like to connect the Caliphate with diplomacy and astuteness, and believed that the Umayyads had degraded Islam from religion to chauvinism and militarism, and thence to pure royalty.

§ 51. Caliphate necessary for an Absolute Despotism.

It is our belief that an absolute despotism cannot be maintained, strengthened, or preserved except by religion or a substitute for it; nor is there any case of an absolute despotism which has lasted for a long time, and gained ground, which has not also had a religious element able to protect it from aspirants, by giving its occupant some superiority over the rest of mankind If religion is to be separated from politics, the monarchy must be strengthened by a council, which produces the best and the longest lived of constitutions ; otherwise it will quickly be dissolved, and it will be sufficient for its dissolution that the occupant of the throne should be incapable and inexperienced : from the hands of such a monarch the power is certain to be snatched by a vizier or general. Anyone who examines the history of the Islamic empire will find that the religious headship had a wonderful effect in preserving it and enlarging it. Thus none of the dynasties which sprang up within the 'Abbásid empire, Persian, Turkish, Kurdish, and Circassian, such as the Búyid, Seljucid, and Ayyúbid, was able to hold out for any considerable length of time, notwithstanding that their monarchs were often men of valour and ability, and notwithstanding that they were supported by the 'Abbásid Caliphate. Whereas, on the contrary, those Arabian dynasties that combined spiritual with temporal headship, such as the 'Abbásids, Fáṭimids, Umayyads of Spain, did hold out and maintain themselves for a great length in spite of the various causes of ruin that attacked them. Among foreign dynasties also we shall find that the longest lived and furthest spread is that which combines the spiritual with the temporal headship. I mean the Ottoman empire. The Umayyads of Syria could never have obtained supremacy had they not taken the title Caliph and seized the spiritual headship. They ruled and confirmed their authority by the religious element which the Caliphate contained. They had the advantage of helpers who were aware that a people can be governed by nothing so well as by religion, and so they made it their business to exalt the Caliphate so much that they even set it above the office of Prophet, calling the Caliph God's Caliph (or vicegerent), with the aphorism that a man's representative in his household is grander than the messenger whom he sends on an errand. (This has been quoted before.) The learned, indeed, disapproved of this principle, and would not accept it. The people, however, were intimidated into obedience, in spite of the doubtful validity of the Umayyad claim.

When the Caliphate came to the 'Abbásids, who did belong to the Prophet's family, and indeed were the people who had the best right to it, the Moslems were more inclined to obey them than they had been inclined to obey the Umayyads. They even thought that the 'Abbásid Caliphate would last for ever, even till the coming of the Messiah;[1] and an idea got implanted in men's minds that if an 'Abbásid Caliph were killed, the order of the universe would be disturbed, the sun darkened, the rain would stop, and vegetation would dry up.[2]

The Caliphs by no means disapproved of these exaggerated ideas of their importance, not even the intelligent Rashíd, in whose days knowledge advanced so much. It is said that he allowed praise to be bestowed on him such as should only be bestowed on Prophets, and made no objection. A poet was allowed to say, "He is like an Apostle after the Apostle."[3] Flattery of this sort was still more rife in the time of the decline, when imagination took the place of reality. At that period, too, the number of flatterers and sycophants was greatly on the increase, and the ruling class made words do instead of acts. When a government has reached its dotage, the rulers stick to the accident and neglect the substance. Naturally, therefore, in the days of Mutawakkil, they would call the Caliph the shadow of God spread between Him and His creation.[4] Or they might use phrases such as that addressed by Ibn Háni' to the Fátimide Mu'izz:

> "What thou wilt, not what fates decree,
> Our God Almighty's none save thee."[5]

§ 52. THE CALIPHS AND THE LAWYERS.

This verse shows what sanctity attached to the Caliphate in the minds of the people, and their deification of the office had its root in religion. For this reason the first Caliphs

[1] Athír, v, 198. [2] Fakhrí, 125. [3] Agháni, xii, 18. [4] Mas'údí, ii, 280. [5] Athír, viii, 245.

had reciprocal relations with the representatives of the Islamic religion, such as Koran-readers, Traditionalists, and Lawyers, and they gave each other mutual support. In other words, the Caliph combined spiritual with temporal sovereignty, was the governor of the nation in peace and their general in war, their leader in prayer, their judge, and their legislator, just as the Prophet had been at the commencement of Islam. As conquest succeeded conquest, and it became necessary to divide duties in accordance with the needs of civilization, the Caliphs took to deputing a variety of officials to discharge these duties on their behalf; and the viceroy was then deputy governor for the Caliph, the judge his deputy for the trial of cases, the general his deputy commander of the forces; the same was the case with the remaining administrative, political, and judicial appointments. The same was the case with religious offices; readers, interpreters, traditionalists, and jurists were all deputies of the Caliph. Just as the Caliph required the help of governors, generals, and judges for the maintenance of his temporal sway, so he required the assistance of jurists and scholars for the maintenance of his religious authority. Therefore we find the Caliphs promoting learned men, especially at the commencement of Islam, when they consisted chiefly of persons who knew the Koran by heart or could read it properly; to these persons the Caliph resorted when religious, judicial, or legal difficulties required solution, and such questions form the basis of the political code of Islam. And since the public in general were very much at sea as to their religion, the jurists had a powerful influence on the government. No important matter was decided without their being consulted, even such a question as the appointment of a Caliph. If the jurists disapproved of such an appointment, the public disapproved it also. The Caliphs in consequence had good reason for cultivating and favouring scholars, and relying on their counsels, at the time at any rate of the Pious Caliphs, while the state was still in its simplicity, and neither statecraft nor duplicity had entered in. At this time, if the jurists forbade the Caliph or governor from following a certain course, as a rule the Caliph or governor gave way.

When the Umayyads aspired to the sovereignty, and endeavoured to secure it by craft and violence, among other principles followed by the Pious Caliphs and neglected by them was the practice of following the dicta of the learned, since, had they continued to follow them, they could never have attained to the sovereignty. At the commencement of the Umayyad period the learned were subject to various forms of torture and coercion, some of them suffering themselves to be forced to give such decisions as the Umayyads desired, whereas others refusing to do so were persecuted and annoyed. This process commenced even in the time of 'Uthmán, when the governors of the provinces belonged to the Umayyad family, and began to prepare the way for the sovereignty of the family by amassing wealth and appropriating the influential posts. The story of Abu Dharr al-Ghifári and Mu'áwiyah Ibn Abí Sufyán gives a remarkable illustration of the courage of the scholars of the time in browbeating the Caliphs, as also of the objection taken by the Caliphs to such conduct.

When the Umayyads became firmly seated, free thought was bound and men's tongues fettered, and no learned man gained promotion without flattering the ruling power; and whereas the Pious Caliphs had been in the habit of doing nothing without consulting the jurists of Medinah, the Umayyads neglected both Medinah and its jurists—all save Omar II, who returned to the practice of consulting them; the greater part of their reign, however, the freethinking jurists remained in obscurity. When, however, the 'Abbásids became supreme, and signified their intention to revive the old custom and to reform religious abuses that had cropped up in Umayyad times, various independent thinkers among the jurists, scholars, and ascetics became prominent, and were favoured or promoted by the Caliphs. They once more ventured to address with boldness those who, they thought, would listen. So, we saw, some one ventured to address Manṣúr, when he was making the circuit of the Ka'bah. Similarly, when Rashíd invited Sufyán al-Thaurí to Baghdad, in order to promote him and do him honour, the latter replied as follows:—"I write to tell thee that I break off all ties with thee, and renounce thy love, and that thou hast rendered me a witness against thee, in that thou hast in thy letter confessed against thyself that thou hast pounced on the treasury of the Moslems, and expended what was therein where it was not due, and sent it to such as had no right to it; and not content with what thou didst at a distance from me, thou didst even write to me to make me a witness against thyself; and such witness do I now bear, as do all my brethren such as saw thy letter, and on the morrow we shall present our witness against thee before God the just judge. O Hárún, hast thou verily pounced on the treasury of the Moslems without their leave? Hast thou for this the assent of those whose hearts are united, and those that are set in authority thereover in God's earth, and those that fight in God's path, and the son of the road? Hast thou the assent of them that carry the Koran in their minds, and the men of knowledge? Hast thou the assent of the widows and the orphans, or of any class of thy subjects?" [1]

This same Sufyán once paid a visit to Mahdí, and refused to salute him as Caliph, without, however, exciting the wrath of the Caliph, who endeavoured to conciliate him; [2] and we read of most of the early Caliphs of the 'Abbásid dynasty, that when visited by jurists or ascetics they would demand of them a sermon, which, when delivered, would cause them to weep till their beards were wetted. There are well-known stories of this sort, especially about Manṣúr, Rashíd, Mu'taṣim, and Wáthiḳ.

The jurists formed the religious intermediaries between the Caliphs and the people just as the governors and generals formed the political intermediaries. Both forms of mediation could be effected by the jurists, because the bulk of the Moslems are ready to obey their jurists implicitly, just as the Christians

[1] Damírí, ii, 188. [2] Khillikán, i, 210.

obey their priests; the 'Abbásid Caliphs therefore required the help of the jurists in order to ensure the subjection of the people and to obtain control over their hearts. The sultans and governors used to do the same for the same cause or others. The benefit was reciprocal, for the jurists by the Caliphs' favour would gain money and position, whereas what the Caliphs obtained from them was yet more valuable and lasting. Respect for the Caliphs became deep-rooted in the minds of the people, and for the sake of religion the people remained faithful to the Caliphs and magnified them.

In religious matters, too, the Caliphs used to gratify the people. Often they were compelled to humour the people in some religious belief or other, even when such a belief was contrary to their own conviction or opposed to facts. So once when a man brought the Caliph Mahdí a shoe which he asserted was the Prophet's, Mahdí accepted it and gave its bringer a reward. He believed it to be a forgery, but was afraid of stirring up popular feeling against himself, as careless of religion, if he openly expressed his disbelief in the genuineness of the relic.[1]

The Caliphs were compelled to make a display of piety and zeal concerning their religious duties for fear of alienating the public and exciting contempt for their authority, however free-thinking the Caliph himself might be. Al-Walíd Ibn Yazíd, a notorious debauchee and loose liver, is said, when the hour for prayer arrived, to have been in the habit of throwing off his dyed and scented garments, after which he would perform the appointed ablution after the proper fashion, and put on clean white garments such as the Caliphs were in the habit of wearing, and then lead prayer in the most approved style, with correct enunciation, and correct pauses, stops, genuflexions, and prostrations. When he had finished he would resume his festive attire.[2]

[1] Adhkiyá, 29. [2] Agháni, vi, 141.

§ 53. THE ISLAMIC DYNASTIES AND THE CALIPHATE.

For this reason those viceroys who managed to make their administration and policy independent of the Caliphs, owing to the latter being unable to repress them by force of arms, were yet unable to assume religious independence, as they were compelled in order to the maintenance of their own authority to render homage to the Caliph. Whenever, therefore, any potentate wished to make his principality independent, having acquired it either by conquest of a country or by founding a dynasty, he would write sending his homage to the Caliph at Baghdad, requesting the latter to forward him a deed of investiture or a certificate that he was governor of the country, or else to send him a robe of honour and some honorific title. Refusal on the Caliph's part was treated by such potentates as an insult, and they would often make war against the Caliph to compel him to assent to their demands.

The independent principalities or kingdoms which were formed in Fars, Khorasan, Turkestan, Mesopotamia, Syria, Egypt, and Africa, prior to the foundation of the Fáṭimide Caliphate in Egypt, were all in the hands of princes who delivered the *khuṭbah* in the name of the Caliph of Baghdad, and who sent him fixed annual payments, although they were in no fear of the Caliph's power. All that they wished was to have the people satisfied with their rule.

The conduct of the Turkish guards and their commanders was similar. Though they had complete control of the Caliphs, and could depose them or put them to death, they did not venture to leave the office of Caliph unfilled for a single day, believing, doubtless, that without a Caliph they could never satisfy the people. Those kings and sultans who took Baghdad and seized everything that it contained, and in whose hands the Caliph was a mere tool, such as the Búyid and Seljucid monarchs, would attack and make war upon the Caliphs with their armies, and then when they had got the victory would themselves render homage to the Caliph, do him honour, and treat him as a superior being. Such was the case of the Búyid 'Aḍud al-daulah, who took Baghdad and made himself autocrat there, being a Shí'ite, and so a follower of a different system from that of the Caliph; and, indeed, he was a fanatical Shí'ite, and convinced that the 'Abbásids had stolen the Caliphate from its rightful possessors, so that there was no religious motive compelling him to do honour to an 'Abbásid; none the less, he paid homage to the Caliph of Baghdad, treated him with high respect, and restored some of its lost dignity to the Caliphate. He commanded the Caliph's palace to be rebuilt and to be filled with furniture, and the same to be done to the palaces of the courtiers and others connected with the court.[1]

On the other hand, the Caliphs were well aware how much the Moslem potentates required their approval, and if any of them misbehaved himself the Caliph would threaten to leave Baghdad, a threat which ordinarily compelled the potentate to give the Caliph satisfaction, for fear the Caliph's quitting Baghdad should anger the mob[2] and encourage them to revolt, since their superstitious regard for the Caliph inclined them to treat him as infallible. Hence there was no way of opposing his authority except from the religious standpoint, whence those who rebelled against the Caliphs would make religion their weapon. They would put on wool, and call on their fellows to champion the right, or else hang Korans on their necks,[3] or adopt some other way of moving the feelings of the mob.

Similarly, if a Caliph wished to conciliate the people he compassed this end by piety. So when Al-Fadl Ibn Sahl promised the Caliphate to Ma'mún he advised him to make a display of conscientiousness and religion, in order to win the favour of the commanders of the troops;[4] and when Abú Muslim of Khorasan saw the Yemenites in Meccah, he exclaimed what a fine army they would make if they

[1] Athír, viii, 257. [2] Id., ix, 213. [3] Id., viii, 208. [4] Adhkiyá, 27.

encountered a man with a dexterous tongue and a ready flow of tears, meaning a person who could move their religious feelings by preaching and weeping.

The independent potentate might often have a grievance against the Caliph of Baghdad, but he would master his indignation, and refrain from violating his oath of obedience, until he saw another Caliph to whom he could render homage. So when the Fátimide dynasty arose in Egypt, many of the countries threw off their allegiance to the Caliph of Baghdad and rendered homage to the Fátimides in Cairo; and when Saladdin became master of Egypt, and the Fátimide dynasty was at an end, the first thing the new ruler did was to pray in the Mosque of Cairo for the 'Abbásid Caliph of Baghdad, and demand investiture from him and a robe of honour. The 'Abbásid Caliphate was at the time at a very low ebb, and Saladdin had no occasion to render it homage; but he was aware that without homage rendered by him to some Caliph the people would not be satisfied.

The same course was pursued by the Mamlúk Sultans who obtained possession of Egypt after the close of the Ayyúbid dynasty; they swore allegiance to the 'Abbásids, and robes of honour were sent to them from Baghdad to Cairo as a formal confirmation of their authority, and when the Tartars stormed Baghdad in the year 656 and killed the 'Abbásid Caliph Musta'sim the Caliphate was suspended and the state of Egypt became disturbed; the Sultans therefore did their best to call into existence a Caliph whom they might do homage to.[1] Had they been unable to lay their hands on a Caliph, it is probable that they would have made one, in order to rule the people by his aid.[2] And, indeed, they made a diligent search after the relics of the 'Abbásid Caliphs of Baghdad until they got hold of these fugitives, summoned them to Cairo, and assigned them stipends, welcomed them with great acclamation, and did them every sort of honour,[3] knowing well that these Caliphs could not help them at all, yet fearing a loss of authority

[1] Abu'l-Fidá, iii, 222. [2] Athír, ix, 119. [3] Maḳrízí, ii, 301.

unless they had them on their side. Similarly, the provincial potentates of Islam in India and other distant regions regularly paid homage to the 'Abbásid Caliphs in Cairo, and requested charters of investiture from them through the Mamlúk Sultans.[1] What could have induced these sovereigns to demand such a diploma from a fugitive Caliph, who could neither help them nor intercede for them, except the notion that such a diploma would produce an impression on the minds of the people? Some of them may, of course, have desired to do homage to the Caliph out of some conscientious motive of their own, but in the greater number of cases the motive was the desire for popularity.

§ 54. The Caliphate lodged with persons not from the Tribe Kuraish.

A point that demands attention and consideration is that the non-Arab Moslem potentates, belonging to different countries, races, languages, such as Persians, Turks, Kurds, Berbers, Circassians, etc., who attained to the possession of vast dominions and powerful thrones, though needing spiritual sovereignty in order to secure their dynasties and ensure the obedience of their subjects, yet never bethought them of seeking the Caliphate for themselves before the transformation of Islam into its second stage of development, after its humiliation at the hands of the Mongols. No Arab, either, outside the tribe of Ḳuraish ever claimed it for himself. The first non-Arab monarch who was proclaimed Caliph was the Ottoman Sultan Selím, in whose dynasty the Caliphate still remains.

It should, however, be observed that non-Arab princes and generals, who grew powerful during the epoch with which we are dealing, often, if they aspired to spiritual sovereignty, or the Caliphate itself, invented a Kurashite pedigree for themselves; this, e.g., was done by Abú Muslim of Khorasan, when

[1] Khaldún, iii, 543.

he believed himself strong enough to found a dynasty, and may have even aspired to the Caliphate. He invented for himself an 'Abbásid pedigree, declaring himself son of Salíṭ son of 'Abdallah son of 'Abbas.[1]

The foreign kings or Sultans who controlled great empires at the close of the 'Abbásid period, seeing the decay of the Caliphate and its retrogression, wished to dispense with it, but saw no way of achieving this except substituting another Caliphate for it. Some, however, tried to obtain religious influence by intermarrying with the Caliph's family. The Búyid 'Aḍud al-daulah (ob. 372) was the first who did this; he induced the 'Abbásid Caliph al-Ṭá'i' to marry his daughter, in the hope that she might bear a son, whom he might make heir to the Caliphate. The Caliphs of the future would then be descendants of his.[2] This hope, however, was not realized.

When the Seljúḳs became all-powerful they slightly altered this idea; the Sultan Toghrulbek determined to marry the daughter of the Caliph al-Ḳá'im. He therefore sent in an application for the hand of the princess, making the *ḳáḍí* of Rai his intermediary. The Caliph was outraged by this request, since till then only peers of the Caliphs in descent had married their daughters. However, the Seljúḳ was all-powerful and the Caliph a nonentity, so the latter tried by humble solicitation to move him to abandon his request. The Sultan, however, was inflexible. A long series of negotiations took place, till the Caliph was alarmed for the safety of his throne, and so was compelled to give in, and the betrothal took place in the year 454. Such a thing had never happened before; the Búyids had never ventured to make such a demand, in spite of the fact that they differed from the Caliphs in religion.[3] It was thought a sufficient condescension on the part of the Caliph to marry the Sultan's daughter; it was not expected that he should go so far as to give his daughters to them. No Sultan before Toghrulbek enjoyed this honour. When in the following year he was admitted to see his bride,

[1] Fakhrí, 123. [2] Athír, viii, 283. [3] Id., x, 8.

he kissed the ground before her, she sitting on a throne covered with gold, and she neither removed the veil from her face nor even rose up. For some days he continued to pay visits in this style, after which he would go away. The marriage was never consummated, since he died in the same year. No non-Arab potentate succeeded in obtaining proclamation as Caliph before the Ottomans. When Sultan Selím conquered Egypt he found there the last of the 'Abbásid Caliphs, who had been invited to Egypt by the Mamlúks, and this person yielded his rights to the Ottoman monarch, in the year 933.

§ 55. Second Arabian Period.

Arabian Principalities and the Arabian Element.

By the second Arabian period we mean the time in which the Arabs obtained a fresh lease of power, and recovered their influence in the empire after the Persians had obtained the upper hand and become autocratic. We saw above how the power of the Arabs declined in consequence of the fall of the Umayyad dynasty and the rising influence of the Persians in the 'Abbásid empire, culminating with the defeat of Amín and the overthrow of Arabian domination. Then there came the accession of Mu'taṣim, who stopped the stipends of the Arabs and deprived them of all government employment. This humiliation was resented by the Arabs, who kept waiting for some chance of recovering their importance, and in consequence they were always ready to aid anyone who revolted against the 'Abbásids, in 'Irák, Syria, or Egypt, Kurd, Bedouin, or Carmathian. Owing, however, to the rising influence of the Turks these revolts helped them but little.

Certain Arab tribes, nevertheless, were able in various ways to establish some small principalities in Mesopotamia and Syria, under 'Abbásid suzerainty, and they were assisted in their schemes by the civil wars between the Caliphs and their Persian viziers and Turkish guards. This was in the fourth century, when the Arabs, seeing the Persians and Turks assuming independence, imitated them. Thus there arose the Taghlibite dynasty of the Hamdánids in Mauṣil, Ḥalab, etc., which lasted from 317 to 394. This was an Arabian dynasty, which restored the Arab culture. Its most famous prince was Saif al-daulah, rendered immortal by Mutanabbi's verse.

In the same century there arose at Ḥalab another Arabian dynasty called Mirdásid, after Asad al-daulah Ṣálih Ibn Mirdás, of the Mudarite tribe Kiláb. This person and his descendants ruled over Ḥalab from 414 to 472. At Mauṣil the place of the Ḥamdánids was taken by the 'Uḳailids of the Mudarite tribe Ka'b; their rule lasted from 386 to 489. During this period there arose a fourth Arabian dynasty, called that of Mazyad, after Mazyad al-Shaibání of the tribe Asad. This dynasty built the city of Ḥillah in 'Iráḳ, and reigned from 403 to 545.

We have to mention two more dynasties founded by Arabs during the 'Abbásid period, which being in a non-Arabian region should rather be called foreign dynasties. They are the Dulafí dynasty, founded by Abú Dulaf al-'Ijlí in Kurdistan, and the 'Alawí dynasty, founded by al-Ḥasan Ibn Zaid in Ṭabaristán. If we add to these the Aghlabí dynasty, which made itself independent in the Maghrib before the other offshoots of the 'Abbásid dynasty, and the Idrísí dynasty, which shall presently be mentioned, the number of Arabian dynasties which arose in the second Arabian period will amount to eight. The following table gives their localities and dates :—

DYNASTY.	LOCATION.	DURATION.	FOUNDER.
Idrísí	Morocco	172–375	Idrís Ibn 'Abdallah.
Aghlabí	Tunis, etc.	184–289	Ibráhím Ibn al-Aghlab.
Dulafí	Kurdistan	210–285	Abú Dulaf al-'Ijlí.
'Alawí	Ṭabaristán	250–316	Al-Ḥasan Ibn Zaid.
Ḥamdání	Ḥalab and Mauṣil	317–394	Banú Ḥamdán.
Mazyadí	Ḥillah	403–545	Mazyad al-Shaibání.
'Uḳailí	Mauṣil	386–489	Banú 'Uḳail.
Mirdásí	Ḥalab	414–472	Ṣálih Ibn Mirdás.

Besides these there were various small Arabian dynasties which arose in Yemen, such as the Ziyári of Zabíd, the Ya'fúrí of San'á', etc.

These dynasties did little towards restoring the influence of the Arabian element or renewing the power of the Arabs, for they all (with the exception of the 'Alawís and Idrísís) acknowledged the Caliphate of the 'Abbásids and paid them homage. We cannot indeed blame them for this, for the Persians, Turks, and Dailemites had made themselves masters of the greater numbers of the principalities of the 'Abbásid empire, and there was a deep-rooted idea that the 'Abbásid dynasty would last till the coming of Christ. Hence the whole East remained under the suzerainty of the 'Abbásids, proclaiming their *khuṭbah* in the mosques and striking coins in their name; the hope of the Arabs, therefore, turned towards the West.

The Umayyads were the champions of Arab nationality and the chief enemies of the Persians and the barbarous nations on their boundaries. The remnant of the Umayyads had established an Arabian dynasty in Spain in the year 138, of which something shall be said presently. Those Arabs, therefore, who desired to see the Arabian element revived, and who were grieved at the decline of Arab power under the influence of the 'Abbásids, migrated westward and settled in Spain, or abode in Africa under the suzerainty of an Arab potentate, and at a distance from the power of the 'Abbásids.

The Arabs who most detested the 'Abbásid dynasty and were most anxious to escape it were doubtless the members of the 'Alid faction, when their hopes in the East had come to nothing owing to the determination of the 'Abbásids to monopolise the Caliphate in those regions, and some of the 'Alid propagandists fled westwards to escape the 'Abbásids at the beginning of their dynasty; these persons founded a dynasty called the Idrísí, after Idrís Ibn 'Abdallah, which lasted from 172 to 375, and whose rulers did not adopt the title Caliph.

There remained in the East a number of 'Alids who hoped to gain the victory with the aid of Persian clients who belonged to their faction. When, after the civil war between Amín and Ma'mún, they found themselves ousted by the 'Abbásids, and presently found the control of affairs assumed by the Turkish guards, who were opposed to both Arabian and Persian elements, they despaired of gaining anything by the help of the clients, and many of them gradually migrated westwards, though some still remained in the East on the watch for some weak point to be manifested by the 'Abbásids, when they might seize the opportunity of attacking them, and to effect this object they cared not whose aid they invoked nor on whom they relied. At times, therefore, they placed reliance on the people of Fars and Khorasan, at other times on Kurds or Dailemites, or other nationalities that felt resentment against the Turks, or on communities who had suffered injury owing to the maladministration of justice and the tyranny of the slaves. None of these 'Alids succeeded in founding a dynasty with the exception of al-Ḥasan Ibn Zaid in Ṭabaristán, who founded the short-lived dynasty that has been mentioned; but at times the injured communities would adopt the 'Alid programme for the purpose of attacking the government. This, indeed, was the method pursued by the chief of the Zanj in 'Iráḳ, who for many years disturbed the repose of the 'Abbásids, with their armies and governors, by gathering together runaway slaves and the Zanjís who were employed in sweeping the offal in the suburbs of Basrah and Kúfah. This person caused a movement among all the blacks, who left their masters, took sides with him, and fought a number of battles against the 'Abbásids, in which two and a half million men lost their lives.[1] Their programme, however, was that of the 'Alids, and their leader an impostor named 'Alí Ibn Mohammed, who professed to be descended from Ḥusain. The revolt finally ended with the death of the impostor and the dispersal of his followers.

[1] Fakhrí, 227.

The 'Alid faction only acquired considerable importance after the rise of the Buyid dynasty (which, as has been seen, was Shi'ite) in the East, and after it had obtained control over Baghdad and the Caliph. The 'Alids, having already established a Caliphate in the West, were thereby considerably strengthened, and pushed eastwards, hoping to conquer the 'Abbasid empire. Coming to Egypt they conquered it in the middle of the fourth century, and stayed there ; their dynasty, called Fatimide, became powerful, and, indeed, was the most important of all that the 'Alids ever succeeded in founding.

When the Fatimide dynasty came in conflict with the 'Abbasid, it found itself supported by the Arabs and Berbers, the latter claiming to be descended from the Arabs. There were great hopes that through the Fatimides the strength of the Arabs might be restored to what it had been at the beginning of Islam, and homage was paid them by the bulk of the Arabs, even those in 'Irak and Mesopotamia ; even the people of Kufah and Mausil paid them homage, notwithstanding that they were so close to the capital of the 'Abbasids, for a time.[1] They were, however, unable permanently to restore the Arabic element owing to the decline of the Buyid power in the East and the rise of the Seljuks ; those Turks took the part of the 'Abbasids, adopted their system (Sunnism), and protected them. For a time, then, there was a balance of power between East and West, the first being Sunnite and the second Shi'ite.

When the Kurds overcame the Fatimides, and, under Saladdin the Ayyubite, rescued Egypt from their grasp, they restored the suzerainty of the 'Abbasids in the year 567. The Arabic element had already grown weak in Egypt before the termination of the Fatimide dynasty owing to the control of the government having been assumed : by Turks, Armenians, and others, as will be seen. The Arabic element therefore perished except in a few principalities in the Arabian peninsula itself, some of which are still in existence.

[1] Athir, ix, 92.

By the second Arabian period we mean the revival of the Arabian element in the West after its decline in the East, and the chief agencies for its revival were the two dynasties, the Umayyad in Spain and the Fáṭimide in Egypt. At the base of both was an Arabian upheaval, which lasted no long time and was without important consequences; after these the Arabs had little weight in the empire of Islam. At times, indeed, some Arab tribes were able to display a certain amount of energy, and start some political or religious movement, as the Wahhábís of Nejd or the Derwishes of the Sudan; and when Mohammed 'Alí Pasha, founder of the Khedivial family, wished to found a great Islamic dynasty at the beginning of the nineteenth century, he desired to press into his service some Islamic national spirit. The chief nationalities in Egypt were the Turkish and the Arabian, and the Turks being devoted to the Ottoman empire, he made use of the Arabian national spirit. He was the subject of great hopes, especially after his war against the Wahhábís and his meeting with the Sharíf of Meccah and other heads of tribes; he also revived Arab patriotism by the schools and presses which he founded and the books which he published. This did produce an Arab awakening, but it helped little towards the Pasha's ends, since the interests of the European Powers in the Islamic empire stood in his way. Still, it was of some literary and scientific benefit to the Arabs, and prepared the way for the renaissance which we are now witnessing. The reports which we read in the newspapers of revolts in Nejd and Yemen should not lead us to expect any important consequences for political reasons which need not be explained in this place.

The Arabic revival of the second Arabian period with which we are dealing left no important effect in the way of restoring the Arabian element. Both the Spanish Umayyad dynasty and the Egyptian Fáṭimide dynasty underwent various political and administrative vicissitudes, a summary of which may well be given in this place, though both were in most matters reproductions of the 'Abbásid empire.

§ 56. POLICY OF THE SPANISH UMAYYADS.

Like other contemporary or subsequent dynasties, that of the Spanish Umayyads took for its model the 'Abbásid dynasty. Its founder was 'Abd al-Rahmán Ibn Mu'áwiyah Ibn Hishám Ibn 'Abd al-Malik Ibn Marwán, a man as energetic as his ancestor 'Abd al-Malik, who escaped from the massacre of his kindred at the court of Saffáḥ in the year 132, and fled from 'Irák westward, with the help of a freedman of his named Badr, who spared no effort to rescue his patron and protect him during his flight over a long tract of country and among people who felt resentment against the Umayyads. When he reached North Africa, the same freedman did his utmost to secure him some partisans, and help him to cross the Straits of Gibraltar to Spain, where there were some 500 clients of the Umayyad family. Informing these persons of the arrival of his patron, Badr urged them to come to his assistance in order to keep the Umayyad dynasty alive in Spain. They obeyed, and succeeded in combining the Muḍarite and Yemenite tribes—a difficult combination at that time—in his favour. After a ceries of fights they paved the way for his assumption of royal authority, and invited him to come over to Spain, whither then he came and assumed administration of affairs in the year 138. He was called "the Immigrant."

At first he governed Spain in the name of the 'Abbasid dynasty, and pronounced the *khutbah* for Manṣur, not venturing for a year to found a separate Caliphate, whilst the 'Abbásid Caliphate lasted, holding that there could be but one Caliph even as there was one Prophet. 'Abd al-Rahmán had a cousin, 'Abd al-Malik Ibn 'Umair Ibn Marwán, who was a vehement partisan of the Umayyads and had great hopes of restoring the Caliphate to them. Owing to his courage and energy he was called the flame of the house of Marwan. He had fought many fights in the cause of his cousin, and thereby secured his position in Spain; he therefore urged his cousin to remove the name of the 'Abbásid Caliph from the *khutbah*, and when he found the monarch reluctant he threatened to commit suicide unless his advice were followed. 'Abd al-Raḥmán was persuaded, but did not at first venture to assume the title Caliph himself; at the first, therefore, the Spanish Umayyads were called *Princes*, and only after a time were they called *Caliphs*.

Meanwhile it came to pass that the 'Abbásid Manṣúr branded with a mark of his displeasure the chief jurist of Medinah, Málik Ibn Anas, he having sworn allegiance to the 'Alids. The Umayyads took advantage of his resentment to get him over to Spain and do him honour. Each party was benefited thereby; in Málik they secured a jurist of great renown, capable of giving religious sanction to their claim and injuring the pretensions of the 'Abbásids; whereas in the Umayyads Málik found a secure refuge and a consolation for the evil he had endured at the hands of the 'Abbásids. From the time of his arrival the Málikite system spread among the Spaniards, who had formerly followed the system of Al-Auzá'i, like the people of Syria. The principle of deciding in accordance with the system of Málik became law in Spain in the Caliphate of Ḥakam son of Hishám son of 'Abd al-Raḥmán the Immigrant.[1]

'Abd al-Raḥmán imitated the methods employed by Mansúr for securing his government, and the two were similar in many points. Each of them was the son of a Berber mother; they were similar in energy, vigour, and capacity; each of them killed his brother's son—Mansúr the son of his brother Saffáḥ, 'Abd al-Rahmán the son of his brother Walíd (Mughírah).[2] The Spanish potentate also imitated Manṣúr's treacherous policy of making away with all those who had helped him to secure his place. Being offended by his freedman Badr for liberties taken by him, 'Abd al-Raḥmán forgot all the faithful services which that man had rendered him, deprived him of his property and honours, and banished him to a place of exile, where he remained till he died: somewhat as Manṣúr put to

[1] Nafḥ al-ṭíb, ii, 799. [2] Ibid., ii, 715.

death Abú Muslim of Khorasan after the efforts which the latter had expended in creating the 'Abbásid dynasty.[1] Likewise 'Abd al-Rahmán put to death Abu'l-Sabáh Ibn Yaḥyá,[2] chief of the Yemenite Arabs, though this person had assisted the Caliph's rise and had rendered him many services. This was like the treatment meted out by the 'Abbásids to Abú Salamah, Ibn Kathír, and others. When the Yemenites in the service of Abu'l-Sabáḥ demanded vengeance for their master, they were massacred by 'Abd al-Raḥmán; and being dissatisfied with the attitude of the Arabs altogether, who harboured resentment against him, he took manumitted slaves into his service in order to obtain their support against his enemies. Sending to the grandees of his kingdom he purchased their rights over their clients, and in general purchased freedmen from all quarters, and besides got Berber allies, sending to them across the Mediterranean and requesting them to come over to him. When a number of them responded to his invitation he paid them high honour, and encouraged them by presents to enter his service; indeed, out of these persons and slaves he procured an army of 40,000 men, with whose aid he got the upper hand of the Arabs of Spain, and thereby obtained a firm basis for his empire, as the 'Abbásids had done for theirs by the aid of the people of Khorasan.

§ 57. The Slavs.

After this the Spanish Umayyads took to employing in their service Slav eunuchs, brought over by slave-dealers from the North of Europe, there being a good market for these slaves throughout the world. The reason why this traffic was so successful was the following. The Slav or Russian tribes at the first period of their existence took up their abode north of the Black Sea and on the Danube, after which they began to migrate in a south-westerly direction towards Central Europe, being at that time a conglomeration of hordes afterwards known

[1] Athir, vi, 5. [2] Nafḥ al-ṭíb, ii. 706.

as Slavs, Servians, Bohemians, Dalmatians, etc. In the course of their migrations they were compelled to fight with the nations that lay in their path, such as the Saxons, the Huns, etc. Numerous prisoners were made on both sides; and it being the custom in those days for prisoners of war to be sold as slaves, numerous trading companies were formed to purchase the prisoners and take them *viâ* France and Spain to Africa, and thence to Syria and Egypt. When these countries fell into Moslem hands the traders did good business. The European merchants and others bought the prisoners of the Slavs and Germans, traversing for that purpose various parts of Germany, from the banks of the Rhine to those of the Elbe and thence to the Danube and the shores of the Black Sea—the Georgians and Circassians down to the present day sell their own children like merchandise—and on their return from their journeys they would drive the slaves before them like sheep, male and female, all of them white and often exceedingly comely, till they came to France, whence they would transfer them to Spain, where the Moslems would purchase the males for servants or soldiers and the females for concubines. The name Slav or Sklav came to be applied generically to these persons, and came in Europe in the form Slave (esclave, Sklave) to signify white bondsman.

'Abd al-Raḥmán the Immigrant had no great partiality for the Slavs, his grandson al-Ḥakam Ibn Hishám (180–206) being the first Spanish Caliph who acquired great numbers. He indeed made large purchases of bondmen, and kept horses tied to his castle gates, and indeed played the part of a tyrant. He was the first who formed a standing army in Spain, and made paid soldiers of his slaves, whose numbers reached 5,000; they were called "the Dumb" owing to their foreign speech. The Umayyads of Spain continued following the same practice, and the Caliph 'Abd al-Raḥmán al-Náṣir (300–350) acquired vast numbers of Slavs, whom he made his army and his personal staff, just as Mu'taṣim the 'Abbásid had done with the Turks. The Spanish Umayyads kept this European empire of theirs apart from the other Islamic dynasties that were in Asia and

Africa, making no attempt to conquer those other empires, breaking off all relations with them, and forbidding their subjects to go on pilgrimage to the two sanctuaries[1] lest they should fall into the hands of the 'Abbásids. Hence none of the Spanish Moslems went on pilgrimage the whole duration of the Umayyad dynasty, and pilgrimage was only resumed when it was over, and the government of Spain had fallen into the hands of non-Arab dynasties.

§ 58. Provincial Kings in Spain.

The best days of Moslem Spain were those of 'Abd al-Raḥmán al-Náṣir, who died in 350. He was sagacious and munificent, wealth increased under him, and his days were like those of Hárún al-Rashíd in Baghdad, days of luxury and prosperity. He was followed by a son Hakam, who, like Ma'ṃún, was a lover of knowledge and a patron of learned men. Spain, therefore, under these two monarchs reached the zenith of its glory, might, and wealth. After him the Spanish Caliphate began to decline; the control over the government was seized by courtiers and soldiers who were Berber or Slav clients of the Umayyads; these played a part similar to that played by the Persians and Turks at the 'Abbásid court.

The Arabs, indeed, occupied the first places at the Spanish court, and were regarded as its firmest partisans, whence they were of commanding influence there; for, as we have seen, the Umayyads represented the Arabic national spirit. When, however, the Slavs and Berbers got the mastery, the power of the Arabs began to decline, and continued to do so till, at the end of the fourth century A.H., Ibn Abí 'Ámir, vizier of Al-Ḥakam, after the accession of Al-Hakam's son Hishám, made himself master of the government, and by treachery produced dissension among the ministers, and got rid of some with the aid of others; he then prevented the ministers from obtaining access to the Caliph. Being himself by origin a Yemenite Arab, he began

[1] Khaldún, i, 238.

to fear an attack on the part of the army, which he therefore endeavoured to disperse. He began with the Slav bondmen in the palace; by a ruse he succeeded in getting them driven out, and then proceeded to make an onslaught on the Slav soldiery. He then dismissed the Arabian ministers and officials from their places, and replaced them with Berbers and members of the Zanátah whom he had summoned from Africa; and from that time the influence of the Arabs in Spain departed.

The Umayyad dynasty continued to decline in power, till at last its dominions were partitioned among the viceroys, Berber and other, even more speedily than the like had happened to the 'Abbásid empire. The reason of this was that the Moslems attached no great value to the Umayyad claim to the Caliphate, and that the 'Abbásids, owing to their connexion with the Prophet, were more firmly seated. So the Spanish empire at the beginning of the fifth century got divided into a number of principalities, governed by petty princes and tribal chiefs, Arab, Berber, and clients; each man secured any province on which he could lay hands, whence there arose a series of independent dynasties of little importance. The best known are the following:—

DYNASTY.	LOCATION.	DURATION.
Banu Ḥamúd ...	Malaga and Algeciras ...	407–449
'Abbád	Seville	414–484
Zírí	Granada	403–483
Jumhúr	Cordova	422–461
Dhu'l-Nún ...	Toledo	427–478
'Ámir	Valencia	412–478
Húd and Tújib...	Saragossa	410–536

These dynasties had, as we see, no long duration, being ousted first by the Al-Moravids, then by the Al-Mohads. Their dominions kept on being partitioned, and their petty wars were unceasing, so that the Franks profited by their weakness and division to regain province by province and city by city, until at last they overcame the Moslems entirely and drove them out of Spain. The last city taken by the Franks was Granada, at that time in the possession of the Banú Nasr, descended from Yúsuf Ibn Naṣr, who flourished about 629, and more than twenty of whose descendants ruled in the place, the last being Abú 'Abdallah Mohammed Ibn 'Alí, from whom it was captured by the Franks in the year 897. Abú 'Abdallah fled, and after him there were no more Moslem rulers in Spain.

§ 59. THE FÁTIMIDE DYNASTY (297–527).

The 'Alid Faction in the West.

We have had occasion to notice the condition of the 'Alid faction in Syria and the number of persons belonging to it who were crucified or otherwise executed in Umayyad times; further persecutions and massacres befell them in 'Abbásid times, especially under Mansúr, Rashíd, and Mutawakkil. These persecutions induced them to flee to the extreme ends of the Islamic empire, and they fled east and west, as we have seen; among those who went westwards was Idrís Ibn 'Abdallah Ibn al-Ḥasan al-Muthanná, brother of Mohammed Ibn 'Abdallah, to whom Manṣúr had sworn allegiance, only afterwards to violate his oath. Idrís came to Egypt, which was then within the 'Abbásid dominion, and concealed himself in a place where he was secretly visited by some of the 'Alid faction, among them the postmaster, who gave him facilities to escape westwards, in the time of Rashíd. Arrived in North-West Africa, he was met by members of the faction, who swore allegiance to him as Caliph, and he founded in Morocco a dynasty known as the Idrísí, which lasted from 172 to 375, of which, however, the sovereigns did not style themselves Caliphs.

The 'Alid faction owed their actual ascendancy to the Fátimides, so called from Fátimah the Prophet's daughter, otherwise the 'Ubaidí dynasty after 'Ubaidalláh al-Mahdí, its founder. Simultaneously with the rise of this dynasty Shí'ism had also begun to assert itself in the East through the Búyids; the period was the middle of the fourth century.

When the Búyids had gained control of affairs in Baghdad, the Fáṭimides had already gained firm ground in the north-west of Africa, and were planning the conquest of Egypt. The Búyids were fanatical adherents of 'Alí and firmly convinced that the 'Abbásids were usurpers of a throne that rightfully belonged to others; it was therefore suggested to the Búyid prince Mu'izz al-daulah that he should transfer the Caliphate to the 'Ubaidís or some other members of the 'Alid family. One of his friends, however, dissuaded him, urging that at present he was under a Caliph whom both he and his adherents believed to have no title to the Caliphate, and whom, therefore, his adherents would readily kill if he ordered his death; whereas if he appointed to the Caliphate an 'Alid whose title was acknowledged to be valid by both him and his followers, the latter would refuse to kill the Caliph if ordered to do so. Mu'izz al-daulah therefore discarded the suggestion.[1]

Nevertheless, the Búyid ascendancy strengthened the 'Alid faction in the East, and the Búyids restored many religious ceremonies that belonged to the Shí'ah, among them the 'Ashúrá or commemoration of the death of Ḥusain.[2] They induced the Caliph to permit the name of 'Aḍud al-daulah to be mentioned in the *khuṭbah*, his being the first name (of anyone save the Caliph) so honoured. From that time mutual jealousies sprang up in Baghdad between the Turks and Dailemites, which found vent in disputes between the Sunnís and Shí'ís, whom these nationalities respectively represented. And in order to annoy the Shí'ís the Turks induced the people of Baghdad to celebrate certain anti-Shí'í festivities.[3]

§ 60. SHÍ'ITES IN EGYPT.

The rise of the Shí'ah in the East doubtless facilitated the conquest of Egypt by the 'Ubaidís, and enabled them to migrate

[1] Athir, viii. 177. [2] Id., viii, 216. [3] Id., ix, 65.

thither. Before that conquest their capital had been Mahdiyyah in Africa. The Caliphs of this dynasty professed to be descended from Ḥusain son of 'Alí; historians, however, are at variance concerning the genuineness of this pedigree. The partisans of the 'Abbásids deny it; we are inclined to believe it, and to suppose that the doubts cast on it were due to the desire of the 'Abbásids to discredit the 'Ubaidí Caliphs.[1]

From the commencement of Islam 'Alí had been a favourite with the Egyptians, who took his side on the day when 'Uthmán was killed; not, indeed, that Egypt played a considerable part in the 'Alid faction, seeing that the 'Alids endeavoured to get help at the first from the people of 'Irák and Fars, as has been seen; and when the 'Abbásid dynasty arose, and Manṣúr persecuted them, imprisoning and slaying, and those that survived fled to be out of the reach of the 'Abbásids, one of the fugitives, 'Ali Ibn Mohammed Ibn 'Abdallah, despatched emissaries into Egypt. He was, however, speedily seized and brought to Mansúr, and disappeared.[2]

With the character of the various rulers at Baghdad the condition of the 'Alids in Egypt varied between stress and comfort: a Caliph who hated the 'Alids persecuted the faction and made their life a misery; in the opposite case the opposite was the result. Mutawakkil, who persecuted the faction fiercely, wrote to his Egyptian viceroy, bidding him expel the 'Alids from Egypt and send them to 'Irák. This was done in the year 236, and when they came to 'Irák they were sent on to Medinah; any adherents of the 'Alids who remained in Egypt concealed themselves. Mutawakkil's governors, anxious to curry favour with their master, showed their hatred of the 'Alids in the most offensive ways. Thus there is a story that a soldier, having committed some offence and been condemned by the Egyptian viceroy Yazíd Ibn 'Abdallah to receive stripes, implored the governor in the name of Ḥasan and Husain to let him off; the governor's response was to increase the punishment by thirty blows. The postmaster sent word of this to

[1] Maḳrízí, i, 349. [2] Id., ii, 338.

Mutawakkil, who sent an order to the governor to have the man beaten with a hundred stripes, which was carried out. This same Yazíd took trouble to trace out the 'Alids, and learning that there was one who had adherents and emissaries, he arrested him, sent him with his family to 'Irák, and had those who had sworn allegiance to him beaten.

When Mutawakkil's son Muntaṣir succeeded in the year 247 he sent orders to his Egyptian viceroy to the effect that no 'Alid should be allowed to farm an estate, or ride a horse, or travel from Fustát to any part of Egypt; they were also not to be allowed to have more than a single slave. If there were litigation between an 'Alid and anyone else, the word of the other litigant was to be accepted without any evidence being required. This caused the 'Alids great annoyance.

When, in the year 254, Ahmad Ibn Ṭúlún became master of Egypt he persecuted the 'Alids, being a Turk and an adherent of the 'Abbásid doctrine; he tracked out the 'Alids and fought several battles with them. Only when the Ṭúlúnids had lost their power in Egypt, and the 'Abbásid Caliphate was declining in Baghdad, and the Búyids had become masters of the metropolis, in the fourth century A.H., did the Shí'í party begin to flourish again; so when Egypt was invaded by the army of Al-Mu'izz lidín alláh the Fáṭimide, in the year 356, under the command of the Sicilian Jauhar, men's minds were ready to accept the 'Alid propaganda, and Jauhar captured Egypt without difficulty, and there delivered the *khutbah* in the name of the 'Alids and raised their ensigns, removing those of the 'Abbásids. He built the city of Cairo, and thither his master Mu'izz brought his belongings. The Fáṭimides formed a series of ten Caliphs, or fourteen, commencing from the foundation of the dynasty in Africa. Their whole duration was, then, from 297 to 567, when Egypt was taken from them by the Ayyúbid Kurds.

§ 61. Policy of the Fatimide Dynasty.

The Fatimides were one of those islamic dynasties that imitated the administration and methods of the 'Abbasids, except, indeed, in religion, since they lent their aid to all devices that aided the Shi'ite system, such as bestowing honour on 'Ali and his descendants and following the opinions of the leaders of their school. The vizer of the Fatimide 'Aziz, Ya'kub Ibn Killis, composed a manual of law based on what he had heared from Al-Mu'izz and his son 'Aziz ; it was divided into sections, and was in bulk about half the size of the Sahih of Bokhari. It contained the law of the Isma'ili sect, and Fatimides took trouble to circulate it among the Moslems ; the vizier himself had audiences in which he read the book out to disciples, seances which were attended by both high and low, and by most of the jurists, judges, and scholars. The book was made the great reference book for legal questions, according to which cases were decided, and it was taught in the Ancient Mosque (Mosque of 'Amr). The Caliphs furhter encouraged its study by offering prizes and rewards. So 'Aziz gave ample stipends to thirty-five jurists who attended the vizier's course, in addition to yearly presents from the royal purse. He also gave orders that a house should be built for them by the side of the Al-Azhar Mosque ; robes of honour bestowed on them at the Feast of Fast-breaking, and they were given mules to ride. All this was to encourage them to propagate the Law of the Shi'ah and its doctrines. Persons were besides appointed to sit in the royal residence and read out the works of the 'Alid family to the people. For it was hoped that by the propagation of the Shi'i doctrine the Fatimide dynasty would be strengthened, owing to the close connexion between religion and politics in those days, as we have seen. Persons who studied other legal works were persecuted and even tortured ; thus a man who was found to have in his possession the Muwatta of Malik was beaten and dragged round the city.

Ya'kúb, the vizier who has been mentioned, was originally a Jew, who adopted Islam and did the Fáṭimide dynasty great service in gaining strength for their propaganda. We are not surprised to read that when this man was ill he was visited by 'Azíz, who said to him, "I could wish you were to be bought, in which case I would have given all my property to possess you."[1]

The successive Fáṭimide Caliphs followed the same method, and did their best to spread the doctrines of the Shí'ah. 'Azíz and Ḥákim both established libraries where men could read and copy, with this object; when Ẓáhir became Caliph in 411 he banished from Egypt all Malekite jurists, as well as others of the orthodox schools; severe orders were issued compelling people to learn the "Pillars of Islam" and "The Vizier's Abridgment," and prizes offered to those who committed them to memory.[2] A rule of the Fáṭimide law of inheritance is that the whole inheritance goes to the relatives, and if there be a single daughter she takes the whole;[3] this principle is meant, of course, to confirm the 'Alids' claim to the Caliphate, as they claim descent from Fáṭimah, who, when she died, was the Prophet's only child.

§ 62. PERIODS OF THE FÁṬIMIDE DYNASTY.

The Fáṭimide dynasty passed through three periods resembling those through which the 'Abbásid dynasty passed. Now we have seen that at the commencement of the 'Abbásid period the influence was divided between the Persians and Arabs, that then it passed in its entirety to the Persians, and then to the Turks. Now the Fáṭimides were Arabs, and the Arabs were the mainstay of their dynasty, with the Berbers, and at the first the power was divided between these two elements; presently it passed entirely to the Berbers, and then to the Turks.

The Berbers are a hardy people, whose home is in the north of Africa. They helped the 'Alid dynasty in North-West Africa

[1] Athír, ix, 32. [2] Maḳrízí, i, 355. [3] Id., i, 111.

just as the Persians helped it in the East. They are a set of nomad tribes not unlike the Arabs, whom the Moslems had great difficulty in subduing. Twelve times did they revolt from Islam, and make united onslaughts on the Moslems, nor was their conversion permanent till the time of Músá Ibn Náṣir at the end of the first century of Islam. When the Moslems resented the Arabian chauvinism of the Umayyads, the Berbers joined the revolt and even ventured on violent courses. The Berbers were delighted at the fall of the Umayyad dynasty, and were grieved at its transference to Spain, which was so near their country; they disliked their chauvinism and helped the 'Alids in order to injure them, though some of them were bought over by the Spanish Caliphs. The Berbers did much to spread Islam in the midst of Africa, even as the Turks did much to spread it in Central Asia, as far as India and China. For when the Berbers were definitely converted to Islam they endeavoured to conquer the parts of Africa that lay beyond them, and to spread Islam there.

While the Fáṭimide dynasty had its residence in North-West Africa it was supported by the Berbers, and especially by the tribes Kutámah, Ṣinhájah, and Huwárah. These tribes helped the Fáṭimides from the time of their rise under 'Ubaidallah the Mahdí, the first of their Caliphs, towards the end of the third century. When he was firmly seated in the year 297, he chose his staff from them and made them his ministers. In the Caliphate of his son Al-Ḳá'im, commencing in 322, and that of Al-Manṣúr binasr allah (334), and that of Al-Mu'izz lidín allah (341), they also enjoyed great favour. They aided the Fáṭimides in conquering all Africa and clearing it of representatives of the 'Abbásid doctrine. In the days of Mu'izz the Fáṭimides conquered Egypt and built Cairo, which they made the seat of government.

When 'Azíz son of Mu'izz became Caliph in the year 365, he wished to imitate the 'Abbásids, and made advances to the Turks and Dailemites, summoning them over in great numbers, promoting them, and taking his staff from them, as though he were afraid of the Berbers ; the Berbers and Turks thus became rivals, and the jealousy between the two was serious. But when, after the death of 'Azíz, his son Hákim became Caliph, he, believing in the superiority of the Berbers, gave them the preference and promoted them at court. They stipulated that the command over them should be given to Ibn 'Ammár al-Kutámí, a Berber, and Ḥákim in consequence appointed him Intermediary, i.e. to an office resembling the vezirate. This person became complete master of the government, and favoured the Berbers, whom he rewarded and promoted, whereas he humiliated the Turks and Dailemites, whom 'Azíz had won over to his cause. These people gathered round an eminent person of their number, originally a Slav, named Burjuwán, who aspired to office, and who set them against Ibn 'Ammár, whom they succeeded in deposing, he resigning the office of Intermediary, which was then accepted by Burjuwán ; Burjuwán then promoted Turks and Dailemites, and gave them offices in the palace. Presently it occurred to Ḥákim to put Ibn 'Ammár to death, and with him he also slew many of his father's and grandfather's officials. Thus the Berbers' power declined and the Turks advanced.

When Hákim was succeeded by his son Al-Ẓáhir li'i'záz dín allah in the year 411, the latter led an idle and debauched life, and his taste led him to favour the Turks and other Orientals, whence the influence of the Berbers declined yet further. Indeed, it continued to decline till it was almost extinguished. When, in 427, Mustanṣir came to the throne, his mother, being a black slave, caused her son to employ many of her compatriots in his army, to the number of one thousand, whilst he also endeavoured to procure large numbers of Turks. His army thus came to consist of two large divisions, between which much jealousy existed, and each of which aimed at securing exclusive influence. The jealousy finally turned into war, which wearied Egypt out, and the Caliph was compelled to call in the aid of Syria, and obtained as an ally Amír al-Juyúsh, Badr al-Jamálí, an Armenian by birth, who organized a great force of Armenians and put the chief ministers to death. From that time the bulk of the army was Armenian; the influence of the Berbers was lost, and they became mere subjects. Thus, after having been the chief persons in the kingdom, they became of no account.[1]

During this period the Seljúḳs had gained the upper hand in 'Iráḳ and Fars, and the Búyid dynasty had come to an end, whereby the influence of the Shí'ah was weakened in the East. The Seljúḳs appointed their freedmen and officers—the Atábeks—governors of the provinces, each one of whom, as we have seen, assumed independence; among these Atábeks was Núr al-dín Zengí in Syria. Among the generals in the employ of this person there were a number of brave Kurds, among them Najm al-dín Ayyúb and his brother Asad al-dín Shírgúh, both of whom obtained high places at his court. Now in the year 555 the Egyptian Caliphate had come into the hands of Al-'Áḍid Ibn Yúsuf, a weak-minded man, whose empire was struggled for by rival viziers till they rendered the country desolate, and the Caliph could do nothing to help. Among the rival viziers was one named Sháwar, who, being ousted, went to Núr al-dín Zengí and demanded his help against his rival for the vezirate. Núr al-dín seized the opportunity to get possession of Egypt, sending as his ally Asad al-dín Shírgúh with an army of mamlúks, who restored the vezirate to Sháwar, who by way of recompense paid a third of the Egyptian land-tax to Nur al-dín.

At this time the Crusades assumed a serious aspect, which caused Núr al-dín yet further to interfere in Egyptian affairs, appointing as his lieutenant there Asad al-dín Shírgúh, with his nephew the famous Yúsuf Ibn Najm al-dín, or Saladdin the Ayyúbí. Shírgúh died in 564; he was succeeded by Saladdin in the lieutenancy.

Saladdin was a very ambitious man, who, when he had been invested with the office of lieutenant (which resembled the

[1] Maḳrízí, ii, 12.

vezirate), wanted Egypt for himself and not for his principal, Núr al-dín. So when Al-'Áḍid, the Fátimide Caliph, died, Saladdin introduced the name of the 'Abbásid Caliph into public prayer, and transferred the government of Egypt from the Shí'í to the Sunní faction; and he assumed complete control of the administration. The Crusades being then at their fiercest, Saladdin performed a series of exploits which still resound in history, of which the most important was the recovery of Jerusalem, and extended his authority over Syria and other countries; he founded the Kurdish dynasty of the Ayyúbids, which followed the Sunní system, and Egypt returned to 'Abbásid suzerainty, which, however, was confined to verbal homage.

Saladdin and his successors procured great numbers of Turkish and Circassian mamlúks for military service, according to the custom of those days, and when these grew very numerous they claimed the right to control all the affairs of state and wanted the supreme power. And when the Ayyúbid dynasty declined they seized the government, and founded in Egypt two dynasties known as the Mamlúk dynasties, the Baḥrís and Burjís, of which the former ruled from 648 to 792 and the latter from 792 to 923. Both these rendered homage to the 'Abbásid Caliph. When the Tartars came and took Baghdad in the year 656, and killed the 'Abbásid Caliph Musta'ṣim, the surviving 'Abbásids fled and took refuge with the Egyptian Sultans. The Sultan at the time was Al-Malik al-Ẓáhir Baibars. The 'Abbásids remained there receiving homage from the Sultans till the Ottoman Sultan Selím the Conqueror came and took Egypt in 923. The 'Abbásid Caliph of the time was Al-Mutawakkil, the last of the line. He paid homage to the Ottoman Sultan, and handed over to him the relics of the Prophet, and thus was the Caliphate transferred from the 'Abbásids to the Ottomans, who hold it still.

§ 63. PERIOD OF MONGOLS OR TARTARS.

Dissolution of the Islamic Empire: from the rise of Jenghiz Khan in the year 603 to the death of Timur-Lenk in the year 807.

We have seen above how, when the 'Abbásid government became rotten and its Caliphs grew weak, the power being usurped by soldiers and servants, the connexion between the remote provinces and the capital became loose, and the empire split into divisions, Persian, Turkish, Kurdish, and Arabian. All these, however, paid homage to the 'Abbásid Caliph at Baghdad, until the Fáṭimide dynasty with an 'Alid Caliph arose in North-West Africa, took Egypt, and struggled with the 'Abbásid Caliphate for the possession of Syria and other countries. Presently the Fáṭimide dynasty was overtaken by the same fate as had befallen the 'Abbásid, and grew decrepit. It was, however, cut off before the other through the Ayyúbid Saladdin, who restored Egypt to 'Abbásid suzerainty.

The 'Abbásid dynasty was, it is true, in a state of extreme weakness at the time, its provinces of Syria, 'Irák, Fars, and Transoxania having been seized by the Seljúḳs for a time, after which they were partitioned between the Atábeks, as has been seen.

When, therefore, the sixth century closed, the 'Abbásid empire was weak and divided, especially in the east, where it was distracted between the Seljúḳ captains and their mamlúks, the most important of them being the Khwárizmís in Khorasan and Turkestan. The Caliphate was at its last stage of weakness and decrepitude and near dissolution. It was only maintained in existence by the provincial rulers, who desired its aid in the maintenance of their own authority; the wide domain of the Caliphs was then struggled for by three nations, who had as it were divided the whole between them: the Seljucid Turks and their captains in the east; the Ayyúbid Kurds in Egypt and Syria; and the Berbers in North-West Africa and Spain, where they had the name Al-Mohades. The Arabian dynasty had finally been extinguished, with the exception of some trivial principalities that remained in Yemen and other parts of Arabia. These dynasties, though of different race and principles, all agreed in paying homage to the weak and decrepit Caliphate of Baghdad, while they were all striving for the mastership in the Islamic world.

When the enemies of Islam that surrounded it saw its weakness and how it was divided, they determined to take vengeance, and attacked it from north, west, and east, each enemy hoping to deal it a deathblow. Georgians, Armenians, and Alani attacked it from the north, anxious to pillage and plunder, at times invading in tens of thousands, and sweeping over Azerbaijan and the neighbouring country, and after slaying and spoiling, bringing home captives and spoils, the Moslem captives at times being several thousands in number,[1] dealing with the Moslems as the Arabs had dealt with them at the beginning of their empire; only these raiders were unable to make any permanent conquests in Islamic territory.

From the west the Islamic empire was invaded by the Frankish Crusaders, anxious to conquer and united to overthrow the empire of Islam on religious grounds, owing to its containing the Holy Sepulchre. They conquered Palestine and part of Syria, and for a time obtained possession of Jerusalem. Had they remained united they might have got much further; but they were divided, and being assailed by the brave, skilful, and astute Saladdin were deprived by him of what they had taken, and driven out of Jerusalem in the year 583, after which they had no firm footing in the Islamic empire.

From the east it was assailed by the Tartars or Mongols in their various tribes and clans. They had still the Bedouin hardihood and strength of frame, and had the advantage of an energetic leader, the famous Jenghiz Khan, who brought them from Central Asia against the civilized world at the beginning of the seventh century. The Moslems had no one like Saladdin

[1] Athír, xi, 128.

on their side, so Jenghiz Khan was able to subjugate the Islamic empire from the extreme east to the frontier of 'Irâḳ, besides making such conquests in India and China that his empire attained a surface of 400,000 square miles.

§ 64. THE MONGOLS.

These were a Tartar tribe whose home was round Lake Baikal in South Siberia, and whose ancient history is obscure, because they only came to the front at the time we have mentioned under Jenghiz Ḳhan; before his time they were like other nomad tribes, living by raids, plunder, and the chase, which last pursuit they carried on in countries that were at a distance from the civilized world, which received neither benefit nor injury from them. They had no national importance till the time of Jenghiz Khan, since till then they consisted of no more than 40,000 tents, or, if we reckon ten persons to a tent, 400,000 persons. Jenghiz Khan with this small number invaded the civilized countries which surrounded his, and in a little more than ten years became master of them, just as the Bedouin Arabs at the commencement of Islam, coming out of the Arabian peninsula, conquered the Persian and Byzantine empires in about the same space of time; in both cases it was a victory won by the desert over the town, for at the time of Jenghiz Khan the Moslems had adopted the town life and got sunk in luxury, besides being divided against each other, as was the case with the Persians and Byzantines at the commencement of the empire of Islam. History repeats itself.

The father of Jenghiz Khan was a governor of thirteen Mongol tribes under the suzerainty of the great Khan of the Mongols, in virtue of mutual contracts. Jenghiz was born in the year 548, and was called in his youth Tamuchin. When he was 14 years of age his father died, and the tribal chieftains, despising Tamuchin, revolted from him, each of them seeking the headship for himself. Tamuchin, however, being from his early youth extremely energetic, rallied his followers, fought with the rebels, and defeated them ; this was his first battle, and won him general respect. Nevertheless, he thought proper to invoke the aid of the Great Khan, who granted it, treated him honourably, and gave him not only the headship which his father had enjoyed, but also one of his daughters.

Tamuchin had passed his early years on horseback, had learned archery and swordsmanship, and all branches of horsemanship. He was hardy, brave, patient of fatigue, hunger, thirst, cold, and pain; he accustomed his followers to similar privations, and they all formed a united body of auxiliaries, absolutely obedient to his will.

When Tamuchin rose high in favour with the Khan the envy of members of his family and others was roused, some of these being grandees, against whom Tamuchin had irritated the Khan ; when the Khan gave them signs of his displeasure these persons in resentment raised a revolt and fought a battle with him, in which he was defeated. He thereupon summoned Tamuchin to his assistance, who succeeded in restoring him to his throne, when he cruelly punished his enemies ; seventy of them were thrown alive into boiling water.

Tamuchin after this engaged in a series of wars, in which he was regularly successful, and attached his captains yet more firmly to himself. A vast assembly met to congratulate him on a plain on the banks of the Selenga, where he stood up, and being a good speaker, made an oration. He then sat down on a rug of black felt, which had been put on the ground for him, and this rug remains with them as a sacred relic. Then some pious and influential persons rose and said, "Whatever power thou hast acquired is from God ; He shall take thee by the hand and strengthen thy loins ; whereas if thou do wrong in thy government thou shalt become like this black felt, and thy people shall discard thee like a date-stone." This speech gives an illustration of Bedouin freedom similar to that exercised by the Arabs towards their Caliphs and princes at the commencement of Islam. Then there came forward seven chieftains who respectfully raised him up from the rug, and going in front of him, set him on the throne and proclaimed him king of the Mongols. Among those present was an old man, believed to be noble and of sacred character, who came forward with no clothing on him and said, "My brethren, I have seen in my dream as it were the Lord of Heaven, surrounded by the spirits, and He began to judge the people of the earth, and decided that the whole world should belong to our master and that he should be called Jenghiz Khan, i.e. the universal ruler." Then turning to Tamuchin he said, "I obey thee, O king; from this day thou shalt be called Jenghiz Khan, by God's command." And after that time he was called by no other name.

When he had sufficiently established his dynasty and trained his army he determined to conquer the world, and went first eastwards towards China, whose Emperor exacted a poll-tax from the Mongols, paid annually. When Jenghiz Khan had become powerful, he refused payment, which was equivalent to a declaration of war; he proceeded to invade China with his army, and made a breach in its Great Wall, and penetrated far within, slaying and spoiling. Now the Chinese of those days had anticipated a number of military inventions, and made use of the Greek fire which the Greeks were in the habit of employing against their enemies. They also discharged against the Mongols balls charged with gunpowder some time before the Westerns were acquainted with their use. Still, these expedients by no means hindered the advance of the Mongol tribes, and Jenghiz Khan continued his invasion till he entered the Chinese capital, Peking, and the whole northern region. This success only increased his lust for conquest, and with his enormous army he turned westward to the empire of Islam.

That empire was at the time in the weak and decadent condition which has been described, being split up into a number of states, Kurdish, Turkish, and Persian. The nearest of these states to the Mongol empire was that of Khwárizm, a branch of the Seljúḳ empire; its prince was at that time 'Alá'u'l-dín Khwárizmsháh, whose power towards the latter period of his life had spread over most of 'Iráḳ 'Ajamí,

Sijistán, Kirmán, Ṭabaristán, Jurján, the mountain country, Khorasan, Fars, Transoxania, and part of Afghanistan and India. The city of Khwárizm was the capital of the empire, whence the prince was called Khwárizmsháh. Jenghiz Khan advanced against the west with an army of about 700,000 fighting men, seized Turkestan and the region beyond, and pressed forward, massacring and plundering in a gruesome way.

His motive for committing these excesses was that when he had brought his army to Turkestan he sent certain Turkish traders, bearing gold, to Samarcand and Bokhara, countries in Turkestan or Transoxania, with instructions to purchase wearing apparel. They arrived at a Turkish city called Atrar, on the frontier of Turkestan, which adjoined the territory of Jenghiz Khan and where Khwárizmsháh had a viceroy. This person, on the arrival of the Tartar merchants, sent news to Khwárizmsháh, who sent back orders that they should be killed and their property seized and sent to him. The viceroy accordingly put them to death and sent their property, which was considerable in amount, to his master, who distributed it among the merchants of Samarcand and Bokhara, taking the equivalent from them in goods. His excuse for this conduct was that the Mongols had raided Kashgar, Balasaghun, and other places in Turkestan, and fought with his armies; for this reason he could allow them no market.

Now when Khwárizmsháh murdered the emissaries of Jenghiz Khan, the latter was furiously angry, and collecting a vast force invaded the Islamic empire, after sending the following message to Khwárizmsháh: "Ye slay my men and spoil their goods. Make ready for war, for I am coming against you with a force which ye shall be unable to withstand."

Khwárizmsháh on reading this epistle slew the bringer of it, and ordered the beards of his escort to be shaved. He then sent them back to Jenghiz Khan to inform him of the treatment that had been accorded his emissary and to bring him the following message from Khwárizmsháh: "I am coming to thee, though thou wert in the remotest parts of the earth, to take vengeance, and to do unto thee even as I did unto thy servants." Khwárizmsháh despised the Mongols just as Heraclius had despised the Arabs when their messages came to him at the commencement of Islam.

Jenghiz Khan thoroughly fulfilled his threat. He brought his army into the Islamic territory, and commencing with Turkestan the Mongols subjugated it, marching westward. They went from city to city, slaughtering, plundering, burning, demolishing, leaving in their rear nothing but heaps of ruins, after a fashion unexampled in the history of mankind. And the Mongol hordes acted very differently from the Arab hordes. The latter spared the countries which they conquered, giving security and protection to the inhabitants and imitating their culture, and adding to it a culture of their own; whereas the Mongols had no idea save to slaughter and plunder like savage beasts. There is no occasion to dilate in this place on the career of Jenghiz Khan; it need only be said in general that he was able in his lifetime to found an empire of a size which had been attained by no conqueror either before or after him, not excepting Alexander of Macedon, Julius Cæsar, Nadirshah, or Napoleon Bonaparte. He founded an empire stretching from the Indian Ocean to the Black Sea, and comprising millions of Chinese, Tanguts, Afghans, Indians, Persians, Turks, and others.

This mighty empire was founded by Jenghiz Khan, who could neither write nor read, which was also the case with most of his followers. For legislation and administration he had to rely on Moslems and subjects of Moslems who came within his jurisdiction, just as the Arabs had at the commencement of Islam to rely for similar purposes on Persians, Greeks, and others. Jenghiz Khan died in the year 624 at the age of 76, after a reign of 22 years.

After his death his empire was partitioned between his sons after the custom of the Mongols at that time, on the theory that the empire being his it was to be divided between his descendants like the rest of his goods. It was therefore split into four, which four divisions were afterwards yet further subdivided. Of these divisions we shall only mention such as were of importance.

The sons of Jenghiz Khan who inherited parts of his empire were four in number: Ogotai, Tuli, Juji, and Jagatai. These four founded dynasties whose rulers bore the title Khakan :—

1. Ogotai : reigned in Zingaria, etc., 603–1043.
2. Tuli, „ Mongolia, 654–750.
3. Juji, „ Kipchak, etc., 621–907.
4. Jagatai, „ Transoxania, 624–760.

The first dynasty had the greatest power, and its first monarch was Jenghiz Khan himself. We are not further concerned with its history. Of the second dynasty we are concerned with one branch which became of importance in the history of Islam, viz., the branch to which belonged Hulagu son of Tuli son of Jenghiz Khan, who obtained some fiefs in his father's kingdom, of which he made himself independent ruler, and took possession of Fars in 654. His dynasty there is known as the dynasty of the Ilkhans, or Mongols of Persia. He began by appropriating the relics of the empire of the Khwárizmsháhs in Persia, and then ventured on an exploit which none of his predecessors had attempted. When settled on his throne in Persia he attacked Baghdad.

§ 65. Hulagu and the Fall of Baghdad.

The cause of this was that the rivalry between the Sunnís and Shí'ís in Baghdad broke out afresh at the end of the 'Abbásíd dynasty, and not a year passed without the occurrence of a battle between the two factions calling for the interference of the Government. And since the Government was Sunní, the pressure ordinarily fell on the Shí'ites, who dwelt together in Karkh, having to endure persecution. Meanwhile the Government continued to entrust members of the faction with important offices, even of an administrative character. The Caliph of Hulagu's time, Al-Musta'ṣim, appointed in 640, was a weak man, and took for his vizier a Shí'ite named Mu'ayyid al-dín Ibn al-'Alḳamí, a crafty and astute individual. One of the ordinary disputes taking place between the two factions, a son of the Caliph named Abú Bakr, who was a fanatical hater of the Shí'ites, called in the aid of the commander of the forces (called the Dawádar), and ordered an attack to be made on the Shí'ites; an assault was then made on Karkh, when many women were outraged. The Vizier Ibn al-'Alḳamí, indignant at this and unable to restrain his wrath, wrote privately to Hulagu, tempting him with the prize of Baghdad, and sent his brother to urge him to attack the metropolis. Hulagu accordingly brought a great army against Baghdad. Musta'sim, hearing of this, sent against Hulagu under the Dawádar such forces as remained in Baghdad, not exceeding 20,000 men. The two armies met at two stages distance from Baghdad, and the army of the Caliph was defeated and dispersed.

Hulagu then advanced till he encamped on the eastern bank of Baghdad, and sent one of his captains to encamp on the west bank opposite the Caliph's palace. Musta'ṣim, having no idea of the schemes of Ibn al-'Alḳamí, sent him to make an inquiry concerning terms of peace with Hulagu, and Ibn al-'Alḳamí brought his schemes to a head by replying that Hulagu meant to leave the Caliphate to Musta'sim and give his daughter to the Caliph's son Abú Bakr. The Caliph thereupon went out to Hulagu with a number of his chief men; these were all bidden to remain in a tent. The vizier then demanded that all the jurists and notables of Baghdad should be gathered there, and when they appeared Hulagu ordered them to be slain. They then let the soldiers loose in Baghdad, attacked the Caliph's palace, and slew all the nobility to be found there, except infants, whom they took and placed with the other prisoners and captives. For forty days Baghdad was pillaged, and then an amnesty was proclaimed. The year in which Hulagu took Baghdad was 656. The 'Abbásid Caliph thus departed from 'Irák through the machinations of the 'Alid faction, as Manṣúr, Mahdí, and Rashíd had feared, who for fear of such a catastrophe had overthrown their viziers and commanders. The 'Abbásid Caliphate was not completely extinguished, as those members of the imperial family who escaped from Hulagu's massacre migrated to Egypt, where they lived under the protection of the Mamlúk Sultans.

After Hulagu had taken the capital of the Islamic world he aspired to conquer the regions beyond, and attacked Syria, which was under the protection of the Mamlúk Sultans after the fall of the Ayyúbid dynasty. They succeeded in repelling him, and he had to be satisfied with what was already in his grasp. His empire indeed extended from Syria to India; he left it to his children, but before a century had passed over it his dynasty terminated (654–750). It split into small principalities, which were in a disturbed and decayed condition till they were subdued by Timur Lenk.

§ 66. TIMUR LENK.

This great commander traced his descent to Jenghiz Khan, to whose family he belonged, though he was not a direct descendant. His grandfather had been vizier to Jagatai, son of Jenghiz Khan. He was born in 736, and when he reached puberty he was set over certain districts in the Transoxanian empire of Jagatai. Presently he was promoted to the vezirate, when he aspired to be king; he therefore ousted his master Mahmúd, and marched against the world as Jenghiz Khan had done before. After a series of battles, in which much blood was spilt, he conquered Fars, and before seven years were out he conquered Khorasan and Jurjan, Mazerindan, Sijistán, Afghanistan, Fars, Adherbaijan, and Kurdistan. He then came to 'Irák and took Baghdad from the Jilaris, who had obtained possession of it after Hulagu. He next directed his forces eastwards towards India, raided Cashmir and Dehli, and afterwards turned westward to raid Asia Minor, which was under the

Osmanlis, whose Sultan at the time was Bayazid. Timur Lenk pursued his career of conquest as far as Ancyra, and in a battle with Bayazid took the latter prisoner in the year 804. He also conquered the rest of the Nearer East as far as the frontiers of Syria, and received the homage of the Egyptian Sultan. He then turned towards China, but died on the way in the year 807, before his empire had been organized, which fell to pieces, the countries falling back into the possession of their former sovereigns. His incursion was therefore without permanent effect. In Transoxania, however, the Timurid dynasty lasted till 906. With the death of Timur Lenk the Mongolian period closes, and therewith closes the first period of Islamic history.

§ 67. SECOND PERIOD:

From the rise of the Ottoman Empire, which still continues.

We have seen that the Mongols founded no permanent dynasty on Islamic territory, and had no influence on Islamic civilization; their only connexion with Islamic civilization was that when the Islamic Empire was in its last stage of weakness and decline, owing to the incursions of Franks, Georgians, Armenians, and Alani, they, the Mongols, came and weakened it still further, and removed the last relics of the 'Abbásid Caliphate in Baghdad. They then went home, leaving the Islamic Empire *in articulo mortis*, being all dispersed, without any living dynasty capable of combining the elements. This task, however, was accomplished by the Ottoman dynasty in the second Turkish period, and the dynasty of the Shahs of Persia in the second Persian period, and these empires compose the second period in the history of Islam.

When, in the beginning of the ninth century of Islam, the Tartars went home, Egypt was in the possession of the Mamlúk Sultans, several of whom struggled for power and fought for profit. Of Syria, part was in the hands of the Egyptian

Sultans, while part was still in the hands of descendants of the Ayyúbid Sultans; indeed, almost each city was under an independent ruler. For 'Irák, Fars, and Mesopotamia there was a struggle going on between Ilkhans, Jilaris, Muzaffaris, Karakoyounlus, Litmuris, and others; whereas Transoxania and Afghanistan were under the Timurid Mongols. Asia Minor was the object of struggles between the Osmanlis and the relics of the Seljúks; for the rest of the Nearer East the remnants of the Tartars and the remnants of the Atábeks disputed. North Africa was divided between the Márínis and the Ḥafṣis. Of Moslem power in Spain nothing remained save the Naṣrid dynasty in Granada. The Arabian peninsula was under a number of small principalities always at war with and raiding one another. Weak and disordered as all these dynasties were, they were united under a Caliph yet weaker than themselves, viz. the representative of the 'Abbásids in Egypt.

Such was the disorder and decrepitude of the Islamic world at the time of the Ottoman conquest; and, indeed, the Ottoman dynasty came when it was needed. The Ottomans took Constantinople, which the Moslems after repeated efforts had despaired of taking; they fought with the mightiest princes of Europe, and pursued them into the Magyar country, besieged Vienna, and exacted poll-tax from the Archduke Ferdinand. They swept the Mediterranean as far as the coasts of Spain, and Europe trembled at their name. They conquered the East as far as 'Irák, then turned to the south-west and conquered Syria and Egypt, where the representative of the 'Abbásids lived, who, as we have seen, resigned the Caliphate in favour of the Ottoman Sultan. In the time of Sultan Sulaiman (926–974) their empire extended from Buda-Pest on the Danube to Assouan on the Nile, and from the Euphrates in the east to the Straits of Gibraltar on the west; all western Islam was gathered, and still is gathered, under the wing of the Ottoman dynasty. And the union of the Caliphate and the Sultanate in the person of its head is the cause of its persisting longer than all earlier Islamic dynasties, for even the 'Abbásids, who reigned so long, so far as actual power went, became a mere name after the third century from the commencement of their dynasty.

On the other hand, the Safawís arose in Fars and Mesopotamia and founded a great Shí'ite dynasty, which united all the countries in which Shí'i doctrine prevailed, and presently their dynasty gave way to that of the Ḳájárs, which still exists. The Islamic world, then, in its second (and present) period is ruled by two great Mohammedan dynasties, the Sunní Ottomans in the north and west and the Shí'í Ḳájár Shahs in the east. And we are not in this work concerned with the policy of these powers.

INDEX

ERRATA.

Page 228, line 1 : *for* Bajkan *read* Bajkam.
,, 293 ,, 29 : *for* Mazerindan *read* Mazandaran.